DATE DUE

GAYLORD   PRINTED IN U.S.A.

ORIGEN
His Life at Alexandria

BY RENÉ CADIOU

TRANSLATED BY JOHN A. SOUTHWELL

B. HERDER BOOK CO.
15 & 17 SOUTH BROADWAY, ST. LOUIS 2, MO.
AND
33 QUEEN SQUARE, LONDON, W. C.
1944

NIHIL OBSTAT

Arthur J. Scanlan, S.T.D.

Censor Librorum

IMPRIMATUR

✠ *Francis J. Spellman, D.D.*

Archiepiscopus

New York, March 20, 1944

Vail-Ballou Press, Inc., Binghamton and New York

PUBLISHER'S NOTE

ORIGEN, HIS LIFE AT ALEXANDRIA, is a
translation of LA JEUNESSE D'ORIGÈNE
by René Cadiou, published by Gabriel
Beauchesne, Paris.

Preface

THE purpose of this book is to give an account of the history of the School of Alexandria during the first three decades of the third century, the period when Origen was teaching there and was formulating its doctrine. Few great thinkers have been the occasion of so much discussion as this man. In the history of human thought he does not belong to Hellenism. But Greek thought and Greek culture formed a great part of his philosophical equipment, and their influence cannot be neglected in any study of the final stages of the ancient civilization.

Because of the fact that on a number of occasions certain opinions of his have been formally condemned, Origen has never been given the title of a doctor of the Church. Yet his influence on Christian thought is comparable only with that of St. Augustine or of St. Thomas Aquinas. The cream of his theological teaching is found not only in the fourth-century Greek writers who were the direct heirs of his learning or in the works of the studious St. Jerome; it is contained also in the writings of St. Ambrose, whose mind was attuned to the obviously practical rather than to the speculative, and in the homilies of St. John Chrysostom, whose education was along lines that ran counter to the spirit of Alexandria.

Nor is he venerated as a saint of the Church. It is true that in his writings he regards God and the soul as the most important of all spiritual entities. It is equally true that in his personal life he showed himself to be a man of heroic mold. But there were two or three periods during his lifetime when he let himself be misled by some rash or unchecked line of thought, a tendency of his Oriental genius which he usually managed to keep under control. Must our verdict be, then, that beyond everything else he was a pioneer whose very mistakes were helpful? Some such appraisal of his errors

v

would go far to explain why the Church's condemnation of them
has always been tempered by the quality of mercy. In any case, he
made his entry on the stage of history at one of those vigorous and
disturbed moments when new ideas suddenly emerge, ideas that no
simple stroke of the pen can readily harmonize with tradition or
with the current norms of thought. With that moment of crisis we
are concerned in this book.

In studying that critical period, we must take still another element into consideration. That element is the Church. To her service Origen dedicated all the vigor of his genius. In his anxiety to
defend her he sought to enrich her with the wealth of his profound
speculations, capable as they were of attracting minds trained to
the technique of philosophical inquiry. Stronger than his scholarly
interest in his studies and mightier than his preoccupation with
the activities of his School, there was an even more powerful influence in his life: the influence of a spiritual milieu that gave meaning and value to his researches, his controversies, his boldest flights
of speculation.

That spiritual milieu did not exert its influence merely now and
then. Its action was not confined to periods of crisis. It was not
content to meet the challenge of his teachings by invoking the
authority of a recognized formula or by pronouncing a judgment
of approval or disapproval. It acted upon him at every moment of
his life, even when it was not defining anything. The intercourse
of the members of the Christian body with one another, their likes
and their dislikes, the manner in which their anxious looks told
him whether he was reaching their hearts or arousing their opposition, his work of defending the faith, his interest in the lists of the
new converts, the violence of the persecutions which he sometimes
bore meekly and at other times courageously challenged, every
such social experience was woven into a Christian mentality by
which even his most revolutionary theories were kept under control. By reason of that stable mentality he was enabled, time and
again, to turn aside from utopian ideas and from the study of mere
curiosa in order to give his attention to the things that really mattered.

This Christian influence operates both from without and from within, usually with gentleness and without force. Its greatest victories are secret victories, manifested by an inner sense of harmony as well as by the free emergence of a process of thought which testifies to the soul's natural aspirations for truth. As soon as the Christian philosopher perceives within himself the mental adjustment that enables him to maintain the unity of his spiritual life even in the strains and stresses of an intellectual crisis, he knows he is within sight of the truth. When the peak of the crisis has been passed, a mental clarity and a kind of joy in the possession of the truth are the signs telling him that his soul is once again in harmony with the spiritual atmosphere in which he normally lives.

The Church is the social body which enables the individual to bring his religious longings into harmony with a higher discipline. No mere examination of prima-facie evidence can give an adequate knowledge of her influence or her activities—an attribute, by the way, which she shares with the majority of other social bodies. She must be studied in her *raison d'être*, in the very principle of her being; and because of that principle she must be acknowledged as more spiritual than other social bodies and therefore more difficult to describe. Yet there is manifold evidence to the mere fact of her existence. As a social organism she has been the object of study by the historians and has been recognized by other social groups; her frontiers have been marked by those who govern her, and she has been known and loved and even rigorously tested by her own children. Membership in her household is neither a necessary result of an exercise in logic nor is it dependent on the rise and fall of an individual's emotions. Whether the alien inquirer acknowledges her claims to be justified or denies them as baseless, the fact remains that the great family of her children can be distinguished from other social groups in the world of men. Things visible to everyone are their rule of faith and the authority which interprets it, their worship and the ceremonies in which they participate. More concrete and more real than any other fact in the history of Christianity is this organized commonwealth of the Church, together with the great body of spiritual truth which inspires it.

The history of the Church is made up of much more than the teachings of her great thinkers or the discussions which those teachings have provoked; side by side with the doctrines there are the less well known writings, the hymns, the ordinary everyday modes of Christian living. Even in the biographies of the outstanding Christian thinkers who seem to have filled the various periods in which they lived and taught, a detailed analysis reveals the influence of a mode of life common to all Christians. Under that influence academic enthusiasm walks hand in hand with Christian discipline, and philosophical study hews fast to the line of tradition.

This great outstanding fact expresses the very persistence of the Christian religion. It is the norm for all the other historical facts, continually present in the thoughts, the lives, and the works of Christians. Those who conform to this Christian way of life see its meaning clearly, and even those who desire to change it are compelled to acknowledge its power.

This fact of a Christian way of life imposes a greater obligation on writers of religious studies than on other workers not to neglect the social aspects of doctrine. It makes it incumbent on such writers to take account of the traditions which a doctrine has accepted either in whole or in part. They must study the various influences, admitted or denied, to which the elaboration of the doctrine has been subjected. They must know the critical works called forth by that elaboration, and must make themselves familiar with the various degrees of assent given to it when it was first formulated as well as with the general verdict of the faithful at that particular time.

Something more is demanded, however, in the study of Origen's life and works. Historians of every shade of opinion, in approaching his teachings for the purpose of criticism, are always halted at the angle of a dichotomy; consequently they have made a practice of analyzing his works from the viewpoint of a more or less justified antithesis. Does his doctrine belong to the East or the West? Was he a heretic or an apologist for orthodoxy? Was he a Hellenist or a Christian, a rationalist or a mystic? The fact that his teachings are always carefully checked by comparison with Christian tradition, even by historians who know little of the implications of that tradition, is a proof of the historical fact that the Church always kept an anxious eye on the progress of the work which Origen set himself to do. While it may be justifiable to assert that he was a rationalist, it must be admitted that his sincere desire was to be a Christian.

It seems to us that in Origen's case this problem of discipline and inspiration, of authority and personal freedom—a problem which is at the very bedrock of the religious consciousness—can be approached more accurately and more comprehensively than has hitherto been done. Our best means was to follow the line of the development of his theological opinions, and the task was made easier for us because we now possess resources that were lacking to our predecessors. On the one hand, we have been able to make use of the masterly edition of the two principal works on which this critical study is based, the *De principiis* and the *Commentary on the Gospel of St. John*; on the other hand, we have derived great benefit from numerous monographs which, by uncovering the origins of Neoplatonism, have made known the aims and the struggles of the philosophical period under review. Certainly, several of the published texts are still of doubtful or uncertain authenticity, and neither the *Commentary on the Psalms* nor the *Commentary on Genesis* has yet been subjected to a rigorous critical examination; the actual editions of these two works fall far short of containing all the fragments preserved by the compilers of the Byzantine period. Besides, included in them are several passages that must ultimately be rejected.

The historian of doctrine must impose upon himself the preliminary task of checking each of his quotations. Often the strongest argument in favor of the authenticity of the text is to be found in the critic's skill in recognizing the special vocabulary of the author under review, but even in this case it is advantageous to check the quotation by comparison with a similar passage. For this reason we usually give a number of references, although as a matter of principle we avoid an accumulation of texts. In the case of an author such as Origen, alert and skilled as he was in blending the various

shades of meaning of a word, the references are concerned mostly
with ideas that prove to be far from identical as soon as they are
read in the setting in which we found them.

Because of these and similar serious handicaps it is only fair that
the historian should enjoy some advantages. Chief among such
helps is the fact that he is protected from numerous errors by reason
of the consistency and coherence of doctrine, two qualities of Christian teaching which were particularly in evidence during the years
when Origen ruled over the Academy of Alexandria. It was the
formative period of his life, when he was engaged in an effort to
reduce his ideas to a systematic form. As usually happens in the
case of philosophical speculations that are watered and fed by a
deeply religious life, the driving force of his mentality made its
influence felt in every minute detail of his teaching. Throughout
his whole system the ruling thought is not an effort to achieve a
logical unity of propositions formally put together. What he seems
always to aim at is a vital unity; and the student of his writings can
perceive the same principles at work in the commentary on the Bible,
in the study of the soul, in his various controversies, and in his interpretation of each of the dogmas which he sought to expound.
This character of vital unity makes a fragment of a few lines easy to
recognize when it has Origen for its author.

The task undertaken by the writer of this book is to revive some
of those studies made by Origen and, at the same time, not to lose
sight of the ruling thought which in spite of divergences and contradictions in matters of detail makes them clear and easy to understand. According to the plan followed in recent studies in the history of Christian literature, we have felt compelled to give a literary
analysis of each of his great works. During the course of our researches, in which we were much indebted to contemporary editors
of his writings, we rarely found it possible to arrange his works according to their dates. The best we could do was to follow indications given us by Origen himself and to divide his publications into
a number of groups. We are aware that the task of establishing an
inner order within each of those several groupings exposes us to
the charge of putting forth a series of hypotheses, but at least we do

not treat as certain any theory appearing to us as no more than prob-able. In our dual capacity of historian and critic we assert our right to pass judgment on each of his great teachings and even to speak on behalf of the philosophical mind which brought them forth. At the same time we have taken every care to keep such judgments apart from our exposition of his doctrine.

It would be foolish for us to think we had said the last word on a problem that reappears more often than any other such problem in the history of Christian philosophy, for it is a problem whereof it can be said with much show of truth that the era of new discov-eries has not yet come to a close. But our purpose will be achieved if we have helped to a better understanding of a great historical period that was decisive for Christianity and for Western culture; if this biography of Origen allows the reader to see in the earthly life of one human soul the interrelations of reason and faith, of Hellenism and the modern consciousness, relations that have been too often reduced to a conflict of mere abstractions. And lastly we have passed on to the reader a little of that fiery enthusiasm which made Origen's life one unceasing inquiry. Every breath he drew vibrated with an intense desire to know. Every item of knowledge he acquired fanned the flames of his impatience. When he came face to face with a mystery, never for an instant did he halt in his stride. The mystery merely urged him to greater efforts to know.

Contents

CHAPTER   PAGE

I.   Origen's Childhood during the Persecution . . . 1

II.   In the Service of the *Logos* 29

III.   Reform of the School 49

IV.   Commentary on the Psalms 66

V.   Commentary on Lamentations and the Treatise on the Resurrection 84

VI.   Gnosticism and Marcionism 104

VII.   Christian Gnosticism 116

VIII.   The New Philosophy 136

IX.   Ammonius Saccas 149

X.   Origen and Plotinus 166

XI.   Origen the Pagan 186

XII.   The Treatise *De Principiis* 209

XIII.   The Three Worlds 226

XIV.   The Effects of the Treatise on Origen's Teaching 266

XV.   The Prologue of St. John 273

XVI.   The Word and the Lamb 292

XVII.   The Conflict 302

XVIII.   The Church 309

XIX.   Conclusion 325

Index 331

CHAPTER I

Origen's Childhood during the Persecution

I. HIS CHILDHOOD

"CLEMENT, having succeeded Pantaenus, had charge at that time of the catechetical instruction at Alexandria, so that Origen also, while still a boy, was one of his pupils." [1] To the master and to the pupil the gift of faith had come by different paths. Leonidas, the father of Origen, was a man well instructed in the Christian religion and, besides, was the possessor of a library of rare manuscripts. The child, thus reared in a Christian home, soon showed an insatiable thirst for the things of religion. While reading the Sacred Scriptures he was always delving more and more deeply into the text, and he grew into the habit of questioning his father about the more difficult passages, often indeed without receiving any reply. When his genius began to blossom, the boy bubbled with an impatience that had to be restrained in public and even to be rebuked.

Secretly, however, his father's heart was filled with joy when he perceived the gifts with which the ardent and promising young soul had been dowered. In the evenings, when he laid aside the grave manner and the cares that had lain upon him during the day as his son's teacher, his paternal love expressed itself in caresses and in endearments. He used to thank God for having blessed his household. There is a story that, when he used to approach the bedside of his sleeping son, he would see on the boy's breast the mark of consecration by the Holy Ghost and would kiss the spot with reverence—a homage worthy of him who was later to describe in a thousand ways the growth of wisdom in the human

[1] Eusebius, *H. E.*, VI, vi, 1. Origen's name suggests that he belonged to the Greco-Egyptian middle class.

heart. Within the walls of this Christian household the boy's questions were already causing that strange mixture of wonder and unrest which would accompany his work for all the centuries after his time. The feelings which the Church has always had toward his memory are the same feelings which he himself aroused in his father's house from the first moment when he began to learn the power of his own mind.

CLEMENT OF ALEXANDRIA

Clement, on the other hand, was a convert. He is assumed to have been a native of Athens. He was led to Christianity while studying the works of the classical authors and the traditions of the various schools of Asia Minor, Syria, and Egypt. Well versed in the teachings of the principal Christian writers of the generation preceding his own, he adhered to none of them. His conversion—or, as he used to say, the act by which his salvation was assured—was the decisive moment of his life. Although the divine goodness calls all men to the Christian religion, the power of choice rests with the individual. At the moment when that choice is made there takes place, in a sense more profound than the Greeks ever dreamed of, the free choice of the wise man and the first step toward the true philosophy. But a man decides for himself, choosing either truth or error.

On the threshold of his life as a Christian the convert makes his profession of faith.[2] This is a free contract which it is sinful thereafter to break. It consists in the acceptance, in the words of a creed, of the abridged knowledge of the basic points of Christianity; and those fundamental truths must never be denied. The baptismal promise becomes, by a succession of free exchanges between God and men, the foundation of all other divine benefits. It even leads the Christian to the knowledge of the perfect life if he finds a teacher to give him an adequate understanding of the truths already known by the light of faith. The Christian thinker who faithfully pursues the lines of study laid down for him finds his ultimate reward in a perfection that can never be lost.

[2] Strom., I, 18.

This was not quite the way Origen had learned how to expound the life of a Christian. His early teachers had told him more about the Sacred Scriptures and about the Holy Ghost than about philosophy, for he had been reared to consider religion of greater importance than knowledge. Clement's academic phrases, even when they referred to matters with which the youth was well acquainted, must have been startingly new to him when he heard them applied to things like baptism and the Eucharist. But the young pupil learned a lesson from them: he learned how the weapons of culture might be employed to develop a more powerful technique of presenting the Christian faith. God had dowered the Greeks with the gift of philosophy to prepare them for the coming of the Savior. If philosophy causes the divine word to fructify in men's souls, has a man the right to treat it lightly? And when the man himself desires to walk the path of holiness, should he ever yield to weariness and sit idly by the wayside?

LITERARY PROJECTS

Then a program of studies, designed to attract the young pupil, began to be urged upon him. On this particular point Clement was the heir of traditions formed at Alexandria in the days of Philo, when the religion of the Sacred Scriptures was first presented in an intelligible form to the Greeks of Egypt. God's wisdom is manifold; and art, knowledge, faith, and prophecy are all a part of it in different degrees. In the city of learning that had grown up around the Museum of Alexandria, how could a man fail to borrow from each line of study whatever was useful in it? Why not take every subject in the curriculum up to the classes in philosophy? And why not go on from there to the study of wisdom? There is not a single line of study which, by stimulating the mind, can fail to prepare it for religion or to make the knowledge of religion grow. A kind of university must be founded for the instruction of men who are destined to become more than preachers, a university for the special training of those who will become, by voice and pen, the heralds of truth to all humanity.

It was a program which, like many another such project, awaited a pupil to translate it into practical terms. Clement was much too busy with the moral training of his younger pupils to undertake the launching of the vast project that he dreamed of. His efforts never passed beyond the stage of collecting sheaves of notes, borrowed by preference from poetry and philosophy; he grouped them together under the form of memoirs, jotted down, as he himself said, as they occurred to his memory. In the beginning he was not very clear about the way the various sciences could be employed, but in the final section of the *Stromata*, written after his departure from Alexandria, he worked out a more accurate idea of what he planned to do. He saw especially that the study of nature "leads the soul nearer to the power of the divine Worker." He also observed that a knowledge of words and of their different shades of meaning could throw a great light on the study of the Sacred Scriptures. Perhaps at a later date, when Origen had entered upon his career as a teacher, Clement heard something of the younger man's experiences in the years when he had first sat at the master's feet. It is not unreasonable to assume that in some such way Clement was enabled to reach a clearer notion of the program he had put forward so eloquently years before.

Origen remembered the various projects—and Clement's lively mind teemed with projects—even more than he remembered the lectures in which he had first heard them. The universal knowledge that Clement talked about proved to be nothing more than a series of false starts and unfinished experiments. But the very insufficiency of the program was one of the best disciplines Origen could have had, for it made him aware of enterprises that were never completed and opened his eyes to the value of some promised books that should never have been begun. For example, Clement announced a forthcoming treatise on nature; it would discuss the creation of the world and would cover the long road from cosmology to theology. In addition to this there was to be a book on the perfect initiation of the Christian which would describe the final stages of the ascent of the human soul. Undoubtedly the two works, together with the *Stromata*, were planned as an exposition of an ascetical system of morals, and Clement himself had promised this exposition to the new converts whose Christian training he had undertaken to complete. It was to be the final stage of Christian preparation for the life of perfection, the last step from faith to the fullness of love wherein the Logos would become the Master who would impart perfect knowledge. Hence Clement proposed to give to the entire work the title "The Master."

Even if Clement had had the time and opportunity for such a task, he was incapable of making the effort required for its successful completion. Drawing copiously from his books of extracts and using the equipment furnished him by his wide reading, he used to talk on a number of themes. He was like one of those Alexandrian tapestries the art of which lies in nothing more than the unexpected variety of colors. In the texture of Clement's life the rich colors blend and mingle without ever falling into any settled design. An academic viewpoint and a particular way of thought constituted the sole legacy he left to his pupils.

One of those pupils, however, would put the great program into operation, would write the books that had been merely empty titles and combine the ambitious projects of study with his own daring efforts of speculation. The treatise on nature by which Clement had planned to bring the human soul nearer to the Artisan of the universe was written by Origen. In the history of Christian thought it is known as the *Tractatus de principiis*. He had more skill than Clement in analyzing the meanings of words, and he formed the habit of studying each word not only in its context and in the subject matter to which it was applied, but also in its history and its inner spirit. Taking all the sciences which Clement used to speak of, he lectured on them as part of the student's preparation for the classes in theology. Clement's notion of a book on the perfect initiation of the Christian was the purpose of his own personal studies from the moment when he first directed his *Commentary on the Gospel of St. John* toward the elucidation of the spiritual sense of Scripture. Clement's great dreams and Clement's ideal of Christian perfection were fashioned by Origen into a method of exegesis, were incorporated into a definite school of philosophic thought, and were used to discover a special vocation for the Christian thinker. In translating into concrete terms the vast projects of his master, Origen achieved much more than Clement had ever dreamed of.

HIS RELIGIOUS TRAINING

Clement's spiritual teachings had an even more profound influence on the development of Origen. It was a definite principle at Alexandria that a teacher should always keep in view the salvation of his pupils. From the beginning of his classes Clement sought to plant in the hearts of his hearers a belief in what he called divine philanthropy. Under the spell of his sweet and penetrating eloquence, justice could be seen to change gradually into mercy. Every punishment inflicted by God is a remedy. God is the friend of man, the philanthropist. Without ceasing for a moment He provokes sinners to repentance by His warnings, His reproaches, His complaints, skilled as He is in a thousand ways of making good come out of evil. He awaits the individual's free choice and begs for it, even beyond the confines of the grave. The sinner's conscience can feel shame even in another world, for no region is outside the influence of God's goodness.

In the atmosphere of this teaching the religion of the prophets became an attractive discipline. It was humanized, so to speak, yet not without the loss of some of its majesty. Clement explained all such difficulties by referring to the action of divine providence. The Word-made-flesh, the partner in the work of divine philanthropy, takes care of all such doubts; and to show how this Word-made-flesh achieves the gradual education of mankind, Clement wisely adopted the tone and the language of St. Irenaeus when he described "the Shepherd who teaches us the highest wisdom." Indeed the exposition soon became a prayer. "Yes, Master, lead us to your pasturage on the holy mountain. Let us lie down within your Church, which has been lifted above the clouds and which touches heaven itself." [3]

The idyllic view of divine providence left such an impression on Origen that, for many years afterward, he had difficulty in believing in the existence of an irreducible evil. We find an echo of that early

[3] *The Tutor,* I, 9.

impression in words like these: "And as God is a lover of men and is ready to welcome, at every moment and under any form, the impulse of human souls to better things, even of those souls who make no haste to find the Logos, but like sheep have a weakness and gentleness apart from all accuracy and reason, so He is their Shepherd." [4]

Clement used to hold up to the eyes of his more enthusiastic pupils the promise of higher and more spiritual teachings to come. Only let them yield to their teacher for a little time, and they would be weaned from the practices of their early life and would find their wholeness in the following of Christ. The years of their academic training were merely a transitory stage, a childhood out of which they would grow into the strength of the perfect Christian.

MYSTICAL ASPIRATIONS

At this period in the history of the early Church a number of Christians, both in the ranks of the clergy and in the body of the laity, gave free rein to the desire to consecrate themselves to meditation and to the practice of the love of God. They used to recite Lauds in the morning, to read lessons from the Scriptures before dinner, to chant psalms and hymns after dinner, and to say other prayers before retiring to rest at night. They read the Sacred Scriptures as a means of preparing their souls for the work of contemplation, but they had no one capable of explaining to them the difficult passages therein. They needed a more solid diet than the milk and honey offered to the new converts by the Good Shepherd. Where were they to find it?

It would be set before them by their Christian teacher. Clement gave his pupils the loftiest idea of a teacher's functions. Did not St. Paul, in his list of Christians favored with special gifts, number the doctors next to the apostles and the prophets? Yes, but the days of the *charismata* were apparently gone forever, although St. Irenaeus had seen some examples of them. Origen's knowledge of the subject was confined to an acquaintance with what he called "scraps and vestiges."

[4] *In Joan.*, I, 29.

It has become the fashion among moderns who study the early history of the Church to consider the *charismata* and the functioning of an ecclesiastical hierarchy as being mutually exclusive, and it is often assumed that the establishment of Church discipline meant the end of individual inspiration among the faithful. The assumption is not justified, for the earliest apostolic authority was contemporaneous with the existence of the *charismata*, and indeed the two were often found in one and the same person. The primitive gifts known as *charismata* never disappeared. They were simply transformed, being absorbed into the religious life and into the study of theology. They became permanent functions, normally filling the role previously held by the extraordinary gifts, the persistence of which, however, they did not exclude. Private inspiration was gradually welded into the Christian mode of life, and the Church, acting in the interest of the common good, laid down rules for her doctors and her mystics, just as she formerly did for those favored souls who enjoyed special gifts from on high.

Now, the true spirit of Christian perfection did not always prevail at the Academy of Alexandria. The desire for the perfect life assumed a new intellectual form, especially in the little groups that had the use of their own libraries and lived according to the religious traditions of an older day. That new intellectual form was a thirst, or what Origen would later describe as a gluttony, for the knowledge of divine things.

GNOSIS

Not without reason did the students who followed the elementary classes at Alexandria long for the special knowledge of God which Clement had promised them. In the common conviction among all the various sects of the day, this special knowledge of God was an assurance of salvation; it was supposed to be mysteriously imparted to special individuals who were born with the gift of unlocking the secrets of the divine. Such special individuals were considered to differ essentially from the common run of men. Something of this notion was picked up from the Valentinian groups at Alexandria by the educated Christians who frequented the classes of the catechetical school. Soon the infected Christians were demanding that the higher learning be given to them, and Clement could not refuse to fan the flame which flickered in their hearts. Faithful to his own program, he yielded to their demands. He continued to train them in the ways of holiness but he also took pains to equip them for the higher knowledge they sought. Thus it happened that, from the day a student enrolled at the Academy, he was taught to regard the life of a Christian as a progressive introduction to knowledge of the divine. He learned to see the Church as a long course in the study of religion, a course which admitted of several degrees. And he absorbed the general principle of the Academy, which made a distinction between the two kinds of Christian, the simple and the perfect.

In the eyes of Origen, as in those of Clement, the Church has its privileged souls; they are the friends of wisdom, and they either cultivate the spirit in lives of personal holiness or dedicate themselves to philosophical research. Beyond this group is the main body of the faithful, content to eat humbler fare. The catechumens and the penitents belong to this latter class, but it was held that the majority of Christians are on the same lowly level. The simple, then, are all Christians who resist the influence of the Academy or who are not tractable enough to its methods. At first, this class of Christians was composed of those who were quite content to practice good works without any participation in the intellectual life. Later the opponents of the Alexandrian system of the spiritual interpretation of the Scriptures were added to this class, as were a number of the Judaizing groups of Syria. Thus the Alexandrian theologians cannot readily be acquitted of the charge of introducing into Christian life the Greek opposition between the learned few and the ignorant multitude. Origen acquired this mentality during his early days at the Academy. He was never quite free from it thereafter. Sometimes he lets an admission of it escape him: "By proudly bragging we mislead the simple, and forget that God made every man in His own image and that He has adjusted men to one another." [5] Clement, as long as he was teaching at Alexandria, took special

5 *Ibid.*, XIII, 28.

care to remind the new students that their baptism had made them perfect Christians. They were perfect absolutely, without any more or less, "because we were illuminated, which is to know God." The first surge of joy and the final happiness are not essentially different. "The perfect Word, born of the perfect Father, was begotten in perfection."

The faith that comes with baptism was the only foundation on which Clement cared to build. For that reason he considered it necessary to assure himself that the foundation was solid before he allowed a student to enroll for the higher classes. There were many candidates, and Clement used to watch them carefully with the eyes of a guardian of morals, noting the forms of speech they used, their ways of meeting a problem, and their general behavior. How diverse those young souls were! Some of them were still infected with the philosophy of Hellenism. Others, like Origen, had grown up in a holier atmosphere. Converts mingled with young men born of Christian families. In each single case Clement strove to make himself a co-worker with God.

THE STUDY OF RELIGION

In the preface of the first book of the *Stromata*, Clement makes his position clear, as he would have done for his audience in the opening lecture of a course at the school. For a Christian, the study of religion is neither an occasion for brilliant speeches nor an opportunity to display his skill in argument. "Men who are studying theology have no time for that kind of empty curiosity with which a sightseer takes notes about the monuments of a city." "A student must not be asked to measure the value of a teaching by a set of arbitrary comparisons." The gift of ready speech and the talent for assembling a multitude of arguments constitute a danger. "But whoever chooses to banquet on faith, is steadfast for the reception of the divine words, having already acquired faith as a power of judging according to reason."

Clement did not require his students to live a conventual life as did the Pythagoreans of his time, nor did he impose any rules of behavior beyond obedience to the precepts of Christianity. But incessantly he was urging them to deeper and deeper study, telling them that later the recollection of their efforts would make their possession of the truth all the sweeter. Beyond everything else, however, he insisted that the student take care of his own preparation by continually exercising his faith and by developing the practice of detachment. With his personal enthusiasm welded into his skill in expounding the intricacies of the subject, he was at his best when he was pointing out to his classes the distant perspectives ever to be seen on this road of Christian learning. Small mysteries opened up vistas of great mysteries. The greater the student's advance, the longer the path that was still to be traveled. Like a distant mirage, the horizon continued to recede more and more every day.

In all this academic enthusiasm Origen had no time for anything like disappointment. Throughout his entire life he was to remain partial to those scholarly elaborations of knowledge and to those progressive introductions to new problems. His own system of theology was to be full of those perspectives of which Clement delighted to talk. At the Academy he learned how to hunger and thirst after wisdom. "The desire for wisdom," as Clement had said, "grows when it is inspired and fed by habits of study, and it grows in proportion to the growth of the student's faith."

Often it happened that Clement, with his Greek love of restraint, tried to hold back those enthusiastic young Egyptians who already thought themselves capable of seeing God and were eager to dispense with the ballast which Clement demanded. "Among us," he used to say, "the philosopher is laden with three obligations: the first is the duty of contemplation, the second is obedience to the commandments, and the third is the education of righteous men. Taken together, these three things are the decisive mark of the perfect Christian."

So there they were—the study of truth, the practice of mortification, and the duty to teach. They were more than a literary program. They were a design for living, and that design was offered to Origen. Later events might sometimes seem to disturb the design, but its bold lines would be visible throughout the entire course of his life, standing forth more clearly for the shadows that fell across them.

II. THE PERSECUTION OF THE CHRISTIANS

A.D. 198 Emperor Septimius Severus, fresh from his defeat of the Parthians, made a journey through Syria. In that province the Christians and the Jews were very numerous, a fact that led the Roman rulers to prohibit conversions either to Christianity or to Judaism under pain of the utmost rigors of the law. When the Emperor left Syria he journeyed all through Egypt, and three years later replaced the prefect Maecius Laetus by appointing Subatianus Aquila to the former's post. His visit was marked by the launching of a violent persecution against the Christians. He took temporary charge of the administration, superseding the local prefects. Those officials were accustomed to administer the antichristian laws according to their own particular disposition; sometimes they were tolerant, but occasionally they yielded to the force of public opinion and applied the laws over brief periods.

When Septimius Severus learned that some of those in his own immediate circle had embraced the new faith, he awoke to the menace of Christianity. He thereupon promulgated the law against conversions. Its real purpose was to prevent the growth of the Christian religion, and its full force was directed against the catechists and the teachers of Christian groups. Clement was a prominent target, for he numbered among his pupils several converts from Hellenism. Soon he left Egypt, and he never returned.

CLEMENT ON MARTYRDOM

After his departure he wrote a short tract on the martyrdom of the perfect Christian. He had already touched on this subject in a casual way by his praise of the martyrs and by his teaching that the conquest of the passions prepares the Christian to give the witness of blood, if need should arise. In that reference to the persecutions his enthusiasm knew no restraint. But now he found himself compelled, like many others, to justify those Christians who had fled for shelter.

"When again He says 'When they shall persecute you in this city, flee into another,' He does not advise flight as if persecution were an evil thing. He enjoins them by flight to avoid death, not as if in dread of it, but wishes us to be neither the authors nor the abettors of any evil to anyone, either to ourselves or to the persecutor and murderer. For He, in a way, bids us to take care of ourselves; he who disobeys is rash and foolhardy. . . . Such is also the case with him who does not avoid persecution, but out of daring presents himself for capture. Such a one, as far as in him lies, becomes an accomplice in the crime of the persecutor. And if he also uses provocation, he is wholly guilty, challenging the wild beast. And similarly if he affords any cause for conflict or punishment or retribution or enmity, he gives occasion to persecution." [6]

He goes on to add that there are in the Church different kinds of perfection and different *charismata*. His esteem for the ideal Christian thinker and Christian contemplative is not at all inferior to his reverence for the martyr. Both thinker and contemplative must acknowledge God. The martyr must preach Him. Besides, if a man understands what Christian perfection is, he also understands that martyrdom is only a more splendid manifestation of it. The proof of the value of the work is the love that inspires it. "Each soul that has lived purely in the knowledge of God, that has obeyed the commandments, is a witness both by life and by word, in whatever way it may be released from the body—shedding faith as blood along its whole life till its departure." Rightly we give the same marks of honor to the martyrs as to confessors of the faith. "We call martyrdom perfection, not because the man comes to the end of his life as others do, but because he has exhibited the perfect work of love." So Clement feels that henceforth he will not permit himself to be called perfect, until the shedding of his blood, poured out in a sacrificial offering of love for Christ, has released his soul from his body.

Since persecution came at the hour fixed by God to put an end to his days of study and prayer, Clement wished it well. But he saw no need for it to turn him from his work. He believed that the prestige of those who had died for the faith should not make the Christians forget that teaching had a value also, nor should it lessen their ap-

[6] *Strom.*, IV, 10.

preciation and esteem for the practice of the lowliest virtues. He made the wisest explanation possible to him in the delicate situation in which the persecution placed him. He wanted for a little time longer his life of mortification and his quiet days of peaceful study wherein he was content "to leave worldly kindred and wealth and every possession in order to lead a life free from passion." Clement had the Greek gift of balancing one notion against another. Martyrdom was something that would come in its own good time, like the laurel crown that was given to the athlete at the end of the games.

Origen was confronted with the same problem, and his conscience met it without difficulty. The persecution broke out when he was seventeen years old, and it helped him to see Christianity as a conflict, demanding an effort of the free will that has been illuminated by the light of faith. In this crisis he drew comfort even from the keen intellectualism of the Academy, and the young student was prepared to carry his Platonism to an extreme before which Clement was still hesitating. The body was a prison, and the soul should be freed from it. He longed for the opportunity to make the supreme sacrifice. The opening lines of his *Exhortation to Martyrdom*, written long afterward, give us an echo of the exaltation which lifted up his mind and his heart in those days of crisis: "A man truly loves God with his whole soul when an ardent desire to be united to his Creator seizes his soul and makes him long to escape not only from this earthly body but from every material thing that can keep him from God."

Exhortations to martyrdom mark the beginning of Origen's work as a catechist and a writer. When his father was in prison, Origen wrote to him: "Take heed not to change your mind on our account." After his father's martyrdom he continued to encourage his brethren who were in prison. He made a practice of visiting them. "When the holy martyrs were led to their death," Eusebius says, "he, with great boldness, saluted them with a kiss." He felt obliged to show the persecutors how little their hate meant to him and he wished to bear witness before God to the beliefs he had learned from the study of His holy words.

ALEXANDRIAN MARTYRS

Soon he was called to the task of preparing Christians for martyrdom. He now became a catechist, and every person who came to him for instruction in the faith was liable to the penalties of the law. Liable also were his more advanced pupils who had submitted to baptism in spite of the imperial edict against it. Several of his pupils were condemned, and he assisted them in their last moments. But in the eyes of the law the born Christian who lived by his faith was as much a criminal as the Christian who made converts of others, and it is probable that Origen owed his immunity to the tolerance of the local administration at Alexandria. It seems to have been the policy of the Roman governors throughout Egypt to spare the leading members of the various Christian communities. It was enough for the administration at Alexandria that good order was maintained in the house where the young catechist held his classes and that too large a gathering of the faithful never assembled there. But for a long time public opinion raged against the Christians, especially at Alexandria, where it had been the policy of the Lagides to develop an official form of worship in an effort to bring unity to a city which had no traditions. Ptolemy Soter had erected a temple to a semi-Greek Serapis and the populace used to worship there. A day came when the mob made a demonstration against Origen, holding him responsible for the deaths of his converts. Word even went forth that he would be compelled to abjure the faith. For a number of years he had to hold himself ready for every eventuality and to keep before his eyes the danger of a sanguinary attack in the streets.

When the danger of further persecution passed away, the memory of the holy martyrs began to be perpetuated in the Church of Alexandria. The Christians who had borne the rigors of prison life were granted places of special honor among the faithful. The names of the dead were preserved, the circumstances of their deaths and the replies they had made at the tribunal were recorded, and they began to be venerated under the official title of martyrs. From the beginning of the third century pious customs were prescribed as a tribute to their memory, although the Christian body was not always unanimous in the observance of those new practices. "In some such way must we suppose the death of the most holy martyrs to operate, many receiving benefit from it by an influence we cannot describe." [7] Since they are victims offered by the Church, we can obtain through their intercession the remission of our sins.

The thoughts that came to Origen in those days of persecution were deeply etched on his soul. His treatise on prayer, written in the year 232 after a long period of peace, contains many allusions to martyrdom, and his enthusiasm glows in them so brightly that we are tempted to believe they were written in the period when the persecution was raging. That, however, is scarcely probable, though Origen always regarded the supreme sacrifice from a fixed viewpoint whether the danger was imminent or not. His entire system of personal mortification dictated that viewpoint. The words of Scripture and the advice he gave to Ambrose, that the Christian scholar has no right to take refuge in a policy of apathy, reflect the same mentality with which he wrote two years later, when his friend was in prison. Mortification and martyrdom are, he held, one and the same thing. If a Christian fails to accustom himself to consider all human life as a testing wherein all his reserves of courage must ultimately be called into play, he is likely to find himself exposed to the danger of apostasy in his hour of trial.

ORIGEN'S LONGING FOR MARTYRDOM

As he grew older, Origen was impatient to make the supreme sacrifice. Time and again he vowed himself to it, but God seemed ever to withhold from him the joy of the martyr's crown. Martyrdom seemed to him to be a means of attaining the perfect purity which even personal holiness was unable to give; it was the final preparation for the right to stand on the heavenly altar. This was the view of martyrdom that he wished every member of the Christian body to have. The Church without martyrs, he used to say, is as desolate as a Jerusalem without victims for the sacrifice in the temple. He was always prone to recall his first years as a catechist, when he prepared his pupils for holy martyrdom at the same time

[7] *In Joan.*, VI, 36.

as he prepared them for baptism. He reached the point where he no longer called the laws against the Christians a scourge; instead, he regarded them as a blessing from God. "When the Christians came back from the cemeteries after bearing the bodies of the holy martyrs to their burial and assembled in the church for prayer, we used to see the evidence of their holiness. The whole Christian body was there, and no member of the flock showed fear. The catechumens learned a lesson in those assemblies when they heard the report of what the holy martyrs had said to their judges and of the steadfastness with which they confessed the faith up to the moment of their death. I know Christian men and women who saw strange things happen in such assemblies, and even real miracles." [8]

In the life of the Christian who devotes himself to the service of God there are critical moments when personal convictions seem to fall into a definite and permanent pattern, and that pattern becomes a viewpoint from which the soul views all the elements of the crisis and is enabled thereby to act with courage and assurance. In the life of Origen such critical moments are indicated by the early exhortations by which he encouraged his own father, his personal friends, and his pupils, to choose the better part which unites the soul to God by a death willingly accepted in testimony of the Christian faith; they are indicated also by the days when he held himself ready to shed his blood for the faith, days when he believed near at hand the martyrdom which he had learned to see as the final seal of Christian perfection.

III. THE GRAMMARIAN

When Origen's father was martyred, the property of the family was confiscated, and the numerous household was left without any resources. In this plight Origen was befriended by a wealthy lady who was a member of the Christian body. With this financial help he decided to follow his father's advice and to extend his literary studies along the lines which were then in vogue at Alexandria.

---

[8] *Hom. in Jeremiam*, IV. Origen always holds that it is licit to flee from persecution. Cf. *In Matt.*, X, 23.

Within a short time he became a teacher of "grammar," and was thus able to take ample care of his material needs.

THEORY OF STYLE

What was called grammar was a part of the group of subjects which constituted a liberal education at that time. In many curriculums it was listed below geometry and music, as being a less learned subject. It belonged to the post-elementary school and was taught there by a master whose duty it was to prepare the pupils for the higher classes given by the teacher of rhetoric.[9]

In dealing with this new subject Origen adhered to the lines of study he had followed in the catechetical school. There was a prejudice at Alexandria against the pedantry of writers who affected the style of the age of Pericles, and in the matter of vocabulary the Alexandrians were definitely anti-Atticist. They left it to those whom they called sophists to appraise the quality of words and to string them together in sentences of musical cadence. They used to sneer at such writers as "hunters of sweet expressions and amateurs of verbal knicknacks." Clement was too much of a philosopher to allow himself the luxury of hellenizing in his choice of words. Origen also was hostile to the use of grandiose language, for he had long been steeped in the simple poetry of the Sacred Scriptures. He had little fondness for the literary weapon that had been beaten with blows of a hammer and sharpened on a rock, as he used to say. He preferred the word of God, which falls from the mountain by its own weight without any assistance from the hand of man.

Origen is one of the founders of biblical romanticism. His words come as if they were inspired, showing no evidence of careful and patient phrasing. His language is like that of an experienced lecturer who delivers a talk without any copy of his lecture before him and who speaks according to good usage, accurately and without any sign of pedantry. Critics have discovered in Origen's writings a

---

[9] The cycle of studies seems to have been: first, elementary classes under the registrar, who was a master and also a kind of doctor; then classes by the professors of grammar and rhetoric; and instruction by the head of the school (*doctor ipse*), who was the professor of philosophy. The grammar course comprised the epic poets, the comic and tragic poets, and the historians.

number of words and constructions belonging to the Byzantine period. His syntax is less classical than that of Clement or of St. John Chrysostom. His grammar, however, shows a number of resemblances to that favored by the Attic school. He looked upon erudition as an instrument for achieving accuracy rather than as an expedient for a display of elegance. He used it to examine a text according to the Alexandrian methods, to weigh the relative merits of a number of different translations of it, and to clarify the meaning of a verb by a study of the noun from the same root.

THE SCIENCE OF SEMANTICS

What claimed his interest most of all in his studies as a grammarian was what is called today the science of semantics, the science that treats of the evolution of language and of the various phenomena marking its growth. Meaning was to be found, he held, in the word rather than in the phrase, but he often verified his analysis of a word by reference to the context where it was employed. When he analyzed a Hebrew word in search of the hidden meanings it might have acquired in the course of its philological history, he usually checked his findings by reference to the Greek lexicons; often indeed he began his analysis by making the Greek lexicon his starting point. It seemed as if his knowledge of the meanings of words were encyclopedic. In his study of philology he was especially partial to the works of the Stoics, and their influence is clearly visible in his ethical system and in the definitions of his philosophy. From the very beginning of his career as a writer he relied largely upon the encyclopedia of Hierophilus the Stoic, for that work contained a list of the various meanings given to the same word in the different schools—in that of Plato, in the schools of the Stoics, among the followers of Posidonius, and in the different coteries of philosophy at the end of the second century. He used also an Aristotelian lexicon, a dictionary of rhetoric that distinguished the meanings of synonyms or closely related expressions, and a sort of encyclopedia that classified words according to their derivation, starting from nouns, which were considered to be the primitive elements in the science of words and their meaning.

If it is permissible to say that Origen's literary technique contained a special device, that device is to be found in his choice of words and in his expressive grouping of them to make a phrase. This skill can be seen in operation again and again, especially in passages where he is using words from Scripture and where he is balancing them in a phrase which shall be at once concise and eloquent. His concern for the meanings of words, even when he writes in the fervor of religious exaltation, causes his style to remind us, even in little details when we least expect it, of the beautiful designs which the Alexandrians of that time liked to see on their lockets and other ornaments. To all this he added a restrained enthusiasm, marked by gentleness and spirituality. His pupils found his manner irresistible. "He was possessed of a rare combination of a certain sweet grace and persuasiveness, along with a strange power of constraint." [10] His eloquence was at once penetrating and sublime, although he disdained to impress his audience by the ordinary expedients of a public speaker. From the moment he began to speak he had the attention of his hearers.

Origen could not have denied that his literary culture had much to do with his popularity as a teacher. His pupils were content with the enthusiasm he aroused in them, but his critics saw a touch of artfulness in this skill of his. He knew how to expound his teaching, how to discuss it in public, and how to meet all objections with an impressive display of learning. Later in his life he was not too well pleased that his clarity of expression, his fame as a teacher, and his philosophical method should all be glorified with little regard for the doctrine he sought to expound. "When I have thus made several conversions and when the superiority of my arguments or my skill in reasoning have been the means of leading a number of pupils to the true philosophy of Christ and His holy religion, I feel like a man who has begotten children of an alien woman or of a concubine." With this reference to the concubines of whom Abraham had children in his old age, the great master of the Academy made his humorous apology for his widespread fame. "It is obvious that advancing years do not hold me back from such alliances or

[10] Gregory Thaumaturgus, *Panegyric Addressed to Origen*, VI, 78; P.G., X, 1072.

from begetting children in such a way. Let us say rather that this manner of acquiring sons, licit though it was in the Old Law, is more fitting to those who are old, as is evident from this passage about Abraham, who was already a grandfather at the time." [11]

IV. THE CATECHIST

Origen's occupation as a schoolmaster did no harm to his growing prestige, for the Christians of Alexandria understood that the learning and holiness of this man whose father had died as a martyr were far from common. In the view of the ecclesiastical authorities it was not wrong for a Christian to hold a teaching position in a non-Christian school if such an occupation were his means of obtaining his daily bread, but it was obligatory on such Christians to make their young pupils see that pagan morals were sometimes evil as well as to teach them that the gods whose adventures they were studying were simply demons. The necessary ecclesiastical approval was all the more readily given in Origen's case, for it was felt that he was capable of guiding some of the young minds in the direction of the true faith as he watched their progress in their studies.

About this time pupils of another kind began to make their appearance in his classes. From the day of Clement's departure and that of the other Christian teachers whose lives were threatened by the persecution of Septimius Severus, there was no official catechist in the Christian community at Alexandria. But now a number of non-Christians appealed to Origen for instruction in the faith. The first to come to him were two brothers, Plutarch and Heraclas, the former of whom was destined to shed his blood for the faith.

The bishop of Alexandria at the time was Demetrius, who had just succeeded Julian. One of the new Bishop's first acts was to appoint Origen as head of the catechetical school, and the young catechist entered upon his new duties just one year after his father's martyrdom. In the Christian communities this particular post was directly under the care of the local bishop, and the man appointed to it was always a Christian of irreproachable morals, who

[11] *Hom. in Gen.*, XI, 2. Cf. *Hom. in Exod.*, XI, 6. Origen borrowed the idea from Clement, but he handled it more wittily.

was experienced as a teacher and who was known to be capable of
expounding the Sacred Scriptures. In ordinary circumstances Origen's youth might have been a bar to his appointment, but the trials
through which he had come go far to explain why the Bishop decided to entrust him with the education of the catechumens. Origen
was not in holy orders, for a catechist had no rank in the hierarchy
of the Church. In the majority of Christian communities the bishop
merely appointed a man to the position without tying his hands in
any way. The catechist usually remained a layman, and at the
Christian gatherings he took his place in the midst of the catechumens. But when the liturgical prayers came to an end and the
baptized Christians entered upon the essential parts of Christian
worship, it was the custom for the catechist to place his hand on
each catechumen's head and to send them all away.

When his appointment as catechist gave him a definite place in
the life of the Christians at Alexandria, Origen decided to revive
the classes which Clement had conducted. His desire was to develop them to the point where they would constitute a real school
of Christian philosophy, and he proposed to borrow from the Greek
academies of the day the custom whereby the master of the school
shared with his pupils his life of study and meditation. His aim was
to impart instruction in a twofold way, by teaching them the word
of God and by giving them the example of a truly philosophical life.
Therefore he gave up the use of wine, he adopted a regimen of fasting, he slept on the bare ground, and he never wore sandals or shoes.
But he laid no obligation on his followers to observe this mode of
life, for he was still the Christian catechist who taught all without
distinction. At this school of Christian philosophy the students did
not wear the philosopher's robe nor were they bound by anything
like the philosopher's secret as were the students of certain other
academic groups in Alexandria at that time.

PREJUDICE AGAINST PAGAN CULTURE

His duties as a Christian catechist did not interfere with his
work as a teacher of grammar, but it was beginning to be felt by the
Christians that the combination of two such occupations was hardly

fitting. Origen, as a Christian who would be perfect, must make his personal life conform in all respects with his official teaching. In the Christian communities a vigorous movement against pagan culture was beginning to make itself felt, a movement which had been gathering strength since the publication of Tatian's *Discourse*. One result of this resentment against everything pagan was that the aims of the Christian apologists met an almost insuperable obstacle. It was recalled that Emperor Marcus Aurelius was a pagan philosopher and had actually founded the philosophical school at Athens; yet this same Marcus Aurelius had been one of the most bitter opponents of Christianity. Thus the writers of works of Christian apologetics were compelled to yield to the storm of criticism, and the opinion became crystallized among the Christians, that there was something unholy in any policy of agreement whereby it was proposed to bring the teachings of the Bible into harmony with the principles of Greek thought.

It was certainly not difficult for the Christians to believe that the heresies had their birth in an unchecked devotion to philosophy. The heretical sects had been quick to make profit from the revival of Aristotelianism and had found there a number of new weapons with which to attack the Sacred Scriptures. Apelles the Marcionite built his book of syllogisms on each verse of the Book of Genesis and found it easier to discover contradictions there than to write a commentary on the sacred text. His enormous collection of objections served as an arsenal for other heretical writers. A pamphlet of the period shows that the heretics were skilled in this kind of polemic, against which even the most learned among the Christians protested thereafter. "And if anyone brings before them a passage of divine Scripture," Eusebius tells us, "they see whether a conjunctive or a disjunctive form of syllogism can be made from it." The traditions that stemmed from that grove in Athens where Aristotle taught constituted the last word for the heretics. Could a method of argument which was glorified by heretics be adjusted to meet the needs of true believers? From the soul of Tertullian the question thundered: "What indeed has Athens to do with Jerusalem?"

The philosophical skill of the Greeks was, it was said, an invention of the devil. It was no longer necessary to follow their custom of writing treatises on this or that subject. What Christians should do was to hold fast to the one thing necessary. This prejudice against the pagan culture was so strong in the days preceding the persecution of Septimius Severus that Clement referred to it in his preface to the *Stromata*, putting forward a plea there, not without some measure of prudence, on behalf of those Christians who felt an impulse to write. He reminded his readers that, to show the weakness of the pagan philosophy, it was necessary to study it; and he remarked that quite possibly it would be found to contain something good.

The lines of this demarcation between learned and unlearned among the Christians were rendered even more manifest by the edict of Septimius Severus, although that law attacked Christianity in its teachings and in its missionary activities rather than in its inner life. The Christian communities had acquired a definite habit of condemning the learning of the Greeks. Clement's view was: "the crowd has the same fear of Greek philosophy as little children have of the bogey-man; our people are afraid of growing up." At the time Tertullian had just launched his thunder against the unceasing search for truth; the Alexandrians, on the contrary, saw this search as a desire for perfection. But the great African put all his argumentative skill and all his rich knowledge at the service of ignorance. "After the coming of Jesus Christ, we do not need to gratify our curiosity; after the promulgation of the Gospel we do not need to study." He proved to be a brilliant advocate in the cause of the unlearned, and the echoes of his plea ring through the entire sixth book of the *Stromata* where Clement refutes them and proclaims the greatness of the Christian philosopher. But the African would not admit defeat, and some years later he published the applications of his theory. They are found in his treatise on idolatry: to teach grammar or rhetoric is to preach the gods of the Gentiles; no Christian may be permitted to open a school.[12]

[12] In his *De praescriptione*, VII, 7, Tertullian appealed to St. Paul: "Whence spring those fables and endless genealogies and unprofitable questions and words that spread

Though not sharing the sentiments of hostility which the great majority of Christians felt toward pagan culture, Origen could not fail to be disturbed by his own employment as teacher of a pagan subject. He was in a position which, viewed from the standpoint of the ecclesiastical regulations themselves, was tolerated only with a large measure of caution. Without delay he gave up the teaching of grammar, deeming it useless and an obstruction to his sacred studies. No longer would he be obliged to discuss the pagan gods, to utter their names, to expound their qualities, or even to refer to the myths concerning them. Then he sold whatever copies he had made of ancient manuscripts, some of which he had executed with elegance and taste, and was content to receive from the purchaser a daily dole of four obols, on which he managed to live.

ORIGEN'S ABJURATION OF PAGAN LITERATURE

Origen's act of rigorous mortification in abjuring pagan culture obviously put his entire mental life to a severe test. His mind was steeped in the learning of the Greeks, but he made the drastic choice with an enthusiasm that flooded his whole being. His enthusiasm was colored, however, by a tinge of bookishness. That strange mixture of enthusiasm and pedantry is to be found in all the great decisions of his life and was his most subtle danger. In this juncture he fell back upon the ethics of Philo, a moral system which he had studied under Clement. Clement was partial to the system because of the sharp contrast it drew between the perishable nature of the material world and the self-denial of the soul that feeds upon thoughts of immortality. Reviving now the interest which Clement had kindled in his youthful heart for the philosophy of the Jewish exegete, Origen read Philo's little essay, *Evil Often Attacks Good*, and he came to the conclusion that Philo's style would have attracted the attention of the Greek philosophers if he had lived in their day.

In addition to this little publication of the man who was known

---

like a cancer. From all these, when the Apostle would restrain us, he expressly names philosophy as that which he would have us be on our guard against. Writing to the Colossians (2:8), he says: 'Beware lest any man cheat you by philosophy and vain deceit.' "

to the scholars of his own time as the Pythagorean, Origen found still another book to help him. That second book was the *Sentences* of Sextus, a work held in high esteem by the faithful in a day when ascetical literature was far from abundant. He was attracted to the book both because it was written in the style of the Pythagorean school and because the author gave certain maxims of the Gospel a Pythagorean rendering. The mystical philosophy of Pythagoras was much in the air at that time. Indeed, in this third decade of the third century the famous sect was enjoying the last of those periodic renewals which had marked its life for more than eight centuries. Under the name of Pythagoras and through the study circles and the meeting places of the Pythagorean school, Neoplatonism entered the world.

With those two books as his guide, if we are to believe Origen's own account of the matter, he performed an act of self-mutilation which showed "that he had the faith of an ardent soul but not a truly illuminated religion." True purity, he says later, does not consist in doing violence to the body, but in "mortifying the senses for the kingdom of God," [13] in receiving the word of life, and in disdaining the advice of fanatical dreamers.

Are we to seek the cause of this act of self-mutilation in the literal interpretation of a verse of the Gospel? At Alexandria, we know, the system of literal interpretation of the Scriptures was held responsible for all the sins of the world. Were the two books not perhaps as much to blame in this matter as Origen's recollections led him to believe? Would his own impatience not have been sufficient to induce him to such an act? The perfect man, he believed, is not content to free himself from the bonds of flesh and of sin; he tears them apart if God gives him this happiness, because his whole soul longs to lead the life of the angels. Only a few years earlier the young catechist had been impatient for martyrdom, body and soul. He had stood beside those who were about to lay down their lives for the faith. So many times he had gathered his energies together in preparation for the supreme sacrifice, and so many times that grace had been withheld from him! Then he had turned to mortifi-

[13] *In Matt.*, XV, 3; P.G., XIII, 1264.

cation. Was not martyrdom, as Clement had explained, merely an exceptional form of self-mastery and of the love of God which the perfect Christian could practice at every moment of his life? "Those who obey the teachings of the Savior are martyrs in every act whereby they crucify the flesh with its passions and desires." Origen had longed to lay down his life for Christ but was not called to shed his blood. Yet he knew that "the system of mortification enjoined in the Gospel really effects a separation of the soul from the body in an offering of thanksgiving." [14] He threw himself upon the evangelical counsels as if to obtain his revenge.

In one of the works he wrote in those early years he says that "there is within us a mentality which we must destroy, to the end that thus it may become a sacrifice to God." [15] All the moralists of his time who were affected by the prevailing gnosis were of the opinion that our human passions are adventitious forces which the wise man entirely rejects; those forces add to the soul "an earthly and material element with all the different properties of evil." This contempt of the body was shared by Origen in a fanatical degree. Only little by little, as a result of his meditations on the Gospel and on the writings of St. Paul, did he reach an understanding of the inner reformation of the human heart and the humble purification of the Christian soul. "In the same way the martyrs bear witness for a testimony to the unbelieving," he says later, "and so do all the saints whose deeds shine before men. They spend their lives rejoicing in the cross of Christ and bearing witness to the true light." [16]

There is, however, another aspect of his resignation from his post as a teacher of grammar. In spite of that resignation he was still a grammarian. True, he sold his books and manuscripts; but in order to expound the Bible he drew upon the wealth of his early education. The literature and the philosophy of the Greeks were part of that wealth, and a radical elimination of Greek culture from the storehouse of his mind was impossible. He had a lively consciousness of what he owed to the Greeks, especially now when certain

[14] *Strom.*, IV, 5. On this episode in Origen's life, see Bigg, *The Christian Platonists*, p. 154.
[15] *In Psalm.*, 2; P.G., XII, 1109.
[16] *In Joan.*, II, 28; P.G., XIV, 89.

breakers of idols were employing against Hellenism the very skill in the use of language which had come to them by inheritance from the Greeks.

But mortification and culture and all such interests became of secondary interest to him. Everything was subordinate to the mighty adventure on which he had embarked, the pursuit of religious truth, the purification of the mind and the heart, the great invisible and mysterious world to be discovered in his studies of the word of God.

CHAPTER II

In the Service of the *Logos*

IN TEACHING the Christian religion Origen used the method by which he himself had learned it: he read a passage of Scripture to his pupils and then made his comments. This indeed was part of his duty as a catechist, but he soon began to wonder if it were possible to develop those elementary lectures to a point where they could be employed as an established means of appealing to the more highly educated Christians.

BIBLICAL EXEGESIS

At first his commentaries on the Bible were directed to the refutation of the Judaeo-Christians or of the Jews themselves in the controversies that raged in Alexandria at the time. The *Dialogue with Tryphon* is an illustration of his interest and his skill in this kind of apologetic. Then the rising tide of the Marcionite heresy forced him to the study of the Old Testament in its significance as a preparation for the Christian religion. In this new activity his procedure was to lay down certain principles of exegesis and then to show how they could be applied to one passage after another taken from a collection of texts, chiefly from the prophetical books. Such a collection of scriptural passages had been made by Melito of Asia, who had been one of Clement's teachers. Melito's book was called *Extracts* from the Old Testament, and it contained a series of explanatory notes whereby the author clarified the figures that foretold the life of Jesus. Origen was familiar with this work. Undoubtedly he was also acquainted with a number of Old Testament studies published by Pantaenus, who had made a careful analysis of the way the prophetical books were written.

Meanwhile the publications of the heretics were steadily growing in number. Apelles the Marcionite brought forth a verse-by-verse criticism of a part of the Old Testament, and Heracleon made a study of the Fourth Gospel, setting forth many of the ingenious and romantic notions of the Valentinian heretics. These and other such heretical publications made a stir among educated Christians, and the ecclesiastical authorities at Alexandria felt the need of presenting to the learned class among the brethren a satisfying explanation of the various texts in dispute. Wherefore Eusebius says: "In the work called Hypotyposes, to sum up briefly, Clement has given abridged accounts of all canonical Scripture, not omitting the disputed books."

But in his *Stromata*, Clement did not dare come face to face with the problem. Realizing the harshness of style in which many of the Old Testament passages were written, he was afraid of their effect upon the unity of orthodox thought. Satisfying himself with the conclusion that a number of the new converts were not yet capable of taking this strong food, he preferred the use of paraphrases. "If among the body of the faithful," he said, "my choice of words is considered to be sometimes different from the actual expressions employed in the Gospel, let everyone remember that my language draws its breath of life from the Scriptures themselves. My words are founded on Scripture, and I claim that they remain faithful to the biblical thought even where they do not reproduce the actual biblical expression." Origen refused to have any part in such apprehension as this. He based his entire doctrine on his commentaries on the Sacred Scriptures. His theology was, above everything else, a system of exegesis. By his technique of spiritual interpretation, he succeeded in making the Bible accessible to every Christian who had any feeling for holy things.

I. SYMBOLISM

The Academy of Alexandria is the cradle of symbolism, an interpretative device that has encountered both success and defeat in literary history. Adopted by the greatest theologians of the West, it inspired the preaching, the mysticism, and the art of the Middle Ages. It was used in the sculptured porches and the stained-glass windows of the great cathedrals, in natural history and in poems, even in the songs of the troubadours lifting the aspirations of the human heart to an ideal of beauty. It may not be an essential part of Christianity, but it is one of its by-products: the crown which cannot be removed without lessening the beauty of the face, and one of the oldest adornments of the civilization inspired by the Gospels.

The period was brief in which Origen was meditating on "the Word of God according to the flesh and the letter, without yet understanding it." [1] Soon he was asking himself if it were really necessary to accept literally the evangelical counsel of not possessing two garments or of girding oneself with a sword for the day of tribulation. By way of answer he told himself that the books of the wise are full of symbols and enigmas. He found the strongest possible reason to say the same thing of the Bible, for it speaks of God, of the Unknown whose inner nature can be expressed by no human word. But Jesus came for the purpose of making God known to men. Therefore there exists a method of discovering God, a technique of study which, with the help of divine grace, must ultimately lead the soul to the knowledge of true wisdom. In symbolism Origen would find this higher technique.

SPIRITUAL INTERPRETATION

From the very beginning of his biblical studies Origen sought the spiritual interpretation because it is of the essence of the mission of Christ and also of the intercourse which the Christian soul enjoys with God. The voice of Jesus can be heard as He talks to the angels, summoning them to assist Him in the work of redemption. Then He is seen turning to His disciples as He calls upon them to hasten the triumph which He has promised them in His holy discourse. The mystical meaning and its moral application become one and the same thing as the Savior proceeds with His instruction.

But definite facts and a recognized history which has often been the subject of human commentaries are also part of the sacred text. They are concrete elements that we cannot afford to neglect. We must preserve the literal meaning and hew close to the line of the facts whenever we can do so. We know, for example, that certain

[1] *In Matt.*, XV, 3; P.G., XIII, 1257.

psalms recount for us David's sin and his unhappiness in the revolt
of Absalom, and we penetrate the surface of those facts in search
of a more mysterious meaning within them. No disciple of Christ
can achieve the perfect degree of faith without a study of the moral
truth or the spiritual meaning enshrined in the facts of the Gospel.

In Origen's early studies of the Bible, the allegorical method had
three definite stages. First, there came the study of the life of Christ;
this study comprised, above everything, the contemplation of His
manifestations of divinity and of what the moderns call His mysteries—His Passion and death, His Resurrection and Ascension
into heaven. Secondly, there comes the application of the lessons
learned from the study of Christ, whose mysteries are variously
reproduced in the drama of every human soul. This, however, is an
invisible world that we are unable to explore at first but that we shall
know better as we proceed, for there are secrets of human destiny
which this method of studying Scripture can make clear to us. Lastly
there is the Church. Being of a spiritual essence, the Church also
must be considered from the allegorical viewpoint. It is the society
of human souls, and the spirit that animates it is the spirit that inspires all real holiness.

This manner of interpreting Scripture is regarded as the discovery
of the Academy of Alexandria. Origen, it must be noted, made
something of a change in it; it became more intellectual in his
theological system and more moral in its applications to the life of
the Christians. In the form which he gave it, it has always tended to
nourish the inner life of the soul. It was not quite what popular
tradition understood by figure or allegory. For example, the old
idea was that certain happenings recounted in the Old Testament
were foreshadowings of the life of Christ, and that certain personages of the Old Testament were imperfect outlines of what the
Messiah would be; the coming of the Redeemer was felt to be foretold in His saints, Josue and David.

METHOD OF SYMBOLISM

This did not satisfy Origen. Symbolism, he asserted, has a higher
duty than that of linking a number of historical facts to the Gospel.

It is not enough to see in Absalom an image of the devil, nor is it sufficient to apply the noblest metaphors of the psalms to the glorious body of Christ.[2] There is a possibility that the biblical exegete may adhere too closely to the literal sense, may become a slave to the historical meaning, and he may even become the opponent of allegory, however surprising this reproach may appear to be. In Origen's view, an interpretation of a scriptural passage was not spiritual if it held fast to the material facts of the Gospel, if it failed to cross the threshold of the world invisible, or if it did not aim at turning men's minds to the contemplation of the things of God.

The prophetical or figurative interpretation compares Moses with the Gospel, with the New Testament. Symbolism, on the other hand, transposes the entire Bible, the books of Moses and the books which recount the history of Jesus, lifting them to a super-terrestrial plane. Studied in this manner, the Bible opens to us riches old and new from the treasury of the Father of us all. "In some way," a critic has said, "it imparts a sublimity to everything: to Jewish history and to Gospel history, to the various events and to the words in which they are told, to all the narratives and to the entire sacred text."

Now, to make any such transposition of the biblical narrative the exegete must know that narrative thoroughly. He should not be indifferent to the fact that David was lacking in vigilance and that his neglect of his kingly duties offered Absalom the opportunity of revolt, since all this is a picture of human souls that yield to sleep and thus fall into sin. He must not forget that when Ezechiel recounts to the Babylonian captives his vision of the dried bones, the meaning of the passage is that souls who have become the prisoners of their own sins can be restored to spiritual life by the help of divine grace. But the spiritual meaning of a text is not always obvious. Some texts seem, at first sight, to present almost insuperable difficulties; they appear to contradict the majesty of God or to be unworthy of it. In such cases the very difficulty of the text compels the exegete to realize that a symbol is hidden beneath the verbal form of the biblical passage; and the further problem of bringing

[2] *In Psalm.*, 18, 16; *P.G.*, XIII, 1244.

any such text into harmony with its context drives him to an effort to find the hidden meaning. The hidden meaning, it must be remarked, is never unrelated to the literal sense.

Such was the method which enabled the Alexandrian School to turn its attention from the mere facts recorded in biblical history and to devote to the minutest detail in the inspired books all the force of its exegetical skill. In that great School no one saw the Sacred Scriptures as a set of cryptograms, a charge often made against Alexandria, or as a collection of cabalistic writings. The student at Alexandria learned to love the literal sense, and to revere the straightforward and wholesome expressions which bore a meaning that was obvious at the first glance; but at the same time he was taught that not one iota must be lost from the full meaning of a biblical expression. Everything—the events, the miracles, the parables—bore within it some vestige of infinite wisdom.

The world of sense, which never leads us entirely astray, thus forms the first stage in the application of the allegorical method. Then there follows the subtle logic of the heart. When a man knows how to listen to the inner voice according to the rules of holy Church, the Bible speaks to him in the language of the saints. The divine light of the Church shines through the obscurities of the prophets, and the Church's own language affords us the best means of understanding the deeply religious meaning of the words of the Sacred Scriptures. In the Epistles of St. Paul there are words that give us the key to a psalm, and "even the smallest penetration into the meanings of such words can open immense perspectives to our eyes." [3] When we read the words of the Psalmist, "I have cried to the Lord with my voice," do we not instantly recognize that cry as being one with the unspeakable groaning which, according to the Epistle to the Romans, marks the prayers of the saints? St. Paul himself tells us that spiritual things are to be compared with spiritual things, and the Bible becomes known to a man as soon as he develops an ability to find more and more of those links between one passage and another. Such parallels often throw light on the meaning of the text, and then "the Word itself shines in our hearts."

[3] *De princip.*, IV, 2, 3.

Analogies such as these are subtle, but they are not arbitrary. Certain modern critics have denounced as a pious fraud what they regard as the procedure of making a text say a thousand things which its author never dreamed of: "Something was found in a phrase or in a word which recalled an idea already existing in the exegete's own mind, but whenever the literal meaning refused to be fitted into the ingenious parallel he wished to establish, he simply refused to see the literal meaning at all. Then the text assumed a symbolical meaning."

ORIGEN'S USE OF SYMBOLISM

Although it is not part of the historian's duty to deliver a verdict on the value of the applications of the allegorical method, we find it necessary to deny that Origen used symbolism in any such way. "And these things will be gathered together when we also read and know and, remembering them, at a fitting time compare things spiritual, not comparing things that cannot be compared with one another, but things which admit of comparison, and which have a certain likeness of diction signifying the same thing, and of thoughts and of opinions, so that by the mouth of two or three or more witnesses from the Scripture, we may establish and confirm every word of God." [4] The fact that such likenesses and parallels are numerous need not cause astonishment, for the Bible is, in its deepest meaning, a unity whereby the sacred books are explained and completed by one another. However detailed a study of the Bible may be, this great basic unity must always be kept in view.

Thus the more spiritual books of Scripture are a help in the interpretation of the others. St. John's Gospel is the key to the rest of the Gospel narratives. The New Testament and especially the great Epistles throw light on the entire Bible. What comes before is explained by what comes after; or, to speak more accurately, the Christian revelation gives us a special example which ought to be our guide in every study of the Scriptures. When we learn how the Word taught His apostles, we learn how He spoke to the prophets. The parables of the Gospel are the final stage in the long process of

[4] *In Matt.*, X, 15; P.G., XIII, 872.

efflorescence. Formerly God used the less perfect forms of the biblical narrative, of the prophecies and the canticles, as a means of imparting His mysteries under different forms to those souls that knew how to ponder the meaning of the message.

The range of this theory of allegory reached far beyond the lines of the controversies of Origen's day. Neither the dangers of the Marcionite heresy nor the attraction of Hellenism can offer a sufficient explanation of its development in the hands of Origen.

When Marcion placed the religion of Jesus in opposition to the God of Israel, the Church had to find a justification for those Old Testament texts which the heretic had twisted into a contradiction of the Gospel narrative. Thus the spiritual interpretation by the heretics was applied to the rites of Israel, to the anger of Jahveh, and to the atrocities of the ancient wars, all with the purpose of destroying the appeal of the biblical narrative. When Origen set his mind to the study of difficult passages like these, he resorted to symbolism on more than one occasion. But to reduce his method of exegesis to this kind of apologetics is merely to see a secondary aspect of it. Origen employed the allegorical method in many a passage of the New Testament which the heretics accepted without reserve, and on the other hand he put it aside when he was dealing with the outstanding problems of the Marcionite heresy. For example, he gave the literal explanation of the anger of Jahveh, relying on his dictionaries for his defense of the literal meaning. His doctrine of providential remedies and of God's guidance of men enabled him to justify easily, without any subterfuge whatever, the harshness of the history of Israel. In the hope of causing embarrassment to the partisans of literalism, he took a pleasure in discovering exegetical difficulties where none had been discovered before. The truth is that in the use of his allegorical method he was not primarily concerned with the heretics. In principle the method was similar to that in use in certain rabbinical schools and in the majority of the heretical sects, not excluding the Marcionism of his time.

THE ALLEGORICAL METHOD

His application of the allegorical method to the problems of the Pentateuch was so successful that the critics of his day might have logically charged him with the hypocrisy of remaining a Christian in spite of his devotion to Moses. Instead, and with more show of truth, they accused him of an equivocation which allowed him to remain a Greek in spite of his professed love of the Bible. They said that in his zeal to convert unbelievers he would have hidden the poverty or the absurdity of the Jewish Scriptures under a fog of commentaries which had no relation to the text. They taunted him with inventing textual difficulties in order to apply a method borrowed "from the mysteries of the Greeks." "Your knowledge," it was said to him, "comes from our culture; your methods of study and your very teachings are themselves the products of our school."

In their use of the allegorical method the Alexandrians, it must be confessed, unwisely yielded to the impulse to multiply textual parallels, and sooner or later their critics would seize upon this practice in order to accuse them of plagiarism. Clement indeed had compared the Greek mysteries with the Christian mysteries and had stated that every religion is founded on the need of a revelation. He used to employ figures of speech familiar to his audiences in the effort to make their ears accustomed to the words of the Christian revelation. "All those, in a word, who have spoken of divine things, both barbarians and Greeks, have veiled the first principles of things, and have delivered the truth in enigmas and symbols, and allegories and metaphors, and such like tropes." [5] In his public discourses he gave his audience the first thoughts coming to his mind and the parallels easiest for them to understand. Hence comes his comparison of Moses and Pythagoras, and also the fable of Prodicus of Ceus about Virtue and Vice. Allegory was, for him, of secondary importance.[6]

Origen took quite a different view. He made the allegorical method an essential part of his theological equipment. His critics

[5] *Strom.*, V, 4.
[6] *Ibid.*, 5.

assert that his plan was to use the Bible as a means of introducing into Christianity a number of doctrines which the faithful would never have accepted if they had known them for what they were. He has been accused of desiring to resolve the conflict between popular tradition and enlightened religion by a sort of philosophical sleight-of-hand, transforming Christian beliefs from within while he took care to leave the verbal formulas intact. In all this he yielded, they said, to the same urge that impelled the Stoics and the Neoplatonists to draw from the Homeric fables and the Platonic myths a moral system, a set of secret dogmas, an entire philosophy. To express the objection in a summary form, the spiritual interpretation was merely a safety valve for educated men whose minds were at once religious and rationalist; such men wished to accept the teachings of Christianity but were embarrassed by religious traditions alien to their type of mind.

In reply to all this, it must be conceded that the Alexandrians were far from hesitant in giving a Christian approval to the cultural inheritance that had come from the Greeks. At the same time their application of the allegorical method to the interpretation of Scripture was something more than a mere trick to tear the Bible from its spiritual framework. In several passages of his *Genesis*, Origen makes no effort to avoid the literal sense, although the creation of the world, of the stars, and of man was a stumbling block to the philosophers of antiquity. The truth is that the allegorical method began to be employed by Christian thinkers as soon as they faced the problem of the destiny of the human soul. Thus Greek notions found their way into Christian exegesis, not as a means of perpetuating the philosophies of the Greeks but rather as part of a technique designed to strengthen the traditions of Alexandrian theology.

It would not have been difficult to Hellenize the Christian teaching, if the Alexandrians had any such intention. At the Academy many religious commentaries were in use which were in agreement with Greek cosmology and other profane sciences. Clement, for example, borrowed from Philo a famous interpretation which represented the ornaments of the high priest, described in Exodus, as a symbol of the four elements. Origen had no love for any such explanations; they pertained to the physical, and they were not spiritual because they failed to lift the mind to the contemplation of spiritual things. "Let us come," he used to say, "to things we can reason about," meaning thereby the mysterious work of Jesus in the hearts of the saints. The symbolism which Origen planned to put into operation was a literary method capable of serving the purposes of Christian meditation and prayer.

Abundant evidence of this is found in his homelies, delivered by him to congregations of the faithful in church. Those popular sermons were as rich in allegory as the learned commentaries written by the little group of his advanced pupils. When he explained the Scriptures to the faithful, assuredly his exegesis was not dictated by a preoccupation over what judgment might be passed upon it by experts in biblical science. But even as he talked before such a mixed assembly, he remembered that the better educated people in his audience had need of a spiritual food to attract them to the Christian banquet table.

ALEXANDRIAN SYMBOLISM AND PAGAN MYTHOLOGY

Without a doubt, then, Alexandrian symbolism is a Christian product. Greek commentaries were concerned with the myths of the gods, and the philosophers of antiquity believed that the purpose of those fables was to cover the sacred learning with a veil or to conceal it with a necessary falsehood. Christianity, however, had the parable, the efficacy of which lay in the fact that it appealed both to the cultured and to the illiterate; and in the hearts of the educated it took root and came to blossom. "Every man is his own farmer. His soul is like a field to be plowed, and the oxen he drives there are the holy thoughts which Scripture has given him. Under the plowshare of the Logos his soul receives the seed of God's grace and becomes, as it were, a new field. On the fertile soil he casts the seed of God's teaching, the seed of the law and of the prophets and of the Gospel, and all such teaching he holds in his memory for his hours of meditation and prayer." [7] Parable is, according to its He-

---

[7] *In Luc., frag.* XXX.

brew derivation, something that stimulates us to think; it is therefore the beginning of a gradual process of divine instruction which
ends by flooding the soul with the light of truth. The Bible in its
entirety is a parable which, in much the greater part, is also a history. "He that hath ears to hear, let him hear." Under the visible
facts of biblical history the throb of God's providential works can
be clearly heard.

A reminder of the ancient parable is to be found in the way certain of the Alexandrians approach the study of the Platonist fables.
They show no desire to reduce these fables either to the historical
meaning or to pure allegory; while seeming to regard the fables as
partly real, they find the fables' chief value in the fact that they ele-
vate the mind above the level of sense to the knowledge of spiritual
things. Used in this way, symbolism readily becomes an instrument
of the mystical life. It helped Origen to discard the material picturizations which several of his predecessors had employed in their
teachings on heaven and on the ascension of the elect. At a time
when the faithful were being offered repulsive stories about the
gods and were being promised a heaven where they would enjoy all
the delights of the flesh, he purified the atmosphere of the Christian
pulpit. He made it plain that the spiritual interpreters of Holy Scripture were primarily interested in the progressive stages of prayer and
contemplation. In his *Commentary on the Gospel of St. John* he
gave special attention to an exposition of the first and final stages in
the illuminative way of prayer. He called this the anagogical meaning of the sacred text, preferring the word "anagogical" to any
other.[8]

These fortunate results were sometimes purchased at too high a
cost. In an age when the Christian revelation was at first sight a
definite fact of history, the Alexandrians were too ready to forget
that history in their enthusiasm for the mystical sense. It must be
remembered in their defense that they opened up many a new path
of Christian study, and it must also be recalled that Christian tra-

---

[8] *In Joan.* The word "anagogical" applies especially to the descriptions of the illuminative and the unitive way. The word "allegory" was that by which the Origenist method
was known and contested at Antioch.

dition has always approved the mystical sense as a nutritious food for souls dedicated to the pursuit of holiness. Discussing the Church's attitude on this matter, Cardinal Newman, who has never been considered hostile to exegetical works of practical research, noted "the disinclination of her teachers to confine themselves to the mere literal interpretation of Scripture. Her most subtle and powerful method of proof, whether in ancient or in modern times, is the mystical sense." [9] To condemn this method of biblical study is to reject an important element of Christian spirituality.

THE OLD TESTAMENT AND THE GOSPELS

Suppose for a moment that the Alexandrian method of interpreting Scripture is merely a systematization of nonsense. How, then, are we to explain its attraction for the millions of saintly men and women who were familiar with the religious teachings of the Bible? It cannot be said that everything in Holy Scripture is the product of caprice or is something without special meaning. Parables are found in the Gospel, and there are parts of the Old Testament that were considered neither as figurative nor as part of the visions of the prophets. Spiritual exegesis, applied to such parts of the Old Testament, is a definite method which consists in probing for the deepest meaning of the text; if such a text refers merely to something historical, its inner meaning is sought in the atmosphere of the thoughts and events to which it has given birth. In other words, a tree is known by its fruits. It has been said by a Jewish critic that "each of the revelations of Christianity realizes on the spiritual plane what in the Old Testament had, and undoubtedly still has, the value of a dead weight of flesh, something of a dulness that is almost animal. . . . The Gospels gave the Bible a new life by delivering the ancient books from their peculiar kind of grossness. . . . The Gospel is merely something that has developed from the Bible, and henceforth mankind reaches the Father through the ministry of the Son." We cannot assume that the early Fathers were ignorant of the historic form taken by this development. St. Irenaeus, in fact, had a definite theory of a progressive education which God

[9] Newman, *Essay on the Development of Christian Doctrine*, p. 342.

gives to mankind. The theory was well known in Alexandria, but Alexandrian symbolism treated it from quite a different point of view. What Origen and his fellow workers did was to place the two Testaments one on top of the other instead of placing them side by side. They considered the Old Testament an emanation from the Gospel, and the two Testaments as an emanation from the transcendent Word of God, an outpouring of the ineffable Wisdom. Thus the entire plan of revelation arranges itself against the background of eternity.

If it is true that the Judaeo-Christian message receives its form by a soul or spirit which proclaims it a revelation unique in the history of religious beliefs, it must be admitted that symbolism is right in principle. In the way Origen used it, the symbolic method gave him a key to more than one difficult passage of the Prophecies and of the Gospels, enabling him to find in those passages different gradations, different spiritual levels as it were, of the religious sentiment. In studies of that nature not even the most rigorous historical analysis has been able to deny his conclusions. One explanation of this is to be found in the intimate knowledge he had of the countries and peoples of the East, whose modes of life in his day differed little from the manner in which the biblical personages had lived. In addition, he was gifted with a mentality both religious and poetic and was therefore quite at home in dealing with the figures of speech employed in religious poetry. Certainly no writer has given a more eloquent rendering to the bitter anguish of the Lamentations or to the repentance and hope of the psalms. His biblical commentaries are remarkable more for their accuracy of detail than for any oddities of expression they contain. Perhaps he fell into many errors of interpretation. Yet his grasp of the inner meaning of the parables of pardon and of God's benevolence ought to remind us that he possessed in abundance a gift of spiritual penetration which many of us may lack. If we take a parable at its face value, are we likely to derive more spiritual advantage from it than if we delve again and again to find its inner meaning? How are we helped by the story of the laborers in the vineyard who came at the eleventh hour if we read it merely as a discourse on the wage system? When

Christ spoke to the multitude in the parable of the talents, was He discussing nothing more than the interest on a loan?

II. THE JEWISH TRADITIONS

The development of Christian exegesis owes something to the learned Jews of Alexandria, for the Bible had been the sacred book of Israel long before it became that of the Christian Church. In their attitude toward the new teachings the rabbinical schools of Egypt had the advantage of an older tradition which was at once national and religious, in addition to which they were equipped with a thorough knowledge of the Hebrew tongue. St. Justin in his *Dialogue with Tryphon* represents a Jewish rabbi concluding the argument by advising his Christian opponent to go back to his studies.

In the course of his biblical studies Origen found it advisable to become acquainted with the leaders of Jewish thought in Alexandria. He had no intention of engaging in controversy with them, nor did he propose to adopt their methods of exegesis. His approach to them shows that an author does not always borrow from his contemporaries what is in harmony with his own type of mind. In spite of his own interest in the allegorical method he did not go to the rabbis for any lessons in its use. He sought from them something he himself lacked: a literal or literary commentary of the Bible.

We have already pointed out that the allegorical method cannot dispense with the literal analysis of the sacred text. Literalism is, in fact, the foundation of allegory. In studying his plans for the lofty edifice he proposed to build, Origen decided that the foundations should be reared on solid rock, however limited in extent those foundations would prove to be. It was a wise decision, typical of that extreme prudence which is to be found in many of the mystics for whom everything has a meaning. In the eyes of the true mystic everything that exists bears the mark of the divine, and Origen saw God's signature in every element of Holy Scripture. When he read one of the holy books he saw a divine message in the life of the biblical personage whose hand penned the inspired words, in the various historical events, in the numbers of characters mentioned

in the book and in their names. He reaped profit even from difficulties and apparent contradictions in the sacred text, for all such
obstacles served only to drive him to further study. Thus Origen's
free and independent methods of study had the unexpected result
of putting him in touch with Jewish publications comparable with
the works of the outstanding philologists of Alexandria.

TRANSLATIONS OF THE BIBLE

Grammatical commentaries on the Bible were no novelty in the
Academy of Alexandria. Pantaenus had written such a commentary, and Clement himself had discussed the authenticity of the
Epistle to the Hebrews by comparing its style with that of the *Acts
of the Apostles*. But in the fashion set later by the humanists of the
Renaissance, Origen planned to go direct to the sources. According
to Eusebius: "So earnest and assiduous was Origen's research into
the divine words that he learned the Hebrew language, and pro-
cured as his own the original Hebrew Scriptures which were in the
hands of the Jews." He is known, however, to have been concerned
with the original texts even in his earlier writings; so it is probable
that he had already picked up some acquaintance with Hebrew
from other Alexandrian writers. But their knowledge of the language must have been far from perfect, and Origen knew less of it
than they did. In this difficulty he studied all the Greek translations
of the Bible available to him as well as the Septuagint, a version
which was popular among the Christians in Alexandria at the time.
In the course of his investigations he managed to obtain the principal Greek versions in addition to those which he had already known.

Every translator is an interpreter, and those Greek versions collected by Origen revealed the most diverse tendencies among the
Judaeo-Greek communities or the Judaeo-Christian groups. One of
those translators was Symmachus, a Judaeo-Christian from Samaria
and a member of the Ebionites. Faithful to the Law of the Old
Testament, he diluted the anthropomorphisms of the Mosiac teaching and produced a work which was full of moralizings. He left behind him a number of notebooks that Origen afterward received as
a gift in the form in which the author himself had prepared them

with a view to publication. Very different was Aquila's version, published fifty years earlier, a few years before the appearance of the Marcionite heresy. The author was a Jew, a native of Pontus, the province that would be the birthplace of Marcion. Aquila's translation was slavishly literal; it rendered each Hebrew word in its principal Greek equivalent without the slightest concern for the general meaning of the phrase in which it occurred. This word-by-word version proved to be of immense value to a man like Origen, who had set himself the task of learning the Hebrew vocabulary of the Bible. Origen indeed used it in preference to other translations. In addition to these versions by Symmachus and Aquila he became acquainted with three other Greek renderings; one of these three was that by Theodotion.

With the help of all this equipment Origen proceeded to explain to his classes the psalms as they were given in the Septuagint, and he soon formed the habit of comparing the different Greek versions and of taking notes on their divergences. Thus it happened that his psalter was enriched with textual variants, to each of which a brief commentary was attached. This was the origin of the *scholia* afterward used by St. Jerome. It was also the preparation for Origen's own great work, the Hexapla.

THE TWO SCHOOLS

In judging the value of those Greek versions, Origen found it useful to check them by comparing them with the Jewish traditions. In this research he was the philologist rather than the theologian, and his purpose in consulting the rabbis was to obtain nothing more than the mere outlines of the traditions and the preliminary notions of the way such traditions were applied to the exegesis of the Bible. From the result of these inquiries it was easy for him to see that there existed two different schools of rabbinical thought. He sought information from some Jewish converts who were in attendance at his classes in the Academy, but their expected contributions were not of the philological kind he required. Their mentality was too richly colored, he found, by the theology they were studying as well as by the allegorism of Philo. He himself recounts for us a remark made by one of those converts from Judaism: "God is not a tyrant but a king, and His kingdom is not based on force. He uses persuasion, wishing His subjects to accept His rule." Origen saw in those words merely a statement of the man's belief in the Alexandrian doctrine of divine philanthropy. Perhaps a similar influence was at work in Origen himself when he was composing his moral exhortations for his *Commentary* on the Psalms and the Pentateuch.

The Jewish allegories had little influence on Origen. His work on Philo, however, shows some traces of them, but we should remember that his interest lay in Philo's system of thought rather than in his exegesis. With his Christian viewpoint he found Jewish allegories cold and lifeless. They lacked what the emerging Christian exegesis possessed, something that would have imparted to them the warmth of life. They needed a view of the Bible as a whole, a general system of interpretation, an ideal that would rouse the ancient texts from slumber, an inspiration that would given them a new sense of authority in the consciousness of a long-cherished hope at last realized.

One of those allegories appears twice in his works, but he takes no trouble to do more than mention it. It is a laborious and prosaic thing. "A Jewish rabbi who had been converted to Christianity asked himself why the king of Moab employed this figure of speech, 'as the ox is wont to eat the grass to the very roots.' The reason was, he said, that the ox in browing uses its tongue like a scythe to cut what it finds. Thus the Israelites use their mouths and their lips as fighting weapons, destroying their enemies by borrowing the words of their challenge and using them for a means of offense."

In place of such unpromising material gleaned from Symmachus and the others, he discovered a literary mine as soon as he became acquainted with the Jews of Palestine and began to study their concise and neat commentaries. Those Palestinian writers rarely used allegory and then only for the purpose of making some moral reflections on the text. Origen found in their works the very thing he needed, derivations of words and concise accounts of their development. During his first visit to Syria he took occasion to consult the patriarch Jullus as well as a famous rabbi, who was probably Rabbi Hoschaya of Caesarea, seeking from each of those two prominent Jews their opinion on some biblical texts and on the authors of the psalms. Another man from whose scholarship he profited was a leader of the Palestinian Jews whom he simply calls the Hebrew without giving us the man's name. From him Origen obtained a number of textual interpretations mainly concerned with the meaning of the words used in the various biblical passages that came up for discussion; the passages were concerned chiefly with incidents of biblical history or with the names of biblical personages.

In the course of these researches in the Hebrew language Origen compiled his lexicon of the Bible by studying the etymology of geographical expressions and by analyzing all the biblical nouns which appeared likely to yield a mystical meaning. He was especially interested in the opening verses of each of the prophecies, for he believed that the inner meaning of the prophetical book was to be found in them. He made a collection of Jewish legends referring to the immortality of the prophet Elias and to the restoration of the city of Sodom. In the course of this inquiry he made ample use of the traditions of the Palestinian Jews.

He became a sincere admirer of the rabbinical custom of comparing different biblical passages with one another and, wherever possible, of establishing connections between them. This was merely one of a number of the exegetical methods in use among the Jews. Origen drilled himself in the application of it, and it later became the principal instrument of Christian exegesis. He himself tells us of a charming figure of speech once used by a rabbi. "The inspired Scriptures are like a house where all the rooms are locked and where there is no key in any door. The keys are actually in the house but are scattered about the corridors and on the stairs, and, moreover, no key unlocks the door near which it is found. Therefore both time and trouble are needed in the effort to fit each key to its own door. In some such way the Bible is a mansion of many locked doors. We have but one way of unlocking the doors and of understanding the numerous obscurities: to apply patiently to one text after another the various principles of exegesis we find scattered throughout the sacred text." [10] Thus spoke the rabbi, but the task confronting the Christian was less arduous. "The divine Logos has David's key," says Harnack; "and when He became flesh, He employed this key to open the Scriptures, which had been locked and closed until the day of His coming."

[10] *In Psalm., Praef.; P.G.*, XII, 1080.

CHAPTER III

Reform of the School

I. THE JOURNEY TO ROME

EVEN while he was devoting his efforts to the study of the primitive text of the Bible, he was eager to go to the sources of Christian tradition. Drawn by the antiquity of the Church of Rome, to which Christians flocked from all parts of the world "to look upon a queen in her garments of gold and her shoes of gold," he arrived in Rome during the pontificate of Zephyrinus. We know that Zephyrinus died in the year 217 and that Origen was in Arabia before the year 215. Therefore his visit to the Eternal City could not have occurred after 214. Another argument for this date is to be found in the fact that, although he had not yet published any of his major works, his name was already known to Christian scholars in Rome; those men accepted him as an authority on the Bible and willingly opened to him their copies of the Greek translations of the Scriptures. The most probable date of the Rome visit is, then, about the end of 210 or the beginning of 211. He met there the most renowned theologian of the time, the Roman churchman Hippolytus. This man's personal life, his methods of study, and his general teaching made such an impression on the young professor from Alexandria that the latter took him for a model in the writing of his earlier works. The esteem must have been mutual, for in the course of an address which Hippolytus gave at Rome on the glory of our Lord and Savior he named Origen as one of those who had been associated with him.

THE EXAMPLE OF HIPPOLYTUS

Hippolytus was a few years older than Origen. His early works gave no indication of the doctrinal differences which were later to incur the disapproval of the bishop of Rome. He was a brilliant speaker and a profound theologian, ever ready to glorify the voice of the Logos and the manifestations of God to men. He preached the approach of the last day and the triumph of Chirst on the Day of Judgment. When he spoke in public his words possessed an ardor which sometimes resembled the burning zeal of a prophet. The swift current of his eloquence was in marked contrast to the spacious dignity of the great concepts he sought to expound. In those great concepts the more contemplative soul of Origen was already beginning to find much to ponder and much to enjoy. But intellectual delights were only a part of what Origen learned to enjoy at Rome. He learned also that he must see things in their objective setting. It was a time when both in the composition of their discourses and in their style of delivery the Roman preachers began to display a definite tendency for realism. This may have been owing to the influence of St. Irenaeus, but it was certainly directed and guided by an Italian sense of objectivity, a sense of balance which, even in the domain of symbolism, takes account of the value of clear and lively observation.

Hippolytus had already published a number of works in which he made use of the allegorical method but which had not yet fallen into the lines of a definite system. Although employing allegory, he did not fail to include a number of concrete explanations in those works. Many of his commentaries, particularly his *Discourses on Daniel*, begin with a historical or literary introduction. The same is to be noted with regard to his *Commentary on the Psalms*, which is properly numbered among his earlier works. It contains a preface, differing very slightly from Origen's preface. Indeed the two writers usually follow the same general method, and the resemblances between them are so close that a critic is easily misled when dealing with fragments that may have come from one or the other commentary. Each of the two writers studies the number of the psalms, their authors and their titles, and the different proofs establishing their authenticity. Each states also what particular psalms are to be attributed to Moses. Each has his own theory of the exegetical principles determining which of the remaining psalms are the work of David and which are the productions of his assistant poets.

In an effort to determine which of the two commentaries was published first, we are inclined to believe that Origen's commentary, which is the more scholarly, succeeded that published by Hippolytus. Besides, if Origen's commentary had come first, Hippolytus was not the man to fail to borrow from the work of an exegete as learned in the Hebrew writings as Origen undoubtedly was. On the other hand, Origen's work on the psalms contains a number of references to opinions already advanced, and one of those references is to a fragment of Hippolytus, the authenticity of which is clearly established. When Origen comes to the discussion of this particular passage from Hippolytus, he corrects it by a comparison of versions that were unknown to his predecessor. In addition to all this, Origen's studies in theology owed much to allegories or formulas which he had found pleasing in the works of the Roman churchman, even when he considered them incomplete or too summary. Many a time the reader can find echoes of Hippolytus in Origen's *Commentary on the Gospel of St. John* or in his books on the Canticle of Canticles.

CHRISTOLOGICAL DISPUTES

In studying the Scriptures from a theological point of view, Origen's main interest was held by passages treating of the eternity of the Logos or of the Incarnation. But he was not satisfied with the conventional manner of describing in subdued and easy phrases the generation of the Logos. That generation was a mystery for him, and he considered himself obliged to probe it. Like Hippolytus a few years earlier, he was forced to make a profound study of the dogma of the Trinity, for the heresies of the period rejected the orthodox distinction of the divine Persons. In the West the anti-Trinitarian heretics professed themselves to be defenders of what they called the monarchy of God, the utter oneness of the divine Ruler of the world. In the East they called themselves the friends of God. But by whatever name they called themselves in the West or in the East, they were afraid of endangering the doctrine of monotheism and of professing the existence of two gods. When the defenders of Christian orthodoxy replied by their distinction of the Logos and by recalling the mission He had received to manifest Himself to men, the heretics who had begun by attacking the Trinity did not hesitate to attack the Church's teaching on the Person of Jesus Christ. Rejecting the divine sonship, they saw in Jesus no more than a Jewish prophet in whom there dwelt the Holy Spirit or the divine power of the divinity of the Father. Against those different versions of the heresy known as monarchianism there was developed, first at Rome and later at Alexandria, a theology of the eternal Word-made-man.

In meeting the challenge of this heresy, Hippolytus and Origen were actuated by one and the same thought: to prove that Jesus, by reason of His divine nature, possesses all the heritage of the Father as well as dominion over all rational creatures and to show Him as the Redeemer who won the victory over sin by His incarnation and by His Passion and death. Without discarding any of the realistically human elements recorded of Him in the Gospels, they insisted on the permanence of the divine nature in Christ. According to them, the Gospel teaches that the mission of the eternal Word is to give sight to the blind and to preach deliverance to the captives, and they held that His divine nature was united to the human elements in Him by virtue of the mission He had received to descend among us. Each of them used the same texts of the psalms to describe the glory of the humanity thus elevated to God. In all this apologetic they employed the mystery of the Trinity to confirm the mystery of the Incarnation, and vice versa. The Logos is the adviser of the Father.[1] The great Voice which has echoed and re-echoed in the works of God since the beginning of the world and which echoes also in the hearts of the saints and of all righteous men, is the same Voice that proclaimed the Gospel by recalling the dead to life.[2]

Thus, at the beginning of this period, notable for its mass conversions to Christianity, Origen listened to the preaching of Hippolytus and made it his own. It was a method of preaching directed far beyond the limits of the immediate audience. It would carry the Gospel message to the sons and daughters of the Synagogue, that

---

[1] This expression, familiar to Hippolytus (e.g., *Contra Noet.*, 10), is often found in Origen.

[2] Hippolytus often calls the Word the voice of the Father (e.g., *Contra Noet.*, 10), an expression that implies a teaching that is effective and energizing. Cf. Origen, *In Psalm.*, 3, 5; P.G., XII, 1124.

spouse over whom so many tears had been shed. It would speak to Gentile nations as they came up from the desert, and the Christian preaching would guide them as a pillar of fire. Origen had already dedicated himself to the service of the Logos, and now he hearkened to the call to arms. In the words of Eusebius: "After a short stay there he returned to Alexandria. And he performed the duties of catechetical instruction there with great zeal; Demetrius, who was bishop there at that time, urging and even entreating him to work diligently for the benefit of the brethren."

II. THE REFORM

Perceiving that his exegetical studies intruded upon his work as a catechist, he divided his pupils into two classes. When Clement had been in charge of the catechetical school, the headmaster had managed to fulfill the dual functions of catechist and teacher of philosophy by adapting his lectures to the three degrees of Christian training. Origen, on the other hand, gave a greater importance to the conventional distinction between the simple and the perfect. Therefore he handed over the classes for beginners to his pupil Heraclas, who was one of his converts from the days of the persecution of Septimius Severus and who had afterward studied philosophy under Ammonius. He devoted his own efforts to the classes in Christian asceticism and theology.

This decision, more than anything else at that time, would direct his future work and guide the lines of the development of his teaching. The Christian life of the common people, the dear days of his boyhood recalled to him by Clement's book, *The Tutor*, days when he labored in ignorance and when he depended more on Christian custom than on doctrine, all that part of his life with its simplicities and its virtues was about to be discarded forever. He will exaggerate its differences from his new life of academic zeal; especially in this first period, he will utter more than one harsh criticism of it. It will seem to him to have one sole function: to protect the religion of the scholar as the leaves of a tree protect the fruit. Such was the cost at which the great works of the School were produced. Origen would never have doubted the meaning and value of popular devotion if he had kept himself more in touch with the beliefs of the simple Christians of his day.

TWO CLASSES OF DISCIPLES

The School was intended for men devoted to the cultivation of Christian spirituality. As Clement had shown, none but purified souls could attain to the knowledge of God. The pupils, therefore, renounced the cares of business and of public life, consecrating themselves to a higher task: to give their attention to the spiritual growth of their own souls, and in a discipline of recollection to see God's mirror in their own hearts, to know the marks of His presence within themselves, and to find there the means whereby they might in some way make themselves godlike. They were also to look on the face of Nature and to meditate on the order of the universe, which moves with an obedience that is intelligent and without sin. These two activities were merely the beginning of Christian discipline. The student must not consider himself already equipped with Christian wisdom; he is obliged to a life of perseverance in the love of God because the purpose of all his studies is union with God by a life of holiness. As soon as he should become established in the ways of holiness, it would be easier for him to practice the virtues and to taste the joy and peace that come from the love of God.

In this great plan of Christian asceticism, profane philosophy had its uses. Origen remembered that the philosophers and poets of Greece had written many true pages, some of them even capable of exciting the Christian soul to greater efforts in the way of holiness. In this mood he returned to the books which he had for some time discarded, but when he opened them he was assailed with new anxieties. The classical authors should be read by the Christian philosopher from a viewpoint unmarked by prejudice; only the atheistic works, those of the Epicureans who denied the existence of God or of providence, must be put aside, because their mere touch soiled the soul. This widespread choice was a safeguard, for the pupil ran no risk of accepting exclusively the doctrines of any one school and thus of resembling a wool from which the dye cannot be washed. In this way the young student was protected against the subtlety of those crafty authors who conquer the weak with one blow, tyrants who insist upon service from the unfortunate youth who has given them even the beginning of an assent.

Origen himself marked out the course of studies his pupils were to follow, warned them of the sophisms they would encounter, and taught them to distinguish error from truth. Among the pagan works to which he gave his approval were, of course, the Platonic treatises so familiar to Clement, the *Phaedrus*, some books of the *Republic*, and the *Timaeus*. He found it necessary to include also works representative of the later Stoicism, of Neoplatonism, and of the recent Aristotelianism. Students whose early education had been neglected were drilled in a special course of general studies as a preparation that would equip them later to follow the ordinary classes.

SACRED AND PROFANE STUDIES

Profane studies at the Academy were soon marked by a freedom and an assurance which the students welcomed as a novelty. It had long been the custom for Christian scholars to read the pagan philosophers merely for the sake of contradicting them, or in order to acquire a quick and agile understanding of their teachings, or to defend the Christian faith, or even with the purpose of showing its agreement with the accepted teachings of every school of thought. This time, however, a scholar with a Christian mentality was meeting the pagan thinkers on their own ground, and his enthusiastic pupils were being encouraged to imitate his breadth of view. Gregory Thaumaturgus was one of those pupils, and he has given us a glimpse of this new departure in Christian teaching. "Nothing was prohibited to us, nothing hidden from us, nothing was placed beyond our reach. We were free to study any teaching whatever, Greek or barbarian, mystical or moral. We could sample all ideas in their turn, and we could gorge ourselves with every type of intellectual food. Whether a certain classical concept was true or whether another such concept demanded our acknowledgment of its truth, there it was, ready for attention, with the marvelous possibility of the most beautiful views." [8] There was no labyrinth

[8] Gregory Thaumaturgus, XV.

too baffling for Origen, no swamp or morass whence he did not guide his pupils to safety, leading them by the hand till they reached firm ground.

In his efforts to grasp the sovereign Good and to learn the eternal Truth, the Christian philosopher is equipped with a special technique which is of the essence of his faith. Wisdom was what Clement used to call this technique. Origen preferred to call it theology. Sometimes, however, he called it religious knowledge, especially when he was employing it against the so-called knowledge of the heretics. It was a nobler kind of knowledge than that acquired through the study of philosophy, just as philosophy itself was nobler than the Greek sciences of geometry and astronomy. Its chief purpose was the development of the contemplative life in a day when pagan writings were the chief source of the ethical training of Christian youth. The Alexandrians did not deny that there were numbers of great thinkers among the pagan philosophers, but they regarded such luminaries as being ignorant of the source of the partial truths with which they dealt. In a world grown negligent and corrupt, passion had so weakened the eyes of men that they could no longer lift their vision to the contemplation of the divine Word. "It is not astonishing that certain writers, who have clear ideas on the arts and sciences and who sometimes display an ability to discuss questions of morals or to solve problems in literature, should remain in ignorance of God. Their intellect is like the vision of a man who can see every object except the sun and who never lifts his eyes toward the sun's rays." [4] Not even the most learned of such men is worth our prolonged study. Our human intelligence is illuminated by the divine Wisdom only when we study the words of Holy Scripture. "Full communion with God, the highest aim of human effort, can be attained only by those who in Christ have grown to the stature of the perfect man in whom the saint and the thinker are blended together in the unity of the Divine Love." [5]

According to the Alexandrians, philosophy at its best was a preparation for the study of the Bible. But when the Christian thinker

[4] *In Psalm.*, 4, 7; P.G., XII, 1164. Cf. *In Gen.*, III; P.G., XII, 89.
[5] Bigg, *The Christian Platonists*, p. 80.

was confronted with the divine mysteries contained in the holy books, he found himself in need of an equipment other than mere learning. Perhaps it was God's will that the biblical mysteries should not stand forth in all their luminous truth at the first view. Perhaps also we ourselves have forgotten how to understand the language of God since we have held ourselves so far apart from Him. Whatever may be the explanation of the soul's lack of comprehension now, the study of the divine Word enables it to become again the intelligence it had ceased to be. But this education of the inner faculties must be the work of faith. "Diligently apply yourself to the reading of the Sacred Scriptures," Origen said to Gregory Thaumaturgus, "with faithful prejudgments such as are well pleasing to God. Prayer is of all things indispensable to the knowledge of the things of God."

ORIGEN'S METHOD

Origen devised his own method of studying the Sacred Scriptures. Using the Septuagint version, he slowly read a verse and then proceeded to make a grammatical commentary on it. He made a comparison of the various translations of the verse. Then he gave the meaning of the words and the sense of the phrase, using for this purpose his many dictionaries and supplementing them from his own wide knowledge. An example of the method is to be found in his definition of the word "principle," wherein he drew as much from his own philosophy as from that of Aristotle. In his dissertation on comparison and parable he reaches the level of the best of the Greeks. When he had thus explained the literal meaning of the verse, he turned to his biblical concordance in search of a number of similar texts. Then he was ready for an analysis of the religious feelings produced in his heart by the words of the text. Besides all this, he made it a habit, whenever he set himself to the explanation of any particular book of the Bible, to include in his preface a study of the title of the book and an examination of the biblical personages to whom the book was accredited. When all this had been done, he addressed himself to the interpretation, the research properly so called. At this early period of his life, the historical sense of the passage was of supreme importance to him, and this he never avoided if it was possible to uphold it; his treatment of the historical meaning of the sacred text always preceded his moral and spiritual interpretations of it.

In preparing his lectures or in writing his books, it was his invariable practice to keep on his desk a number of notebooks in which he wrote his observations or *scholia* suggested by this or that passage. He would use many of those notes in later years, when he was busily writing at Caesarea. His notebooks on the Book of Daniel, on the Epistle to the Romans and the Epistle to the Corinthians were soon absorbed into his *Stromata*. In his controversies with the Marcionites, who had corrupted the text of St. Paul, his notebooks furnished him with an arsenal of weapons with which to establish the authenticity of the Pauline writings. It is possible that, even at this early date, he had already annotated the Psalter. Be that as it may, when St. Jerome was writing his commentaries on the psalms more than a century and a half later, he made use of the homilies and notes which Origen's hand had penned.

Even while he was lecturing to a group of his students his own mind was busy with new aspects of the topic under discussion. Often he would take a theme familiar to his hearers, probably some truth hidden beneath a symbolism which he had already explained to them. But every such renewal of a lecture was embroidered with new beauties; the later studies "were in agreement with the earlier ones but had not quite the same spirit." [6] During this first period of his professorial activities, his initial lecture on a biblical theme was likely to contain a number of rash ideas, especially on the occasions when he was not concerned with the mere exposition of the sacred text. From the steady stream of his words a new theory would seem to emerge, dazzling his pupils like a mirage of the Egyptian sun. But when he spoke on that same subject a second time, the nebulous glow had already vanished and the outlines of a new aspect of truth could be clearly seen. Just as at eventide the sun's white glare gives way before the enchanting colors of the spectrum, even so the inner beauty of this man's loftiest thoughts

[6] *Contra Cels.*, V, ii. Cf. *In Joan.*, V, 5; *P.G.*, XIV, 192.

did not shine forth till the sun of his life was near its setting. Then it began to be evident that he was gifted with an unfaltering instinct for the truth and that his mentality was far less rash and much more acute than his earlier critics had supposed. Unlike many men who are skilled in extempore discourse, he was never known to use an awkward expression or to stray from the subject. If the critic seeks something at which to cavil, he must go higher than the level of this man's everyday life and penetrate into the realm of his thoughts. Scientific criticism of his system reveals the fact that at the root of the teachings associated with his name there was a mentality which was both intrepid in its method of attack on an intellectual problem and receptive of every logical deduction the problem evoked.

Gregory Thaumaturgus refers to him "as being himself a skilled and most discerning hearer of God. . . . Perhaps it is better to say that that Leader of all men has honored this man as He would a friend, and has constituted him an expositor of these same oracles. . . . These things, moreover, as I judge, he gives forth only and truly by participation in the divine Spirit: for there is need of the same power for those who prophesy and for those who hear the prophets. . . . Now that greatest gift this man has received from God, and that noblest of all endowments he has had bestowed on him from heaven, that he should be an interpreter of the oracles of God to men." [7]

The sense of rapture, that mark of inspiration which is present in every word of the sacred text, was generated at the Academy as much by the common routine of daily life as by the natural charm of Origen's eloquence. Origen introduced a new kind of spiritual training, that of the soul purifying itself and refining its faculties in order that it might contemplate to better advantage the world of the invisible; he considered this a more efficacious system of mortification than that of fasting and sleeping on the bare ground. In Clement's day the pupils used to make only one daily meditation on Holy Scripture, just before dinner. Origen, on the other hand, began his classes in biblical lore early in the morning and kept them going till the hour of high noon, the hottest period of the day. In

[7] Gregory Thaumaturgus; P.G., XV, 174-83.

addition to this, one of the pupils was appointed to read from the Holy Scriptures during the dinner hour; there was also a spiritual reading in the hour before retiring. The day was always closed with prayer.

Alexandria lacked, however, two elements which were to be found in the other great theological centers of early Christianity: a certain degree of reverence in the study of a mystery and a definite Christian tradition. Origen's method of teaching was undoubtedly responsible for this twofold defect. In lecturing to his classes he began with the enunciation of a philosophical principle or, more often, with the reading of a difficult passage from Holy Scripture; in each case he proceeded to build his explanation upon notions borrowed from the Greek philosophers rather than upon a feeling for the sanctity of Christian tradition. It was a rare thing for him to start from the common beliefs of Christianity, or the unanimity of the Christian Churches on the point under discussion, or the right of such Churches to interpret God's inspired word. Instead of relying on what we call the mind of the Church, he presented Christian beliefs merely as further illustrations of a larger truth. As a natural result his teaching was subject to no controls save those imposed by his own mind. Invariably his lecture opened up new philosophical problems or evoked a number of questions from his pupils, and the discussion of those problems or questions was of far more importance to him than the attitude of the general body of Christians on the matter in hand. He had no idea that the Church, by giving a direction to the teaching of religion, had also mapped out a program for that teaching, rigorously excluding things that had no reference to the worship of God. It was not unusual for him to lecture on the soul of the stars or on the astronomical changes of a future period in the history of the world.

In this early period Origen had no realization of the fact that his duties as a teacher of the Christian religion imposed upon him certain restraints. He was barely conscious of the principle that human thought is not the measure of all things, or of the opposite principle that the study to which he was committed was the measure of human thought. Mystery, for him, was never the unknowable, never God's secret as Christianity has always viewed it; for him it was a challenge, too often the hidden treasure which he was impatient to discover. He had yet a long way to walk along the road of contemplation before he learned to understand that the study of Holy Scripture was merely the first step in a journey, a journey requiring the guidance of unceasing prayer and ending only in eternal life and in union with God.

UNBRIDLED ENTHUSIASM

In those early years there was yet another danger which he was quite unaware of, the danger inherent in the unbridled enthusiasm aroused in his pupils by his own extreme intellectualism. His students were all too ready to seize the less certain elements in his teaching and to push them to extremes. Under the spell of his eloquence every enigma was instantly solved for them. The historical facts that were veiled in God's communications to man or the coming events that God had revealed through the prophets became, in their eyes, the clearest of doctrines. In their feeling that they were divinely inspired, their minds seemed to be lifted, even in this life, to the level of the angels; even before they had achieved union with the perfect truth, they seemed to know what that perfect truth was.

When a man has experienced even in the slightest degree the mystical knowledge that comes to the saints of God, he is often tempted to neglect the slow progress of tradition. Origen at this time was far from being thoroughly acquainted with Christian tradition, in spite of his own studies and of his various pilgrimages to other centers of Christian learning. From what he tells us of his library we know that it contained the first epistle of Clement of Rome as well as the *Pastor* of Hermas, works familiar to his own teacher, Clement of Alexandria. There were also the various exegetical works of Melito of Sardis, the contemporary works of Hippolytus including the Roman's commentary on the psalms, probably the writings of Bardesanes, and of course the works of Clement of Alexandria. Of these last named, his favorite was the seventh book of the *Stromata;* its influence was quite marked in Origen's first spiritual writings, and indeed he relies upon it throughout his life.

Origen does not quote from the works of St. Irenaeus, although he must have studied them. However, the Irenaean system of theology belonged rather to the schools of Antioch and of Asia Minor than to the school of Alexandria, where it certainly did not wield the authority it had elsewhere. This fact had not deterred Clement, in his effort to prove how we are taught by revelation, from making a careful digest of the teaching of St. Irenaeus in the fourth book, chapters 37–39, of his treatise against the heretics. In neglecting the idea of a progressive manifestation of the Logos, Origen not only showed himself less eclectic than his master but also deprived his own theological system of the most fertile thought which the Christian literature of the second century had expressed. More than once in this first period Origen's theology was notably lacking in the equipment he might have had from his predecessors in Christian learning.

Among the Christian apocrypha he had read the Epistle of Barnabas and the Acts of Paul; he quotes from the latter at least three times. Probably he had studied the *Preaching of Peter,* the authenticity of which he considered dubious; also a work attributed to Clement of Rome and called the *Periodoi,* from which the young Alexandrian quoted a number of passages that are identical with the text of the *Recognitions* as later translated by Rufinus. Besides these works, he freely consulted the Jewish apocrypha which he collected from the various synagogues in Egypt. He knew a number of legends that had been born of the Jewish studies on Genesis and Exodus, things like a manuscript known as *Joseph and Aseneth,* which was written in Egyptian characters, and especially the *Prayer of Joseph,* which relied on astrology and taught that human souls had a previous existence under an angelic form. This last-mentioned work, popular at the beginning of the third century, was widely used by the Jews and was regarded by Origen as worthy of his attention. Other Jewish works appealing to him were the *Ascension of Moses*, a book that Clement had used before him, and the *Apocalypse of Baruch*. In general we may say that he liked apocryphal works because of their interest in antiquity and in mystery, and he readily yielded to any book seeming to promise him what he longed for above everything else, the key to the secrets of the happy life which had been lived and would be lived by souls emancipated from the claims of this world. His interest in the theory of pre-existence was nourished by this sort of fantastic writings much more than by his philosophical studies; indeed they helped to keep that theory in his mind when Plato's authority was no longer strong enough to do so.

In spite of their attraction for him he was always careful to distinguish such writings from the books of the Christian canon, steadfastly refusing them the authority of inspired works, even when the Bible seemed to make mention of them. "We may suppose," says Harnack, "that the Apostles and the Evangelists, filled as they were with the Holy Ghost, knew what to accept and what to reject in such writings; but we, who have not received the same abundance of the Spirit, are not permitted to take such a risk." In some words written by Origen about the year 238 there is something like a note of regret: "Books which are outside the canon of Scripture ought not to be used by him who seeks to confirm a doctrine of the Church." But in the years with which we are concerned here his insatiable curiosity impelled him to grant to them a high degree of importance "without admitting that they can constitute a secret tradition such as is reserved to the Christian gnostic.

Philo, he believed, must not be listed among the profane authors, for the man was not a Greek philosopher although his own contemporaries had known him as the Pythagorean. Clement had already made extracts from his ascetical works and from his treatise on the virtues, and now Origen pays tribute to his genius. With a keenness for ethical truth, matched only by his interest in theology, the young Alexandrian professor drew much from Philo's *Allegories on the Laws* for his own theory of evil and used the *Quod Deus immutabilis* as part of the foundation for his definition of freedom.

CONVERSION OF AMBROSE

Thus deeply immersed in his personal studies, the head of the Academy began to forget his official position as a catechist. Pupils came to him for his theological teachings. A certain Ambrose, one of the leading men of Alexandria, became an enthusiastic admirer of his activities and thereupon renounced the Valentinian heresy and returned to the Church. Then there was one Denis, member of a wealthy pagan family, a man of culture and elegance, who was deeply affected by certain elements of Origen's doctrine. His new pupils also included Ammonius, the future bishop of Thmuis. So rapidly did his reputation grow that it soon extended to the episcopate itself.

The friendship of Ambrose would greatly influence Origen's work, for the reclaimed convert was master of a great fortune and was one of the prominent figures in the political life of Alexandria. He was a man of good education, well versed in the symbolism of numbers. Like many other well-educated Christians of the day, he believed that the simple faith of the common people should be supplemented by an esoteric doctrine; he desired a higher form of Christianity, that would make known to him the mysteries of God and of the world. Convinced that this higher Christianity must ultimately lead him to the possession of the mystical love of God, he joined the Valentinian sect and undoubtedly professed that heresy for several years. Then, using the measure of intelligence with which the Creator had endowed him, he awoke to the fact that mankind's cardinal sin is a failure to go to God through the Logos, who is the Redeemer. Under Origen's influence he soon renounced his former opinions. His years in heresy left their mark upon him in the form of a restless curiosity, and he regarded Christianity as primarily a school. Twenty years after his conversion he was still disturbed about the objections of certain heretics to prayer. He encouraged Origen to meet the heretics on their own ground and to confront them with a system that would be an anti-gnosis, and was the moving spirit in Origen's decision to publish his *Commentary on the Psalms* and to write his *Commentary on the Gospel of St. John.* He instantly became Origen's devoted follower, one of those ardent pupils from whose enthusiasm the master had to protect himself throughout his entire life and to whose importunities he had sometimes to yield. Thus it happened that the great Christian teacher whose own soul throbbed with a resistless enthusiasm was forced to restrain the ardor of those around him. On one famous occasion he finished a dedication to Ambrose with a prayer, reminding his faithful disciple that God alone is perfect and that we must pray to Him for the grace of a twofold understanding, the understanding to discover truth and the understanding to demonstrate it.[8]

There was a day in the year 233, during the persecution which Maximinus launched against the Christians, when Ambrose was torn from his children, cast into prison, and threatened with death. On that day he felt that he was about to realize his longing to see God face to face, more closely even than St. Paul had thought of. But in 247 he was still in the company of Origen's devoted friends, and the master summed up their great friendship by calling him his "noble and holy brother."

In this academic environment, peopled by students who tested his patience as well as by others who yielded to his slightest word, Origen wrote the great commentaries that mark the Alexandrian period of his life. They are scholarly works emanating from a definite school of thought, a school where discussion of every kind was welcomed and where ambitions for a life of holiness were warmly encouraged and fostered; for the knowledge imparted in that school was intended, with the help of grace from heaven, to lead the faithful student to the full and unobstructed vision of God.

[8] *In Joan.*, X, 1; *P.G.*, XIV, 308.

CHAPTER IV

Commentary on the Psalms

As WE have already noted, Ambrose prevailed upon Origen to publish his first commentaries in which the master had written his interpretation of the Book of Psalms. No part of the Old Testament was more familiar to Christians, both learned and simple. It was habitually used in the public prayers of the faithful, and the fact that certain psalms were already a part of the liturgy of the Eucharist was not without influence on their interpretation. The Psalter was also a source of personal piety. Simple souls found there the promise of a kingdom soon to be established here on earth, the sole obstacle to its coming being the weakness and sin of mankind. When the unlettered Christian recited the verse about Him who showeth us good things, he felt that the moment was at hand.

To the spiritually minded, all hopes of this sort were rude and barbarous. What they sought in the psalms was the key to the contemplative life, for it is clearly mentioned there under various symbols. "Who shall ascend unto the mountain of the Lord: or who shall stand in His holy place? The innocent in hands, and clean of heart." Clement had regarded this verse as a description of the goal of him who seeks perfection. "The prophet describes briefly, I believe, the true gnostic," he wrote. Written for seekers after wisdom, the Psalter would become also the guidebook and the favorite reading of the spiritual exegete, for in that book the prophet draws the image of Christ, speaks about Christ, and makes Christ speak to angels and to men.

I. DATE AND COMPOSITION

The publication of the Commentary could not have taken place before the reign of Caracalla. If we are to accept the account given by Eusebius, Ambrose was converted after Origen's return from Rome. But he was a pupil of Origen's for some time before the latter dedicated his book to him. Many a time he had urged the master to avoid the mistake of so many of his contemporaries and not to leave his doctrine to the merely oral tradition of his school. He begged him to follow the example of Hippolytus, and perhaps of the heretical writers of exegetical works. It is probable that, as a former student of the heretical gnosis, he knew of the existence of the Commentary on the Psalms of which Clement had already published some fragments. Those heretical studies, one of which was published as the work of the gnostic Hermogenes, were part of the Alexandrian tradition because of the welcome the Alexandrians accorded to the Jewish apocrypha, such as the Book of Henoch, because of their treatment of cosmology, and because of the numerous philosophical opinions mixed with their exposition of religion. According to Ambrose, a real knowledge based on Christian holiness was the only thing that could destroy the attraction of the ambitious phantasies presented by all those heretical works. It is certain that the Psalter teaches the way of Christian perfection, but it must not be forgotten that the soul encounters the Savior on that way of perfection and that the psalms speak of Him in terms of symbolism. To interpret the psalms from this angle was a work worthy of Origen.

The master was quite aware of the dangers and the errors lying in wait for the exegete; consequently he had long been deaf to the pleadings of Ambrose. Perhaps his hesitation was increased when he reminded himself that the Christian suspicion of literary men was not yet entirely dead. But, according to Eusebius, Ambrose offered him a friendly agreement of collaboration which he was unable to refuse. "He dictated to more than seven amanuenses, who relieved one another at appointed times. And he employed an equal number of copyists, besides girls who were skilled in elegant writing. For all these Ambrose furnished the necessary funds in abundance." Because of his promise to prepare the work, Origen felt that he was under an obligation to his friend and was bound to honor the agreement.

Being thus urged to publish, he wrote with undue haste. His collection of lectures soon grew into a book, not without danger to him. Everything was treated in the book, both long grammatical explanations and the rapid stream of thoughts that came to his mind in the course of his work. Such a method was often a source of annoyance to the writer whom it was supposed to serve, but Origen was one of those authors who write for their contemporaries rather than for posterity.

"This vast enterprise," he writes to Ambrose, "is truly beyond me and my strength. I am forced by your lively curiosity, together with the confusion with which your goodness and your tolerance fill me, to descend into the arena. For a long time I held back, knowing the danger, which would still be very great if, instead of discussing the Holy Scriptures, I wrote commentaries to be left to posterity. But you bewitched me in a thousand friendly ways. Now you have led me to this point as if by an initiation into the knowledge of divine things. You will be for me a witness before God. At the same time that He examines my whole life, He examines the dictations I now give and the feelings with which I give them. Sometimes I find the true meaning and sometimes my interpretation is rather forced, or perhaps I give the appearance of putting forward a definite opinion. But truly I have analyzed the words, not forgetting that when we speak of God we are judged by God, a maxim that is well stated; nor have I forgotten the adage that even to speak the truth on the subject of God is not without danger. Nothing can be beautiful if we separate it from God, especially the meaning of the Holy Scriptures which have been inspired in order to lead us to Him who is the Father of all things, through our Savior and High Priest, the only-begotten Son. Therefore I beg of you to pray for me that there may be granted me from the very beginning the grace to search well. Those who search have already the promise of finding; and undoubtedly those who fail to approach Him as they should are not considered by God as belonging to that class of men who duly search for the principle of all things." [1]

This commentary was the first work that Origen decided to publish outside the narrow circle of his own followers. In the general

[1] *In Psalm., Praef.; P.G.,* XII, 1077.

introduction to the study of Holy Scripture, with which the book begins, no mention is made of any earlier work published by the author, although it was Origen's practice to link each of his publications with the books or essays he had already given to the world. In this instance, however, his only reference is to the comparison which he had already written between the Hebrew text and the four chief versions in Greek. Strangely enough, this introduction contains an interpretation of the second psalm which is to be found in the opening pages of the *De principiis*.

THE DATE

We cannot fix, with any degree of accuracy, the date when this great champion of Christianity went forth to battle for the first time. According to Eusebius, he began to publish about the year 222. We cannot accept this date, for it would mean that the numerous works which poured forth from his pen before he left Alexandria must be crowded into a brief span of seven years. A greater difficulty arises when we consider that in this first published work Origen gives no indication of several problems that would become of intense interest to him at a later date. For example, cosmology and the history of the soul are scarcely referred to at all; and, besides, the work contains a number of opinions that had no place whatever in the great system which Origen subsequently developed. The *De principiis* must have been composed at an appreciable interval after the publication of the *Commentary*, because its viewpoint is quite different from that of the earlier book.

The lateness of the date assigned by Eusebius to Origen's group of Alexandrian publications is, according to Harnack, probably owing to an erroneous reading of the *preface of the Commentary on the Gospel of St. John*. Eusebius must have regarded this study of St. John's Gospel, which was written during the reign of Emperor Alexander Severus, as Origen's first work. Eusebius was led into this error by the fact that Origen calls it his first fruits. But what Origen means by this expression is that the work marks the resumption of his task after he had been absent from it for some time. All the

available evidence points to the conclusion that Origen's first publication was released much earlier than Eusebius supposed. Critical
study reveals the date as being between the years 214 and 218.

This first part of the *Commentary* was published, then, at Alexandria. It discusses twenty-five psalms only, and there is no evidence
that its various parts were all published at the same time. But, since
Origen refers to the merits and the defects of his work, his preface
must certainly have had attached to it a number of commentaries, if
not indeed the entire first part. This hypothesis enables us to consider the majority of the fragments of this first publication as the
earliest examples of his doctrine, an interpretation of them which
becomes the more cogent when we reflect that the book was originally written with the help of his *scholia* and of his notes from
lectures delivered by him to his pupils in the Academy.

The introduction enables us to see the general impression made
upon Origen by the works of Hippolytus, by what he had gleaned
from his conferences with the Jewish rabbis, and by his comparative
study of the various Greek versions of the Bible. It contained a discussion on the authenticity of the Book of Psalms, on their various
titles or epigraphs, and on their arrangement. It was preceded by a
mystical exhortation, according to the fashion at Alexandria at that
time, for this first work was written for the learned, as indeed were
all the works that followed it. This preliminary essay on mysticism
made use of Holy Scripture to elucidate the ascetical precepts which
Clement had formerly given to those of his pupils in whom he dis-
cerned a real aspiration for the contemplative life.

II. ORIGEN'S SYSTEM OF SPIRITUALITY

As usual in books that are the product of an inner life, the opening paragraphs indicated clearly the scope of the doctrine which
the subsequent pages expound. The creature depends upon the
Creator in the totality of his being. God communicates to the creature the Good; and the creature is, only in the degree in which he is
good. Expressing these relations in terms of knowledge, we say
that God knows the righteous and does not know the unrighteous.
He does not know the unrighteous because it is not fitting that

God should know evil, and therefore sinners are as nothing in the eyes of God. The good, on the contrary, belong to God. He is their way; more accurately, His Son is their way with the result that the Father, who alone shares the knowledge of the Son, knows them in Him.[2]

Religious life is founded upon this sharing of goodness, and consequently on the sharing of being. To share means to receive imperfectly, in a manner at once contingent and free. No virtue, no perseverance, is immune to the possibility of change unless it is of Christ, whose human soul chose the good without any resort to that *libertas indifferentiae* which would have confronted Him with a choice between good and evil. This is true for men, for angels, for every creature. Creatures are divine in that degree only in which God is present within them, and, "in the absence of divine Wisdom, they are counted as nothing." Their goodness does not belong to them, and only through trials and afflictions do they obtain perseverance. We cannot speak of self-control or of indifference to suffering without remembering that they come "from the grace of God, to which are added the efforts of man."[3]

HIS ASCETICAL TEACHING

Clement had imposed three duties on Christian philosophers: contemplation, the observance of the commandments, and the obligation to teach. Of the three, the first was held in highest esteem by him during the years of exile when he was engaged in writing his great works. He called it by the seductive title of *gnosis*. In his hands it became a sort of quietism. To know God, and through this knowledge to become equal to the angels; to attain an almost complete indifference to suffering; to suppress within ourselves every desire by the assurance that we are already in possession of unchangeable bliss: these were the dreams which Clement's soul welcomed without restraint and which he portrayed in the last books of the *Stromata* written in Cappadocia or in Syria.

Almost as soon as they were published, those writings in Clem-

[2] *Ibid.*, 1, 6; P.G., XII, 1100.
[3] *Ibid.*, 17, 21; P.G., XII, 1232; cf. *ibid.*, 1, 1; P.G., XII, 1086.

ent's closing years were in the hands of Christian scholars in Egypt. So well did they express the Alexandrian spirit and so strikingly were they in harmony with the academic fashion of the day, that they soon were being studied by the new head of the Academy. But in the years that had passed since his predecessor left him, Origen had assisted the holy martyrs in their last hours, had risked his own life for the faith, had practiced the most rigorous asceticism, had challenged the hostility of the heretics, and had achieved a measure of fame as one of the great defenders of the Christian message. He had seen his own faith grow and had witnessed the birth of faith in the hearts of his disciples. And all this experience had been marked by a distress that still bore heavily on his soul. Man must pass through the gates of sorrow to reach the knowledge of God.[4] The life of the man who has harvested wisdom is less an ascension into heaven than a daily struggle in which the result remains always a matter of uncertainty.

This was the Origen for whom the Psalter chanted tales of struggle and sang paeans of victory unto salvation. Was not David's prayer the song of a repentant sinner whom God in His mercy had pardoned? The sin, the falling by the wayside, the movement of the repentant soul in the direction of God, all those inner elements in the drama of David's story would cast their shadows and their glories on Origen's world. He would draw from them more than a system of theology. In them he would see the whole history of mankind, the entire drama of salvation, in which souls fall and rise again. Interpreted in this manner by a man of intense spirituality and written for souls whose longing for God's love was akin to his own, Origen's commentary on the psalms suggests, long in advance, the history of the human soul that later fills the pages of the *De principiis*.

Clement's ideal of the perfect Christian as one who is both active and contemplative was now being taught to the students at the Academy in a new way. The Christian gnostic of the *Stromata* had been a man utterly devoted to prayer, unblemished in all his thoughts and actions, sharing in some measure the mind of God. In

---

[4] Cf. *ibid.*, 4, 2; *P.G.*, XII, 1137; *ibid.*, 24, 17; *P.G.*, XII, 1273.

Origen's hands, that lofty ideal was transformed, being fashioned into something real and concrete; the gnostic became the ascetic and the contemplative, the first model of what was later to be the Christian monk. From this time onward Origen touched Alexandrian idealism without reforming it; he borrowed from it and sometimes even contradicted it.

Clement had said: "Certainly the elect race justified by the precept says: 'Seven times have I praised thee.' Therefore not in a specified place or selected temple, or at certain festivals and on appointed days, but all during his life, the gnostic in every place, even if he is alone by himself, and wherever he has any of those who have exercised the like faith, honors God." [5] The program was certainly attractive, but Origen wisely observes: "When we meditate on the law of God we must not forget the different applications of that holy law. In the same spirit we must not neglect prayer on special occasions, because prayer, like meditation, consists in fulfilling the law of the Lord in everything." [6] In Origen's view, the contemplative prays at the rising of the sun, and before retiring to rest at night he examines his conscience.

Origen was even more severe in his criticism of another utopian ideal. The philosophical students of the Academy, in their dream of surpassing the ethical teachings of the writings of the Stoics, forgot that temptation is the great law of progress in the inner life; they believed, like their Greek prototypes, that even here on earth are to be found spiritual athletes who, having already vanquished the enemy in life's arena, need only to await the ceremony in which they are crowned with the laurels of victory. Origen did not hesitate to denounce this error:

"If we are spiritual athletes who are more advanced than others in the way of perfection and who are therefore nearer the end of the period of preparation and if we are no longer required to struggle

[5] *Strom.*, VII, vii, 35. Cf. Bardy, *Clement d'Alexandrie*, p. 298. At the beginning of the Quietist controversy, Fénelon composed a memoir entitled *Le Gnostique* in which he invoked many passages from Clement of Alexandria. This manuscript is to be found in the library of the Seminary of St. Sulpice at Issy. It has been published by Father Dudon, *Le Gnostique de saint Clement d'Alexandrie*.

[6] *In Psalm.*, 1, 2; P.G., XII, 1088. Cf. *ibid.*, 5, 5; P.G., XII, 1169; *ibid.*, 4, 5; P.G., XII, 1144.

against the call of the flesh and the heat of the blood, we are still threatened by the principalities and powers, by the princes of this world of darkness and by the evil spirits. None is exempted from that kind of temptation. How is it possible to imagine that men escape the spiritual difficulties with which each soul is filled from the moment it first learns to reason? And at what period of a man's life can the individual soul boast of its immunity from the struggle against sin?" From the need of that struggle the desert is no refuge nor even the hours when we are immersed in prayer. "Even that soul is not free of temptation who meditates day and night on the law of God and puts forth every available effort to fulfill the precept: the mouth of the just shall meditate wisdom." [7]

The program of the young master in the ways of asceticism was far from being as mild as his praises of the divine philanthropy might lead us to believe. He held that the soul must endeavor, not to isolate itself from sin, but to destroy sin utterly. We must study the tactics of spiritual science in the school of Christ if we would annihilate sin and crush within our hearts the carnal temper and the passions which cling to the soul, no matter how wholesome their activities may seem to be.[8] The choice is between sacrificing oneself and becoming as nothing: there is no other alternative. Obviously a mind more troubled than that of Clement dictated those pages of Origen's first published work.

ACTION AND CONTEMPLATION

Contemplation, like activity, is a matter of effort. It completes and rounds out knowledge, the *gnosis*, a hoary and magical word which in Origen's vocabulary loses the meaning it always had in the heretical sects. He does not use it as the name for an instantaneous communication of the divine; for him it means religious knowledge, the interpretation of difficult texts of Holy Scripture, and

---

[7] *De oratione*, XXIX, 2. Origen already distinguishes, according to the classical doctrine, three sources of temptation: the soul, the flesh, and circumstances. Cf. *In Psalm.*, 10, 5; P.G., XII, 1192. A division which is similar, but more theological, is to be found in the *De princip.*, III, 11: the devil, the body, the thoughts. Cf. *infra*, chap. 9.

[8] *In Psalm.*, 2, 9.

the theological conclusions that flow therefrom, all of which things are acquired only after much effort and are granted to the virtuous man exclusively.

Origen recognized no boundary between contemplation and action. Holy reflections have their own work, a ceaseless inquiry in which the sense of the invisible world is sharpened and without which the soul's grasp of God's truth becomes weaker and weaker. "But his will is the law of the Lord, and on His law he shall meditate day and night."

The observance of God's law is only the manifestation of this inner discipline. The active side of the religious life resembles a simple melody in comparison with the magnificent music we call contemplation, but Origen makes it play its part in the gnosis. An action is born of every genuine thought. "The soul that meditates on the law of the Lord is not a soul that undertakes to review in memory the words of the law apart from the works of righteousness which are in agreement with the law; but it is the soul that succeeds in doing the works of righteousness from continually meditating on them. By reason of this continual meditation on the works prescribed by the law, the soul acquires a certain facility in fulfilling all the obligations that can bind the man who lives perfectly according to the law. This is the way the soul becomes capable of meditating on the law of the Lord day and night." [9]

The totality of the religious life consists of recollection: not the recollection of a mind withdrawing from the world of sense in order to follow a demonstration in geometry, but the recollection of the soul. This recollection is a necessary condition of prayer as it is made in the hearts of the saints, the prayer by which "the Spirit Himself asketh for us with unspeakable groanings." Our active part in this prayer of recollection has a kind of voice. When the thoughts within our hearts become focused on the things of God, that voice becomes the voice of our own intelligence speaking to us on the plane of pure contemplation. All that is needed is that we focus our thoughts, enter that upper chamber which is in our soul, and close

[9] *Ibid.*, 1, 2; P.G., XII, 1088.

the door of the senses in order that the current of our meditation may be cleansed and purified from the debris that comes from earthly things.

Recollection is also the necessary condition of virtue. By fixing our thoughts on the Good by means of persistent concentration, we annihilate evil thoughts, which are the proximate cause of sin. If we neglect to practice recollection and allow our minds to wander to the things of earth, our souls become as weak and as feeble as the diet on which they feed; we become as the dust of the pavements and as the wind that blows it away.

In thus emphasizing the active element in contemplation, Origen's system of spirituality gave their proper place to a number of inner acts which, being erroneously regarded as passions, had been held in little repute at the Academy up to this time. For example, this spiritual teaching gave new life to the active virtues of prayer, such as fear, hope, and joy. He distinguished fear from servility and called it reverence, for he held that a Christian at prayer is not necessarily motivated by the notion of punishment.[10] He was especially interested in restoring the virtue of hope to its due place in the Christian plan of life, for Clement had rejected that virtue in one of his last portraits of the Christian gnostic when he wrote: "Established already by the love of God in the good things which he shall possess, having left hope behind him by reason of the higher knowledge which he now has, he longs for nothing since he already is in possession of any and every object his heart could desire." Origen, on the contrary, argued in favor of this virtue of the strong, remembering St. Paul's saying, that charity hopeth all things: "not to lose hope of any of the good things that can be stored up for the reward of holiness, is the act of that soul alone which is clothed in perfect charity." Hope was, in his view, a hunger and thirst after justice, a longing for the kingdom of heaven, an intense desire to obtain God's mercy in the hour of death, and a perpetual eagerness for the realization of all the mysterious promises which God, who does not deceive us, made to His saints.

[10] *Ibid.*, 2, 11; P.G., XII, 1116.

He pointed out that the joy of the heart is very different from the joys of the flesh. That joy is nourished by the bread and stimulated by the wine to be found in the practice of contemplation. It is a spiritual joy, the light that shines forth from a soul in which virtue glows, a joy inspired by the hope of the things of eternity. The hearts of those who are immersed in the things of earth are too heavy to know this joy, which is the only joy that is real and lasting; they know nothing of the holy zeal of the Christian soul rejecting all human interests,[11] and they are ignorant that the Good and the Real are one and the same thing.

III. THE CHRIST OF THE PSALMS

Origen's *Commentary on the Psalms* shows his desire to enlarge upon the teachings of Clement and to make them more human and at the same time also more Christian. But when this first part of his Psalter is compared with the majority of the other works he published later during this Alexandrian period of his life, it shows in many passages the work of an influence earlier than that of Clement. Its theology of the Logos, for example, indicates that in this book Origen was following in the footsteps of Hippolytus, but in this theological domain the sweep and accuracy of the pupil's thought carry him far beyond the stand taken by the master.

The relations of the Father and the Son are based, not on the inner life of God as they would be in later books, but on the missions with which the Son is charged. Origen's theological argument rests almost entirely on the principal mission of the Son, that of redeeming mankind and of ushering in the Gospel period of human history. Jesus is given the title Son of God because of His birth in time. The expression "This day have I begotten Thee" refers to "the Savior's humanity, considered in terms of time and begotten in time. The Savior exists as man as long as there is a today, because in the duration of mankind's today, men will always need the help He can give them." Later in his life he gives quite another interpreta-

11 *Ibid.*, 4, 8; *P.G.*, XII, 1167.

tion of these words. Further study taught him that "the beginning of His birth is not found, as neither is the day of it." [12]

In his inclination to discuss together the eternal rights and the new rights of the incarnate Word, he follows Hippolytus. The Roman, seeing even in the life of Jesus the immutable relations of the Trinity, had employed the Gospel narrative as a mirror in which to study the reflected plan of that mystery. Origen follows the same line, regarding the Son as the sharer of the Father's purposes and as His right hand in the work of creation, and also as possessing already, in virtue of His divine nature, the world He is to conquer by His human nature. "Consider, then, how the Son will be able to be elevated in His flesh to the possession of those goods that already belong to Him by reason of His divinity; for those who are in the world, since they belong to the Father, can be considered to belong, in a certain way, to the Son, the sharer in the Father's purposes. How, then, can He receive from the Father the order to demand that the nations be given to Him for an inheritance and that His possessions should extend to the ends of the earth? The reason is that man, to avoid serving God, has risen in futile revolt against God; and the Father, who is the Creator of all beings, in His wish to redeem mankind has sent into this world the Logos, His only-begotten Son, to the end that the Son might be made flesh and go forth, without changing His divine nature, to preach deliverance to the captives and to give sight to the blind. Therefore we say that the Son receives His kingdom and is recognized as being established as the heir. But, although we can say this because of the human nature which He has assumed, we must be on our guard so as not to misunderstand the inner structure of the mystery of the Trinity." [13] These are the words and the thought of Hippolytus, showing Origen's care and alertness to unite the Logos to the eternal dignity of the Father. The entire passage displays Origen's doctrine long before it blossomed out.

Let us now turn to his commentary on the Fourth Gospel and see

---

[12] *In Joan.*, I, 32; P.G., XIV, 77. "This day" denotes a sort of indefinite duration, coexistent with eternity, which later theology would call *aevum*.

[13] *In Psalm.*, 2, 8; P.G., XII, 1108.

the teaching in full flower. We find a passage that might have been penned by Bérulle: "Jesus knew that the Father had committed all things into His hands. The Father had committed all things into the hands which laid hold on the universe in order that the universe should be truly in those hands. Or we can say that God has committed everything to Him, placing everything in His hands in order that He should do a certain work and in order that He should fulfill a certain beautiful plan? My Father acts up to the present moment, and I act with Him. The things that have gone forth from God have remained outside God; and He who had never the wish to go forth from the Father, or to be separated in His essence from the Father, also went forth, in order that He should receive into His hands what had already gone forth and that thus there might be fulfilled the eternal plan of leading to God the creatures that follow Jesus and that, because they have followed Him, shall be near God." [14]

INFLUENCE OF HIPPOLYTUS

Another evidence of the influence of Hippolytus is to be found in the fact that, in this first part of his Psalter, Origen refers only incidentally to the eternal kingdom of the Son and fails to make the procession of the Logos the core of his theological system as he begins to do later when he is writing the final chapters of the *De principiis*. In his *Commentary on the Psalms* he extols more often the victories of Christ's earthly mission, that "glory of Christ" which had made such a lively impression on him under the spell of the eloquence of Hippolytus. He sees the nations outside the faith, the tribes that are in schism, the kings of this world in the persons of Herod and Pilate, as being all joined together in a vile conspiracy against Jesus. But the Father will not abandon the Son to the mercy of evil powers and men who are leagued against Him. Rather He will establish Him in the glory which He had at the beginning, although He was not glorified in this world. Escorted into the heavenly Sion by legions of angels, the Savior will receive the peoples of the earth as His inheritance. Indeed His triumph begins here below,

[14] *In Joan.*, XXXII, 3; P.G., XIV, 748. The unity of operation of the Father and of the Son is frequently affirmed by Origen. Cf. *De princip.*, I, ii, 10.

in the Church on earth, for the Church is the dwelling place of the Lord. Origen sees all this as a victory that is just and good and real, for it is obtained by sweet persuasion, by that gentle teaching of Him who is the Good Shepherd. Threats and anger may mark His words, but they are calls to conversion. His rod of iron is soon to be put aside in favor of the rod that came forth from the root of Jesse.[15]

IV. THE ARCHAISM OF THIS TEACHING

The most diverse colors blend in this work of Origen's early years. Clement and Hippolytus have the leading parts in the drama of the narrative. The former's theories of the divine philanthropy soften the ruder expressions of Hippolytus. The Roman theologian, being more objective than Clement, dispels the utopias of the Alexandrian and proclaims as Leader of the Church militant the Master who had triumphed over suffering and death. Between these two masters, Origen gives us hardly a glimpse of what later becomes his own great theological system. Although often describing the stages of contemplation, he shows us little of the relations between the Logos and intelligence, nor does he discuss the divine act of illumination which would become, in the works written by him in later years, the essential episode in the process of salvation. He knows only that the divine Wisdom, according to its real or hypostatic substance, is identical with the Logos, and that the Logos, from the moment of His first appearance in the world of men, has blazed like a fire sent down from heaven to destroy the illogical and foolish teachings that intoxicate the minds of men. He also calls the Logos the crown that imparts dignity to human reason and elevates it to its pristine state of union with God, but he fails to push such ideas to further conclusions, for those ideas were the common property of the Alexandrian theology of the time.[16]

One definitely new element stands out in Origen's thought at this time, if we may trust the fragments of this work that contain mention of it. Clement had already called the Logos the face of

[15] *In Psalm.*, 2, 9; P.G., XII, 1109.
[16] *Ibid.*, 20, 4; P.G., XII, 1249.

God, the mysterious revelation of His majesty. Origen, following this thought, now began to seek in the Logos the secrets of divine providence. The mode of God's knowing was a problem that bulked large in the theological thought of the day. Does God possess within His own divine being the why and the wherefore of mundane occurrences? When we speak of the face of the Father, are we referring to this scroll of human history as being ever present to the mind of the Creator? We can contemplate the face of God in two ways or on two levels. If the contemplation is restricted to the level of this world, we can know nothing more than the history of the ages that have passed; this gives us a view of God's face, as in a glass darkly. The other level, whereon there is granted to us a knowledge both of the past and of the future, belongs to the kingdom of heaven. On that level everything falls into harmony in the beneficent plan of providence in which even the apparent enemies of God have their assigned place. In regard to the souls of the saints, they are exempted from the trial of various incarnations; they enter paradise behind the soul of Christ and approach it by degrees, thanks to the practice of contemplation.

This summary of views from the first part of the *Commentary on the Psalms* makes it quite obvious that the work lacked a definite teaching about the soul and the world. The lack could be explained by the incomplete transmission of the work as well as by the censorship exercised on it by successive compilers. Those scholars had the habit of composing passages to fill up gaps in the argument, each according to his own taste and his own reactions to the context. However, the number and the volume of the existing fragments, to which we may add those recently discovered, are sufficient to enable us to form a fairly accurate judgment of the character of this first part. A number of long fragments, the authenticity of which has been established by various arguments which are independent of each other and in which the flow of Origen's thought appears to be free of gaps, offer conclusive evidence that Origen had no definite theological system of his own at this date. Those fragments contain several passages where he would not have neglected the chance to put forward his own theological doctrines if he had written his *Commentary on the Psalms* a few years later, and there are other passages where a theological system of his own seems far from his thoughts.

The unedited fragments contain also some brief commentaries that show him as already preoccupied with the problem of the origin and restoration of human souls, but they give no warning of the theory of successive incarnations or of his belief in universal salvation, two ideas that he later put forward in his *De principiis*. For example, when the psalmist declares: "I have slept and have taken my rest," Origen thinks this may be a reference to the torpor which seizes a soul and makes it clothe itself with a body; and after death the soul descends into limbo from which, according to the traditional teaching, Christ has released the souls of earlier times who were imprisoned there.

MASTER OF THE SPIRITUAL LIFE

At the time of the publication of this first work our theologian had not yet begun to feel the ambitions that later made him the founder of a theological system, the head of a theological school, and even the leader of a party. At the outset of his career he was by nature a master of the spiritual life, a title he had yet to earn in the eyes of men after the brilliance and the sorrows of his last years in his native city. One day the storm that rages around his name will die down, and we shall see again the commentator of the psalms, yielding himself entirely to his studies of the soul, studies that were never really out of his thoughts even in those days when he was hoping to unlock the secrets of the universe. Origen was, above everything else, a man devoted to the things of the spirit. From the time he began to publish, he was always careful, beneath a manner that was still somewhat dry and bookish, to use his intelligence to guide him along the various stages of mysticism. To that habitual care he added the all-pervading enthusiasm which had filled his heart when he was describing for the first time the repentance, joy, and confidence inspired by the practice of holy religion as well as when he was making Jesus speak in the role of the prophet-king.

The book is therefore to be recognized as having come forth

when Christian contemplation was in its adolescence, in the days when the Church was still young. It is a bud of promise that will blossom forth in many other commentaries, whose authors are to learn from Origen how to meditate on the happiness that comes with holiness and on the mysteries of the suffering Christ. The most enduring thoughts are perhaps the early meditations that come from the mind of a master who is still a stranger to the grandeurs of the Spirit and who dedicates all his powers, disdaining the use of argument or theory, to the loyal and sincere service of the Word that was from God.

CHAPTER V

The Commentary on Lamentations
and
The Treatise on the Resurrection

AFTER the death of Septimius Severus an interval of peace came to the Christians, and the early activities of the head of the Alexandrian Academy began to receive public attention. In the year 214 or 215 there occurred an incident which testifies both to the personal influence which the young theologian wielded at that time and to the favor with which the Roman administration in the East regarded this representative of a doctrine condemned by imperial edict a few years previously. Throughout the various provinces of the Roman Empire the anti-Christian laws were not always administered with the same degree of uniformity. In certain provinces, especially those in Asia Minor and other parts of the East, Roman officials accepted the end of the persecution as an opportunity to initiate a policy of tolerance that was not without unsuspected elements of protection. Thus it happened that one of the officers of the garrison at Alexandria visited Demetrius, bishop of the see, and also waited upon the prefect of Egypt, bringing to those two men letters from the Roman governor of Arabia who had his headquarters at Bostra, a town where Origen was later to be hailed by the clergy for two great defenses of the Christian faith. Eusebius tells us that the Roman governor, interested perhaps by the theological discussions carried on by the Christians within his territory, requested that the head of the Alexandrian Academy should be sent to him as soon as possible "in order that he should communicate his doctrine to him."

I. ORIGEN'S VISIT TO PALESTINE

EMPEROR CARACALLA

On returning to Alexandria after a short absence, Origen found his native city decimated and terrorized by Caracalla. Although it lay on the border of an ancient land that had long been peopled by men devoted to the routine of peace, it was a city that knew little of the spirit of tranquillity. It had often been the scene of sudden riots and disturbances. The diverse racial elements making up its conglomerate population never blended into a social whole, and jealousy and suspicion divided class from class as if they were so many castes. Against the background of a countryside that was ignorant and unlettered, it was the most scholarly city in the world of that time, and possibly the most sophisticated. Its citizens were quite conscious of this superiority, and the knowledge of it gave them a feeling of their own independence of other men and other manners. Its half-Greek and half-native middle class was notable for a quality of bitter irony and did not hesitate to employ the weapon of ridicule against the Emperor without any thought for the conventions imposed by the rules of Roman decorum. They gave Caracalla the title which Alexander had borne with honor, vanquisher of the Getes; they called him the Getist. On their lips the epithet became a term of opprobrium, for it kept before men's minds the fact that Caracalla had murdered his own brother Geta. At a later date they contemptuously nicknamed Alexander Severus "the Syrian priest."

It did not take long for Origen to discover that Emperor Caracalla, on his way to winter quarters at Antioch, was making a brief but decidedly punitive halt at Alexandria: aliens were being expelled or imprisoned, schools were closed, and the entire city was being looted by the imperial soldiery. Men who were prominent in any walk of life were being marked for petty persecution, and an order was issued for the dissolution of the philosophical societies known generically as the "table companions." Origen wisely decided to leave the city at once. He returned to Palestine, and resumed his conferences at Caesarea. The bishops of the Church in that country requested him to preach and expound the Scriptures publicly, although he had not yet been ordained a presbyter. In his performance of this task he won two new friends; they were Theoctistus, bishop of Caesarea, and Alexander, bishop of Jerusalem.

ALEXANDER OF JERUSALEM

Alexander, formerly bishop of a diocese in Cappadocia, had known Pantaenus. During the persecution of Septimius Severus he was cast into prison, but he obtained help from Clement who was in Cappadocia at the time. Shortly before his release from captivity he wrote to the Christians at Antioch and entrusted his letter to Clement, "this blessed presbyter, a virtuous and esteemed man," whom he regarded as one of his spiritual advisers. When Caracalla first became emperor and initiated a policy of tolerance toward the Christians, Alexander made a pilgrimage to Jerusalem; he desired to become acquainted with the Holy City and to pray there, as Melito of Sardis had done before him. The Christians of Jerusalem would not permit him to return home, for a number of them had had revelations at night wherein they saw him as their bishop, chosen for them by God Himself. By the common consent of the bishops of the neighboring sees, he was named auxiliary to Narcissus, then the bishop of Jerusalem but already advanced in years. Soon he was being called to settle the disputes among the Christians at Antinoe, for they recognized him as wielding the authority of the Church of the Hebrews.

He was affable and conciliatory in the discharge of his episcopal duties, but capable of firmness in the defense of a friend. His kindly demeanor was in striking contrast with the severe eloquence of Origen. The great Alexandrian, whose pupils were always quick to praise his gentle and penetrating methods of teaching, allowed himself certain elements of rudeness as a preacher. When he compared his own ideals of Christian perfection with the routine practice of the faithful or with the cupidity and laziness of certain members of the clergy, he was as unable to control his impatience as any other such intellectual Christian might be under the same circumstances. A certain sharpness began to appear in his style of preaching, and

he himself acknowledged it in one of his homilies given at Jerusalem. "Do not expect," he says, "to hear from me the gracious
words that you hear from your Bishop Alexander. I agree with you
that he is outstanding in the charm which marks his gentleness, and
I know you have been accustomed to enjoy those delightful exhortations that pour forth from his fatherly heart, vivified as it is with the
spirit of charity. But in my garden the herbs are of a sharper taste,
and you will find them salutary remedies when you come here to
pray." [1]

Alexander's friendship with Origen continued to be unbreakable
and became even warmer and stronger with time. He was bound to
Origen by his recollections of Pantaenus and Clement, those
"blessed and memorable men" whose successor he saw in the young
Alexandrian. He shared Origen's enthusiasm for theology and his
dream of attracting educated men to a contemplative form of life
which would draw its strength from the Christian faith. It is not im-
probable that Origen's advice was responsible for his subsequently
establishing in Jerusalem the first great Christian library. He was
far from patient with the fact that the great genius within his young
friend's soul was not consecrated with the oils of ordination to the
priesthood, for he perceived the resources of scholarship from
which he could draw in his eagerness for the instruction of his Christian flock. In his own study of Holy Scripture he preferred to hew
fast to the line of historical interpretation and to solve his biblical
difficulties by the use of that method. The allegorical interpretation
interested him also, but he was drawn to it by reasons very different from those which were bringing it into fashion at the Academy
of Alexandria. Far from seeing it as a scholarly technique destined
for the education of privileged souls, he regarded it as a means
of drawing from Holy Scripture moral lessons applicable to all
grades of Christian life. [2] He knew that at Alexandria it was held to
be a truism that only in the contemplative life of the most perfect

[1] *Hom. I in Sam.* (*I Reg.*); P.G., XII, 995: The *Homilies on the Book of Kings* were
delivered at Jerusalem.
[2] *Hom. II in Sam.* (*I Reg.*); P.G., XII, 1013. In the *Stromata* Origen begins to show
a great desire to communicate his knowledge to the faithful. Cf. St. Jerome, *In Dan.*;
P.G., XXV, 581; XI, 105.

souls can the parable come to full flower. But his own thought was that the parable is, first of all, the art of reaching the hearts of the simple and unlearned.

Since Origen was Alexander's guest and since Alexander enjoyed the primacy of honor among the bishops of Palestine, Theoctistus appealed to the primate to allow his guest to come to Caesarea and to preach to the faithful there. With Alexander's approval Origen accepted the invitation and preached in the Christian assemblies there, giving explanations of Holy Scripture, although he was but a layman. He followed the same program at Jerusalem itself.

His friendship with those two prelates gave Origen the opportunity to visit the chief places of interest in the Holy Land. For the first time in his life he was able to walk in the very footsteps of Jesus and the prophets, and to linger in those sacred places whose mysterious names had given him food for meditation over a number of years. Probably he penetrated the countryside as far as the river Jordan. It is quite certain that he visited Jericho, because we know that he discovered in that city a Greek translation of the Old Testament; he later incorporated that translation in his Hexapla, where it reappeared in the sixth column. At the village of Hebron his guides showed him the tomb of the patriarchs in the double cave of Machpelah. When he saw Jerusalem, he felt that its mere appearance proclaimed the almighty power of God.

JERUSALEM

At the period of his visit, Jerusalem was known as Aelia. It was still the principal city of Palestine but would soon lose that honor in favor of Caesarea. Although it had fallen from its high estate and was nothing more than a small and impoverished Roman colony, it enjoyed a prestige which the neighboring towns were jealous of. Reached by any one of a number of lonely roads, it stood on the hill of Sion; and, if the visitor came to it from the higher ground, it appeared to be set on the very crest of the little hill with a system of roads radiating from it to other towns. This plan of it, as the hub of a giant wheel, was the sole reminder of its former greatness. In the bleak and untilled lands lying around it a few shabby buildings could be seen here and there. But in the entire picture there was nothing to remind the traveler that he was approaching the site of a capital city.

This was the fallen Sion as Origen saw it for the first time: an abandoned and desolate queen holding forth her hands in supplication, as the prophet had foretold. The whole aspect of the city and its surroundings reminded him of the relaxed and idle hands of laborers whom no master has hired. The mighty palaces were gone, and the lofty walls that had been part of their glory lay in ruins. Gazing on those pitiful reminders of the greatness and the glory of Jerusalem's past, he heard all about him the weeping and groaning of a motley crowd of Jews, in none of whom could he discern the marks of king or prophet or chief. The presence of the Jews, contemplating the memories of their former glory by permission of the Roman authorities, brought home to him the destiny of this fallen people, living in perpetual exile even in the land which had been its own. And when he walked among the poorer classes who dwelt in Jerusalem's ghetto, he recognized the bitter fact that they had lost even the knowledge of their own abasement.

The sight of the ruins and the memory of the disasters that had befallen the chosen people led Origen to meditate on the invisible history of a fallen soul. Up to that time he had always preferred to consider the ideal life as one of inner spiritual victories bringing joy to him who struggled successfully for the palm. Evil, he had always held, was not a real thing. In his Alexandrian optimism, which had been fed by the fruits of a robust spiritual discipline, he had considered evil an emptiness, a lack, a dust carried away by the wind. But here this evil, this nothingness, was real enough to leave ruin and devastation in its wake. That ruin was lasting, and its effects at Jerusalem were age-long. God's absence was written on the face of the conquered land. This lack of God and this dreadful silence in which God's sustaining word was no longer heard were, for Origen, the last phase of the history of the Jews. What then is the desolation into which a human soul can be plunged by sin?

THE COMMENTARY ON THE LAMENTATIONS

Now, he reasoned, God cannot abandon a soul, for He has created it to know the reasons of things, to contemplate. We know further that He has reserved in the hearts of His saints a place of retirement where He can rest and receive the worship of an intelligence that has been purged of all dross and is at peace within itself. In the creation of a soul God does not produce an unfinished or imperfect work.[3] The created soul, however, has within itself the power to turn away from God, the power to abandon truth for falsehood, and reality for illusion.

Considered from this angle, evil assumes a new aspect, which manifests itself in the first culpable negligence of God and in all that follows in the train of that primary fault. Understood in this sense, evil is called sin, and Origen saw the abasement of the soul as nothing but the logical result of this turning away from God. God's help, he reasoned, is lacking to the soul that has broken the bond holding it to God. Such a soul, widowed and desolate like Jerusalem, readily becomes the prey of its enemies. Indeed, its distress only adds to the strength of its foes. As progress in virtue on the part of the soul weakens the devil and dissipates his power as the wind carries away the dust in the road, so sin on the contrary encourages him and makes him daring. He then hurls himself at the noblest part of the soul and despoils it. Thus confusion takes the place of order in the life of the soul. My sins, says the sinner, weigh heavily on my shoulders and my strength is gone. Sin takes possession of the soul and rules it completely.[4] The soul is thus held in bondage without ever being able to realize commensurably its own desires or to satisfy them in any degree. Origen began to view evil as boundless, and passion as a kind of infinity.

But God's love for man never loses its rights, and misfortune is

[3] In the first chapter of the *Commentary* there is a history of the fall of the soul, although all suggestions of myth are carefully eliminated. The primitive state is described as contemplation, which is intuitive and discursive. Cf. I, 608 f., 619, 621, 624; a state of vigilance, I, 612. Cf. *ibid.*, I, 625; *De princip.*, I, vi, 2.

[4] The state of sin is compared with the confusion of Babylon. The word σύγχυσις was applied by certain religious philosophies of the time to the unity of body and soul, and expressed an interior state of that union; *Selecta in Threnos*, I, 612.

useful in guiding men toward holiness and in exalting the virtuous life. From the ruins of Jerusalem there came a cry of hope. "I am abandoned to my sufferings," she said to the nations of the world, "in order that you should find your place. Because of you I have become an enemy of God although He had chosen me to be His beloved because of my fathers. Hear my sigh and understand why I weep. . . . Blessedness is primarily the avoidance of sin, but in the second place it is the confession to God of the sins we have committed. When the rest of the nations of the world will be saved, I in my turn, Lord, shall obtain salvation according to Thy just judgments." [5]

Even in the midst of its darkness the soul that has sinned is not without its intuition of the peace that comes from God, and Origen saw some hope for the Jewish people and for the city that was sunk in despair. *His Commentary on the Lamentations*, besides being a penetrating and abstract study in the realm of psychology, recorded some of his impressions of Palestine wherein he uncovered, as it were, the reverse side of the joyous pictures he paints in his *Commentary on the Psalms*, his view of sin as the complement of his view of perfection. But even on this other side of the picture there was light and mercy and consolation. Origen did not forget that the Lamentations end with a prayer to divine providence.

We need have little hesitation in believing that during this first visit to Palestine he consulted the Jewish patriarch and the learned rabbis of the country on various exegetical problems that had been puzzling him. Certainly he must have discussed with them the titles of the psalms, for at that period he was deep in the study of this problem in preparation for the introduction to his *Commentary*. Soon, as Eusebius tells us, he was summoned home by his own bishop. "Demetrius sent for him by letter, and urged him through members and deacons of the Church to return to Alexandria. So he returned and resumed his accustomed duties." There were reasons, other than the short-lived persecution of Caracalla, to induce him to prolong his stay in Palestine. But he was prompt to

[5] *Ibid.*, II, 632. The numerous similarities between the *Com. in Lament.* and the *Com. in Psalm.* suggests that the two works belong to the same period.

obey, although he had enjoyed his newly found liberty and was already drawing richly on the kindness of his new friends and on the encouragement they were giving him for the elaboration of his doctrines. Perhaps the good Bishop of Alexandria was disturbed when he heard of a layman being officially authorized to preach in the Christian assemblies. If such was really the cause of Origen's recall, Demetrius allowed no sign of his anxiety to appear at the moment when he welcomed home the incomparable catechist who was such a glory to the Christian community over which he ruled.

II. THE DOCTRINE OF THE RESURRECTION

Assured of the protection of his two friends in the episcopate of Palestine, Origen soon began to stand forth as the leader of a theological party. The friendly enthusiasm with which they had surrounded him had been evoked as much by their interest in his scholarly enterprise as by the courtesy and charm of his behavior. They looked to him as a Christian thinker capable of devising a theological system that would appeal to the minds of cultured men, many of whom were beginning at that time to show an interest in the doctrines of Christianity. Indeed that interest was becoming more manifest every day. The two bishops regarded Origen as a scholarly genius who would know how to solve the problem over which they fretted and how to safeguard the traditions on which Christianity was nourished without depending on the gross concepts and the flimsy notions into which the childlike beliefs of the simple Christians of an earlier age had been permitted to grow.

THE RISEN BODY

The first sign of the new technique in the study of Christian tradition came with Origen's treatment of the dogma of the resurrection of the body after death. Christian belief on this subject was in direct and startling contrast to the fashionable Hellenism of the day, and Origen had already given it a passing consideration in his commentary on the first psalm. Christian apologists were content, for the most part, to teach with the Church that the risen body will be identical with the body in which the individual lives his earthly span, except for the fact that the risen body will be incorruptible. In explanation of this new element of incorruptibility, they said that nothing is impossible for God. Other Christian writers were called in mockery "friends of the flesh," because they sought to explain the resurrection of the body as involving a second coming of Christ and His establishment of an earthly kingdom in which the risen would live in the midst of abundance and be surrounded with pleasures of every kind. In general the pictures that Christian apologists endeavored to paint of the resurrection of the body after death served only to evoke laughter from their adversaries. But, laughter or no laughter, the question remained: Why did the Christians take such pains to denounce this earthly mode of existence as vile and carnal although, at the same time, they were so eager that it be prolonged into the realm of immortality?

Now, Christian tradition teaches that the body will rise again. Origen held that this dogma is to be interpreted in the light of the knowledge we have, aided by the word of God. Thus, we must not attribute to God any power that is absurd and unworthy of the divine dignity. We know that our bodies are not substantially the same from one day to another. A continual process of renewal is ever at work in the flesh and the tissues. But over against this, there is, even in physical life, a principle of continuity or an individuality. That continuity or that individuality is made evident to us by a totality of external characteristics, by one form proper to Peter and by another form proper to Paul. Despite the ceaseless process of renewal, there is a definite persistence; particularities, personal marks, even scars are involved in that persistence.

What is to be revived after death? Is it the physical characteristics which, in this earthly life, distinguish one man from another? Consider the physical organs of the body. They are the instruments of the soul; and if they become useless, they must either disappear altogether or adapt themselves to a new environment. The spiritual world is a new environment. The body becomes refined there, being made spiritual and being rendered capable of understanding things which it has hitherto been unable to grasp.

Origen did not consider it necessary to accept literally the Scriptural metaphors, such as the parable of Lazarus or the story of the just man. He held that the *materia prima* of the body does not rise from the dead, at least not in its entirety.[6] In spite of that fact, however, the risen individual is recognizable, just as Jesus, Moses, and Elias were recognizable after death.

Origen's use of those three great names as part of his argument was quite enough to startle his public, and he found it expedient to give a further explanation of his theory. This explanation appeared in one of his subsequent commentaries. "I affirm, with an absolute faith, that Christ was the first to ascend into heaven in His flesh." He further stated that, in the ascension, the body of Christ was already purged of all human weaknesses at the heavenly altar. It is to be noted that he made no such assumptions in regard to Enoch or Elias.[7]

From the first moment of its appearance this new theory of the resurrection of the body evoked such a storm of criticism that Origen saw the need for a careful and scientific exposition of his views. He was further led to this decision by the fact that Christian beliefs about the life after death were beginning to seize the attention of thinkers outside the Church. Possible explanations of this change of front in the non-Christian philosophical world are to be found in the growth of Aristotelianism, the emergence of a philosophical outlook that was not wholly Greek, and the reverence that Christians were beginning to pay, openly and without any effort at concealment, to the relics of the holy martyrs. Besides, Tertullian had already written on this subject of the resurrection after death. Hippolytus would soon do the same, at the request of Empress Mammaea, who was not a Christian. In view of all these considerations, Origen determined to write a theological treatise on the problem. Known to literary history as the *Treatise on the Resurrection*, it consisted of two parts.[8]

[6] *In Psalm.*, 1, 5; P.G., XII, 1092.
[7] *Ibid.*, 15, 9; P.G., XII, 1215.
[8] *The Treatise on the Resurrection* is known by quotations given by Pamphilius in his *Defense of Origen* and indirectly by the criticism of Methodius.

TREATISE ON THE RESURRECTION

In the first part Origen made his confession of faith: we shall rise from the dead with our own bodies. In the case of a holy martyr who suffers the torments of prison life, of the scourgings, of the conflicts in the arena, or of a death on the cross, will such a witness for the faith be recompensed in his soul only? Consider also the martyrdoms borne by the Christian soul in a life of daily mortification. All such sufferings concern the body more than they do the soul, because it is by the passions of the body that we are subjected to temptation. In the body, then, merit is acquired. In this first part of his work Origen did not hesitate to employ several of the traditional arguments which had already been used by Tertullian and by the majority of the Christian apologists.

After making his profession of faith in the Christian tradition of the resurrection of the body, he proceeded, in the second part, to his justification of it. He knew that his task was to expound a Christian belief to men who were not Christians. Hence he took care to adjust his exposition to the intelligence of his audience. The First Epistle to the Corinthians gave him his starting point. In the comparison used by St. Paul, the seed which the hand of the sower casts on the earth seems to die, dissolving in the elements in which it is concealed. But soon its root (seminal force) manifests itself in concrete form—life invincible asserting its right to self-development even within an environment of death. It proceeds to push its way through the ground which encloses it, becoming, as it were, a new creator. It forms for itself its own special set of qualities, its own size and dimension, its own very appearance. Nothing can halt the progress of that creative force, neither water nor air nor earth nor fire. It continues to grow. Ultimately it lifts its stalk and its ear of grain to the light of the noonday sun. This triumph over death is the symbol of the resurrection. Note that the ear is not the grain. It is, however, an essential phase of the process by which the grain arrives at existence.

Consider the resurrection of the dead. The state of glory is the environment uniquely favorable to the development of the germ of resurrection. That germ is already hidden in the matter of which our physical being here below is constituted—the seminal force of eternal life, analogous to the seminal force that causes plants and all living things to grow. The living being endowed with the power of self-movement and self-nutrition possesses a psychic force superior to that of the vegetable. Man's biological equipment possesses also its own special psychic force, its own proper power of ultimately conquering death. That power moves into action under the drive of man's spiritual destiny, as soon as that destiny is finally delivered from the environment which encloses it. Better than the old theory of an individual type and a universal ocean of life, Origen's notion of a germ of the body's restoration already implanted in the living human being made it a little easier to understand how eternity can play a part in the development of a being which, if left to its own proper order of existence, is always perishable.

In support of this view Origen relied on Scripture, but he warned his readers not to be too ready to give to the biblical passages concerned the first interpretation that comes to mind. As a case in point, he took issue with the partisans of an integral resurrection of the body after death, a school of thought which basing its arguments on the famous prophecy of Ezechiel about the dried bones that will live again. They held that in the resurrection our bones will be reassembled, that muscles and flesh will adhere to them, and that a skin will cover them.

Against this theory Origen held that we cannot rightly interpret any prophecy, even in a spiritual sense, without taking account of the circumstances in which the prophecy was originally uttered. The dried bones of Ezechiel's vision represent the people of Israel, in whom the vigor of life had been exhausted by years of captivity, by disappointments, and by troubles of every kind. To that sorely smitten people God promised a return from their exile, a return that was to be a sort of glorious resurrection for them. It might be objected that any such promise is not applicable to the Jews, for their entire subsequent history was marked by a series of disasters. Origen met this objection by saying that the subsequent disasters of the people of Israel are precisely the reason why an exegesis of this passage must uncover in it ideas loftier than the ambitions of a material prosperity. He held that in our interpretation of Scripture we must learn to see the work of the Spirit in all its glorious amplitude. Before giving life to the body, the Spirit opens the unholy tomb wherein the sinner lies shrouded in his faults. There are pardons which can be considered the sign of an ultimate resurrection.[9]

A second objection was based upon the apparition of the risen Jesus in the upper room with the wounds in His feet and hands and the opening in His side. Was not this a proof that the body will rise from the dead in precisely the same condition in which it left this earthly life? Origen met the objection by asserting that the Savior, in view of the fact that His full glory had profoundly dazzled His apostles in the Transfiguration on Thabor, caused that glory to be diminished for them on this later occasion. The plan of the Incarnation was not yet fully achieved. In heaven our Lord no longer bears the wounds of His passion, but He wished to leave to His followers the memory of His bruised and humiliated flesh. At that time their souls were not advanced enough in the path of His love to see Him as He really was in the splendor of His glory.

At this point Origen warned his readers of the prevailing habit of using the word "flesh" in discussions on the resurrection of the body. He held that in such discussions the word should be understood in a broader sense. It must not be forgotten that the state of glory is like that of the angels. In that higher life the body does not sin, for it is no longer subject to the infirmities or the corruption that mark our life on earth. It becomes, in the resurrection, a flesh with which we can please God. The Apostle, desiring to tell us that after our departure from this life of misery we shall be called to glory, says that "all flesh shall see the salvation of God." Pursuing this line of thought, Origen remarked that we speak of the flesh as dust because of the lowly element from which the flesh comes.

[9] Origen always insisted that the historical and moral sense of a scriptural passage should be established before proceeding to the spiritual interpretation. Cf. *In Psalm.*, 1, 5; *P.G.*, XII, 1096.

CRITICISM OF THE TREATISE

Returning to his non-Christian audience, Origen explains to them that the spiritual germ, the very marrow of all human life, is not at the mercy of the elements into which the body dissolves. From any state whatever and from any condition whatever the body can rise again. The reason of this is that the soul, whether in a high state of development or not, expresses itself in the resurrection. When the Apostle enumerates the list of living things (I Cor. 15: 39–42), he gives a picture of the difference that separates the sublime life of the righteous from the unhappy and miserable condition of sinners.

The *Treatise on the Resurrection* offended Christian opinion. Its subtle theories were imperfectly grasped in other theological centers which adhered closely to Christian tradition and which lacked, at the same time, the strong metaphysical tendency that marked the life of the Academy at Alexandria. More than one great Christian writer belonged to the class of those whom Origen complained of as closed minds and advocates of the short view. Indeed, the majority of Christian apologists, even Tertullian himself, belong to what were known as the simple. Those conservatives, including good writers, could point to famous treatises written by their own champions. Their verdict on the second part of Origen's work was that it was chimerical and absurd.[10] Who could recognize, they said, the great doctrine of the resurrection of the body in this unreasonable disguise? What is this ethereal life where the body, translucent and ghostly, is reduced to a minimum of matter which can be put at the service of the mind?

While the orthodox were charging him with boldness, certain of the heretical sects accused him of cowardice. Chief among these critics were the Syrians, who subscribed to the doctrines of Bardesanes. Adhering to half the formula which they had received from all the ancient creeds, they asserted that they believed in the resurrection from the dead. They denied, however, the resurrection of

---

[10] *De princip.*, II, x, 2: "Some take offense at the Creed of the Church, as if our belief in the resurrection were foolish and altogether devoid of sense; and these are principally heretics."

the flesh. The soul could unite itself, without danger of debasement, only to a sort of quintessence or ethereal matter.

At this juncture Origen decided to strengthen his teaching on the resurrection by making a place for it in his *De principiis*. He had no difficulty in blending the new theory into his general system of cosmology which made the world of bodies depend on the world of spirits. The *Treatise on the Resurrection* taught that, with the unique exception of God, no spirit is utterly incorporeal. The soul always possesses the virtualities of a physical life proportioned to its needs. Besides, the physical organism always tends to adapt itself to the function or set of functions which it has cultivated. The gross and earthly condition of the soul, as we know it here below, is the result of a diminution of spiritual activity. If the primary union between God and the individual intelligence is re-established, the entire body sees God, understands Him, and knows Him. Every step taken by the soul in the direction of such a re-establishment makes it more capable of contemplating the goodness of God.

INFLUENCE OF PSYCHISM ON MATTER

Against the two criticisms of his treatise, Origen employed this doctrine of total progress in the spiritual life. It was a tenuous argument, but he followed it with his usual logic. Against the orthodox, the friends of the flesh, he relied on St. Paul and affirmed that matter is plastic and that a higher and more developed psychism modifies the lower functions of the body. Against the heretics, the friends of quintessence, he maintained that no spiritual progress is possible without the permanence of the individual and that the holiness of the soul has its roots in the spiritual opportunities of this earthly life.

This sort of argumentation gave rise to a number of new problems. If spiritual beings can discard their weight of flesh, is there anything to curb their drive toward the divine? If, on the other hand, there always remains within them some element of matter to prevent them from ever achieving a perfect likeness to the divine object of their love and of blending themselves with Him, is the union to which the divine promise calls them to remain always imperfect? Here was a dilemma that challenged Origen's bold theological genius. Striving to escape from it, he fell back upon the thought of a final transformation whereby all souls would be ultimately reunited in one dwelling-place, in the holiest of the heavenly worlds. Even this solution was discarded as soon as he proceeded to examine the principles on which it rested.

Something of a record of this theological storm was preserved at the theological school of Caesarea. In its library there was found many years later an apocryphal document known as the *Dialogue of Adamantius*. The latter part of this little work contains an account of a disputation between Origen and the heretic Marinos, a disciple of Bardesanes. Although at least one passage of this report is undoubtedly written in the style of Eusebius, the opinions attributed to Origen are quite in harmony with what we know was his doctrine on this theological problem. The style is definitely like the way Origen talked and wrote, but there is no theological rashness. In this connection we should remark that the head of the Academy of Alexandria had his moments of strict orthodoxy. An example of this was the first part of the *Treatise on the Resurrection*, where his statement of Christian principles was most correct, an attitude that was to be expected in the case of an author who was endeavoring to build his theological system on no other foundation than the common faith of Christendom. The *Dialogue* has several other reminders of his orthodoxy. Also reminiscent of Origen's technique is the way the unknown author of this little work employs a certain exegetical skill in his interpretation of passages written by St. Paul. In each instance his approach is philological as well as spiritual, just as Origen's approach would have been.

We are not far wrong in assuming that the principal parts of the *Dialogue of Adamantius* are derived from originals that were authentic. Probably the originals were notes giving accounts of one or several disputations held by Origen during his journeys through Syria. Eusebius was in a position to discover such notes at the library of Caesarea. He could have worked over them and completed them by editing them in the convenient form of a dialogue, a method enabling him to strengthen the weaker parts of the theory outlined in the notes by contrasting them with the more orthodox passages from the *Treatise on the Resurrection*. In the final revision he added some ideas of his own. Judged in this way, the *Dialogue* must exonerate Origen's memory from the many errors and contradictions with which Methodius of Olympus assailed him a few decades later in a thoroughgoing criticism which the good Bishop's deferential manner was a poor disguise for the bitterness of his attack. Years after Origen's death a *Fourth Book on the Resurrection* was discovered, containing a number of new arguments in support of the original theory. We are safe in believing that this apocryphal work had the same history as the *Dialogue of Adamantius*, being similarly derived from a series of scattered notes.[11]

INTERPRETATIONS OF THE DOCTRINE

Origen's theory of the resurrection of the dead had a mixed success. As we have just seen, it was the occasion of the first great attack on his orthodoxy. Even when the storms of that academic warfare had passed, the greater part of the leading theologians of the Church at that time rejected the theory as being coarse and absurd. This almost unanimous dismissal of Origen's effort to solve the problem of the resurrection of the dead came at a time when the golden age of the first theologies of the East had become little more than a past that was hidden in obscurity, a period when Origen's fruitful genius had been whittled down to a number of absurd propositions on which certain monks in Palestine were satisfying their curiosity. As we come into the relatively modern period of Christian theology, we find that the theologians tended to disregard the excesses of the theory and judged it as being incoherent rather than blameworthy. They even found that it could be reconciled with the dogma of the Church, except in small matters that were of little account. Many theologians, however, neglected it entirely, their verdict being that Origen had not been able to fit into his system of theology the tradition of the resurrection of the dead.

Our own judgment is that the history of this Origenist theory is the history of the whole theological system which Origen en-

---

[11] Jerome, *Ad Pam.*; P.G., XI, 97. Eusebius and Rufinus knew only two books of the *Treatise on the Resurrection*. St. Jerome mentions four books.

deavored to build. Here are the typical weaknesses and the typical strength. Origen is sometimes too much in the clouds. He is often unduly scornful of the flesh and always unmindful of the ways of the world of living men and women. Yet he is keenly logical and manifests an ability to grasp that strange inner force which, in the case of souls dedicated to the life of the spirit, transfigures even the body.

Besides, the history of the treatise is not without its special meaning for us. Although the entire episode took place in a remote center of theological study, it offers us an eloquent example of what the Academy at Alexandria attempted to do for Christianity. One day the master pauses at a verse in the Psalter and summons philosophy to his aid. In the early phase of this new technique of interpreting the psalms, what comes to his mind is merely an ordinary proposition from Plato, familiar enough to the learned pupils to whom he is speaking. He delivers the words of Plato, words which express the contrast between the fleeting appearances of things and the unchangeable type. Remember that he is lecturing in a school which upholds the idea of the individual. Then we come to the next phase, in which new theories begin to take shape and to manifest the vitality that has given them birth. He must analyze them in a philosophical setting. They have come to his mind hastily and incidentally, without being a part of any philosophical system. Well, he will construct a philosophy for them. Better still, he will adjust them to a Christian philosophy. In the epistles of St. Paul he will seek a way of directing this pagan wisdom, now at last turning toward the truth. He will learn to meditate on the ascent of the soul wherein the atmosphere of the Spirit envelops the entire human being. Then will come the time to compare other scriptural texts, both the texts that offer support to the new theories and the ones that present objections. When all this has been done, a new theory can be released from its nest within his mind and can be trusted to try the strength of its own wings. When he comes to the writing of the *De principiis*, he will report, in chapter after chapter, the philosophical researches of several years.

In that picture of his life in the lecture-room, we have the story of Origen. In that limited domain we can watch the rise and fall of the graph that records his development. When he comes to the great task of knitting his theories into one great theological system, we shall see the tracing of the same graph but in a broader and heavier line.

As he stood up to lecture to a class of pupils, many of whom were converts that had grown up in the doctrines of the traditional philosophy of the Stoics and were imbued with its notion of a comprehensive system of thought, he felt the need of a definite body of doctrine. He would feel that need even more keenly during the theological controversies which so often interrupted his academic life.

CHAPTER VI

Gnosticism and Marcionism

I. GNOSTIC INFILTRATIONS AT ALEXANDRIA

THE academic atmosphere at Alexandria was marked by no sullen hostility toward views alien from its own. Indeed, it was readily admitted that before becoming wise and holy a man must have tried other philosophical systems. Origen, however, had Christianity in his very blood and never subscribed to any such tolerance. Even as an orphan seventeen years old, when he was enjoying the financial help of a great lady of wealth and distinction who treated him as an adopted son, he refused to compromise in any degree, according to Eusebius: "She was treating with great honor a famous heretic then in Alexandria, a certain Paul of Antioch. Origen could never be induced to join with him in prayer . . . and, as he somewhere expresses it, he abominated heretical teachings."

But he could not ignore them, for they infiltrated in many ways the atmosphere in which he lived. They were a source of disturbance to the faithful because of their astrological teachings. Astrology was in great favor and enjoyed the patronage of scholarly men as well as that of the poor and lowly. Its devotees, to protect themselves from the slings and arrows of destiny, had the habit of engraving prayer formulas on jewels and amulets. In those invocations no power was forgotten, neither the God of the Hebrews nor Christ nor even the daemons that were supposed to rule the heavenly spheres. The prayers were usually followed by a series of petitions in the matter of corporal or external goods. Origen denounced all such invocations and requests as "empty words which shattered at one and the same time the unity of God and the simplicity of Christian prayer." [1] The poison of magic was in the atmosphere in which the pupils of the Academy were striving to learn the philosophical foundations of the Christian faith.

[1] *De oratione*, XXI, 1 and 2.

THE ALEXANDRIAN PUBLIC

Another source of danger at the Academy was the presence of hecklers, attracted to the classes by the renown of the young teacher. In Origen's earlier works there was preserved the record of several of the discussions to which those hecklers gave rise. When a difficult passage of the Bible was under consideration, they used to take pride in throwing light on the problem by opposing to the Artisan of the universe a higher principle of action. Christian gnosis at Alexandria relied on biblical interpretation to a greater degree than at any other theological center. At every step the student of Christian exegesis was confronted with objections on the part of the heterodox.

In their fever for something new, heretics poured into Alexandria. What attracted them was the spirit of the city itself rather than the atmosphere of the Academy or the ideals of its head. Even the heretical preachers were not slow to feel the effect of that spirit. An example is the heretic Apelles. On his arrival at Alexandria he so far forgot the teaching he had imbibed at Rome from Marcion as to admit the pre-existence of souls and a sort of procession of them. In the preceding century the son of the gnostic Basilides had come to Alexandria and soon yielded to the influence of that center of learning; he was not slow to accommodate to the more sophisticated scholarship of the West the crude legacy of gnosticism he had inherited from his father. It was in those years at Alexandria that this man succeeded in translating the gross metaphors of Syrian gnosis into a system of psychology that was at once more elegant and more classical than he had ever before known. This city of Alexandria was the stage on which Philo had once received such acclaim as being perhaps greater than the Greek philosophers themselves, and biblical knowledge was held in higher esteem there than anywhere else in the world of learning. Biblical lore was regarded as a preparation for that Wisdom which transforms the soul and as a step toward the mystical life. Every heretical sect aspired to a knowledge of the Bible. In studying the ebb and flow of those early scriptural controversies, the critic is struck not so much by the differences separating the various schools of thought as by the common feeling of a great body of scholarly and daring thinkers who continually sought in the mysteries of the holy books the secrets of eternal life.

When the philosophy of Greece was in full flower, the local religions of antiquity remained in the twilight. As Greek tended more and more to become the universal language of the civilized world, those religions began to reappear. They were in slightly disguised forms, of course, but they had the prestige of centuries of existence behind them. When crude and unscholarly translations of their teachings were circulated, even their crudeness attracted the general public, for it was a time when people were in love with mystery and were weary of the shams of the Attic school. In such an atmosphere Hermas, the shepherd of souls, reveals to the initiated the reason of his existence on earth, teaches him that the life here below is an evil, and delivers him from it by a sudden rebirth on another level of existence, that of perfect purity and total knowledge in a heavenly world. The gnosis of the Egyptians claimed to transform the soul and to render it impassible.

Such are the mysteries. Such is that occult philosophy "by means of which false knowledge is introduced into the minds of men, and human souls are led astray, while they imagine that they have discovered wisdom." [2] The Egyptian goddess Isis is given the Greek name for wisdom and represents a wisdom that is of the princes of this world, a wisdom of those evil spirits that set traps for credulous souls and control by their unholy influence those who preach their accursed message and those who practice their nefarious arts. This is the verdict written by Origen at the end of his De principiis where he sums up the results of his long struggle with the gnosis in vogue in Egypt. His study of its origins led him to the discovery of the ultimate cause of the gnostic scandal of his day; he found one temptation common to every form of gnosis, the temptation to mistake magic for truth. He lived in a city swarming with all sorts

[2] De princip., III, 3; De triplici sapientia, 2: "The wisdom of the princes of this world we understand to be such as the secret and occult philosophy, as they call it, of the Egyptians."

of heresies. With the lower forms of Egyptian gnosis he did not concern himself, nor did he manifest any interest in the fakirs of its filth or the adorers of the serpent or any of those charlatans who pandered to the superstitious tastes of the populace. It was as if his inquiring mind halted at the frontiers of that strange and twilight country of fraud and chicanery. What really evoked his interest was the fact that a number of the leading heretics professed to take their stand on what they claimed to be the doctrines of Christianity.

Those champions of a Christian gnosis appeared to him to show neither the progress nor the vitality to be expected from Christian scholars. He saw them as men set firmly within their own systems of thought. Under the ever-changing aspects of their teaching and under the apparent concessions they were repeatedly making to whatever opinion prevailed at the moment, their profound tendencies were always the same. Even their public disputations, in which they never failed to show their opposition to the mind of the Church, showed those veteran leaders of heresy to be mere doctrinaires incapable of progress. From time to time they might shift their ground, but such changes gave no evidence of a vital development in the direction of truth. The gnostic had passed beyond the phase where a man sought truth.[3] He had already found it and was in the highest degree of initiation where the soul finds repose. Despite all that, Origen saw every gnostic of his day, whether his name was Marcion or Apelles or Valentinus, caught and held fast by the two fallacies that were of the very essence of all forms of gnosis. The first of those fallacies was a theological error: to regard the author of this world as opposed to the Father revealed in the Gospel. The second was a moral error: to believe that evil is something as old as the world itself and to teach the natural predestination of the elect.

ORIGEN'S ACQUAINTANCE WITH GNOSTICISM

The general impression of gnosis which Origen maintained at this early period was something he had acquired in his conferences against the heretics. In the course of those lectures he had found,

[3] *In Psalm.*, 1, 6.

time and again, that a number of diverse heretical doctrines, linking themselves one with another, formed a common antichristian front. This was particularly the case at Alexandria because many of the philosophies of religion which flourished there had no strong tradition behind them. Origen had not been reared in the atmosphere of gnosis or even in the similar atmosphere of the Greek mysteries, as his predecessor, Clement, had been. Gnosis was a world that existed outside him. In a general way he was acquainted with some of its aspirations, for he was a man of his time and his mind reacted readily to the currents of thought that moved through the atmosphere around him. But gnosis, as a definite philosophy, was something he needed to study and analyze.

Evidently he took the earliest opportunity to consult the heretical literature, sometimes Valentinian and sometimes Marcionite, referred to in the pages of the *Extracts from Theodotus*. This was a manuscript collection of notes jotted down by Clement in the course of his reading as a memorandum of points to be refuted or, as often happened, to be worked over in his writing of the *Stromata*. But a young professor of Origen's enthusiastic type has rarely the patience to study his adversaries line by line before he makes known his reply to them. Besides, the literature of heterodoxy was immense, and Origen had no time to do more than study it little by little.

Two works, however, were distinguished from the mass of heretical literature on account of their length, their importance, and their popularity. One of them was the work of the gnostic Heracleon, the most illustrious pupil of Valentinus; it consisted of notes in which the famous gnostic commented on passages in St. John's Gospel and also probably on passages from St. Luke. The author of the other was Apelles, the outstanding pupil of Marcion. It consisted of a series of syllogisms arguing against the Mosaic account of creation on the ground that it had not been written under divine inspiration. It is probable that Origen had already answered this objection while composing certain paragraphs of his *De principiis*, but he certainly would refer to it at a later date when he discussed Adam's free will in his treatise on the Book of Genesis. Similarly, when he was engaged in preparing his *Commentary on the Gospel of St. John,* which he wrote for the benefit of his dear friend Ambrose, he became accustomed to discuss Heracleon's chief interpretations, making his criticism in verse after verse and setting it forth as an addition to his own commentary. This habit gave him a more precise acquaintance with the teachings of the gnostics and a firmer grasp of the principles that separated him from them. In his *De principiis* he had demolished the basic theses of gnosticism but had unwittingly adopted, on more than one point, the mentality that had given them expression. By making himself better acquainted with the foundations of gnostic thought, he shook himself free from that baneful influence. Such an influence was inevitable at first, for it came of the unsuspected tolerance of a master toward his public, of a champion of orthodoxy toward the adversary who confronted him, of a young thinker in face of the public opinion of the day.

The findings of critical research enable us to reconstruct some of the elements of the Alexandrian gnosis with which Origen became acquainted through his activities at the Academy. He fought the heresies of Marcion and Valentinus, because he found them adequately set forth for him in the *Extracts from Theodotus,* the random collection of notes compiled by his predecessor, Clement. From the documents at our disposal we know that the gnosis which was in full bloom at the beginning of the third century was a combination of those two heresies. In the pages of Origen's works we can see today something of the power and vigor of that gnosis. We know how subtly it was preached in public conferences. We understand how persistently it worked its way into the scriptural exegesis of the time. Origen's ceaseless struggle against the gnosis of Alexandria throws no small light on the history of the two great heresies which then menaced Christianity.

II. THE TWO EMPIRES

Textual criticism has long since discovered that the last part of Clement's collection of *Extracts from Theodotus* had nothing in common with the main group of fragments of the original manuscript. The little book was really a treatise on fate. In some passages it becomes a kind of preaching, full of dramatic violence. To the menace of fate it opposes the protective effects of baptism and gnosis. The kingdom of the stars and the spirits no longer exists for the soul that has entered into the kingdom of Providence. Such is its main theme. It lacks the mystical poetry and the lyrical music of Valentinianism, and its entire vocabulary belongs to the Marcionist school. Origen stated this doctrine of salvation in a certain passage of the third book of his *Commentary on Genesis* and even adopted one of its orthodox expressions in the *Commentary on the Psalms*. The Marcionite treatise on fate, as read by the Christians in Clement's book of *Extracts*, was an alert piece of propaganda. It represented a well-known adversary whose strength and whose weakness Origen put to the test.

ASTROLOGY AND BAPTISM

The Marcionites held fast to the dominant notion that gave their heresy its simplicity and its popularity. They regarded the world as divided into two empires, and human history as sharply broken into two periods by an unforeseen event. The unexpected happening that caused this division was the coming of a new God. The star of Christ, something utterly new in this world, had risen to crush the fate of the ancients. The age-long struggle between man and fate had been intensified by astrology, which gave to all men the consciousness of their own weakness to deliver themselves from the power of the planets and the stars. But when the good Shepherd came and dwelt among men, all the spiritual powers, both hostile and friendly, which had been struggling to possess the souls of men, were soothed and subdued.

"The Lord came to make peace between man and Fate. That peace was the peace which comes from heaven to beings who dwell on this earth, the same peace which the Evangelist speaks of when he makes the angels announce glory to God in the highest and on earth peace to men of good will. And so He rises as a star that is utterly new, a star that shatters the entire arrangement of the planetary system. Being baptized in God, He has received from on high the power to trample underfoot the scorpions and serpents, that is, the powers of evil." [4] The religious emotion which had agitated public opinion when Marcionism first appeared was still in full vigor at the beginning of the third century.

Marcionism had still another superiority over its sister heresies: it knew how to do without the pagan myths. Its theological system was based upon the Gospels and upon St. Paul. It is true that it quoted from that scriptural source with a diluted enthusiasm, yet it professed to live on the principles of the New Testament. It preached a doctrine of salvation, and the Christian rites were given a place in its system of worship. Like the majority of the heresies of the time, it preserved the rite of baptism. In the Valentinian sects such reminders of a Mother Church were not unlike the family objects which the emigrant takes with him into his exile but which become useless and sentimental ornaments in a new climate. In listening to the preaching of the Marcionite the populace could recognize the well-known formulas of the catechism and the baptismal liturgy. "Baptism means the death and the end of the old life." It introduces men to "a life according to Christ, who is the one Lord." "The changes it can effect take place not only in the body but in the soul." And they were taught, above everything else, that baptism delivers a soul from the power of the devils.

In spite of its Christian terminology, all this doctrine was regarded by Origen as opposed to Christian truth. He denounced it as substituting a higher sort of fate for a lower. A favorable star leads the convert to believe in God! So, if we desire to preserve the plan of salvation, the sufferings of the Savior and the hardships borne by the apostles in establishing the Church by their preaching of Christ are all supposed to depend on the movements of the stars.[5] In each case, the sacrament of baptism must operate under the drive of a system of influences or energies that are determined by the nature of things. In other words, baptism has a magical efficacy.

[4] *Excerpta*, 74, 1 and 2; 76, 1–4.

[5] *In Gen.*, III; P.G., XII, 52: Christian sacraments do not operate in virtue of the universal sympathy, which would bind all beings together. They operate in virtue of a design of providence according to which all believers are in sympathy with Christ and receive the efficacious sign of that sympathy. This controversy indicates the fundamental difference between the two notions of the operation of the sacraments.

It was objected that this verdict was simply a snap judgment, not unlike the argumentative summary a man might use in a public debate. In speaking of a new star, the Marcionite was quite aware that he was supposing the convert to pass from the empire of fate to the kingdom of Providence. But he was talking of the establishment of a new order. "Before baptism, fate is truly in command. After baptism, astrological predictions have no longer any value." Origen's reply was that, if this is true, "the Christian is emancipated from the life of fate and is delivered from every astrological influence." [6]

This was a view of salvation in which neither Clement nor Origen was able to see the teaching of Christianity. The difficulty remains unsolved if we regard the world as divided into two empires, or human history as split into two periods. How are we to explain the passage from one empire or from one period to the other? How are we to define the power of baptism or the moral transformation caused by that power? How are we to escape from the laws laid down by the Artisan of the world and imposed upon us by the stars? Or would the demiurge himself equip the faithful soul with this Word which would make it know the higher God? Does fate give birth to salvation? If so, we are again in the difficulties of accepting magic as the dominant influence in the lives of men. Or have we already within us this Word, this higher soul, and is it merely necessary to set it free? If such is the case, we divide man rather than transform him. If we have within us two souls and if salvation consists in setting apart the better soul, where is our free will and what is the inner change that takes place in a life which is, at one and the same time, continuous, developed, and re-created? [7]

When a powerful intelligence grapples with a hostile doctrine, it leaves upon that doctrine the imprint of its power. The controversy against Marcionism became, for Origen, a problem in the psychology of religion. Is not salvation, he asked himself, a return of the soul to its primitive condition? Is it not a rebirth of the intelligence, a renascence in which the soul achieves a union with the divine Idea

[6] *Ibid.*, III; P.G., XII, 53.
[7] *De princip.*, III, iv, 4.

from which it originally came and to which it must ultimately return?

BIBLICAL INTERPRETATION AND REVELATION

Marcionism presented Origen with a problem of religious psychology; it also confronted him with a parallel task in the domain of exegesis. The heretics divided the soul and the history of man, but the cause thereof was the fact that they had already divided the Bible between two deities. On the one hand, they spoke of the demiurge of Genesis, the cruel Jahveh of the Jews; on the other hand, they invoked the Father, the beneficent God of Jesus. Irenaeus had already refuted that error by teaching that the Logos, before being made man, had spoken through Moses and the prophets and had thus carried on, little by little, the education of humanity. There was a logical sequence and a definite progress in revelation, as there is in the course of a man's life from infancy to mature age.

In dealing with Marcionism, Origen refused to employ the method used by Irenaeus. The heresy itself had changed, if not in tendency, at least in technique. No longer did the Marcionites contrast pure Semitism with pure Christianity in a series of comparisons. Instead, their passion for minute criticism drove them to chop up the Bible into a number of small parts and to classify those parts as being marked by inspirations that were either good or bad or even indifferent.

By reason of his eagerness to show the fallacy of this technique, or rather by reason of his philosophy, Origen put aside all notion of progressive revelation and set himself to defend, above everything else, the divine inspiration of even the briefest passage of Holy Scripture. His allegorical method enabled him to safeguard the difficult passages, for it had taught him to be patient in seeking the immutable Wisdom beneath every word of the biblical text. But his task was more complicated than this, for he had to collect the debris in order to restore a statue which the Marcionite methods of criticism had reduced to dust. He conceived of the Bible as a whole, a *totum*; and he regarded it, not as something that progressed from past to future, but as a message that began with the letter and reached its full meaning with the spirit. Hence, to reach the inner-most idea of the Bible, he substituted for the Irenaean concept of a progressive revelation a new concept of his own. This new concept involved the progressive application of critical logic to every passage in the Bible.

But the handwriting of divine Wisdom is not equally easy to decipher in all the inspired writings. The providential attribute which is called inspiration is one thing. Quite another thing is the value of the lesson, or the revelation, contained in the various books of Scripture. This latter biblical element is markedly unequal in context after context. The four Gospels are the premises of the entire Bible. Yet even in those four books it is possible to discern other premises. Those other premises are the Gospel of St. John.

To make his argument clearer, Origen resorts to a comparison. It is admitted that the skill and intelligence of divine providence extend to all living things. But there are certain living things—the basilisk and other noxious animals, for instance—in which we encounter difficulties in our effort to discern the work of providence. There are degrees in the mystery of Nature. The operation of providence is more obvious in the order of the heavenly bodies than in the bodies and souls of animals. Yet beings that have not been endowed with the light of reason are equipped with a definite property and an inner skill enabling them to foresee, as it were, all their activities and to protect and preserve their own powers. But the greatest obscurity of all is to be found in the happenings of human life. However, the existence of this unknown factor does not permit us to say that divine providence is in fault, at least if we understand the problem as we should.

In the same way, when we encounter obscurities in Holy Scripture we are not to assert that Scripture itself is in fault. It is a Book that is to be measured, not by our limited knowledge, but by the knowledge of God. Our poor and feeble human mode of speech is incapable of coping with its profound thoughts, and the techniques of human rhetoric are insufficient to express a wisdom that has a supernatural meaning. When a man proceeds to make a commentary on Scripture, it is well for him to refrain from rash adventures of speculation, for the inspired word presents a number of difficulties that can be resolved in no human way. If such obscurities continue to exist, even when a person has renounced his apostasy and has embraced the truth, the man who is truly religious will refuse to deny God in favor of any other principle.[8]

Origen's reply, then, to the Marcionite preacher was to the effect that conversion is a process by which the neophyte passes, not from fatalism to the mastery of his own destiny, but from a condition of degradation to one of restoration. His advice to the exegete was that a deeper knowledge leads the understanding, not from the demiurge to a higher divinity, but from mystery to Wisdom; that Wisdom is at first veiled, then becomes less obscure as the veils are drawn away, and finally is manifested as it really is. In the providential ways of Him who is the God and Father of all things, there is no interruption. Religion is a progress of the soul.

Such are the first victories of Origen: an idea of salvation, a doctrine of biblical inspiration, a technique of exegesis. With those three ideas he established his domain.

[8] Origen gave two successive expositions of this doctrine. In Psalm., Praef.; P.G., XII, 1091; De princip., IV, i, 7.

CHAPTER VII

Christian Gnosticism

MARCIONISM was a little Church confronting a great Church, and it was necessary either to acknowledge its existence or to demolish it. The character of the Valentinian schools of thought was quite distinct, and Origen's acquaintance with them from the days of his youth made him realize that the heresy associated with the name of Valentinus presented a problem very different from that of Marcionism. We can readily understand his lively reactions to the challenge of Marcionism. But this other heresy was far more subtle. Its tenets were but vaguely defined, and it carefully avoided all conflict with Christian tradition.

I. THE VALENTINIAN HERESY

Its method of propaganda was almost imperceptible. It promised to the neophyte an esoteric knowledge and the possession of the divine substance without imposing any obligation on him to renounce Christianity or Christ or the Gospels. The existence of the Catholic Church assured the Valentinians of a continual supply of recruits of a spiritual cast of mind, for it was their contention that the Christianity of the simple and lowly, that of faith and good works, should precede the state of perfection. They held that a man must be justified, must belong to the body of Christ, and must live in the practice of good works before he aspires to the highest degree of Christian life.

In demanding this as a preliminary to the neophyte's entrance into their ranks, they did not mean that any transformation changed the simple and lowly Christian into a spiritual soul. As soon as the neophyte becomes a servant of the gnosis he knows that he is already a spiritual man. The chosen soul possesses within itself, hidden in the recesses of its being, the germ of the esoteric life. He is saved by right of his birth and by the fact that he belongs to a race different from the ordinary mass of the faithful. During the years of his elementary education he shares the life of the vulgar, like a young prince who is unaware that the blood of royalty is in his veins. But the moment comes when the gnosis asserts itself within his soul, and in that moment the germ of perfection begins to come to blossom. Initiation into the life of the school, accompanied sometimes by the recital of certain incantations, is then sufficient to help the process of germination unto perfection. There is no need to renounce the holy practices of his early years. Simply, he has passed beyond them. He may still use the words and even the rites of the Church; but those words and those ceremonies now have another meaning, a much deeper meaning than before. Christ gives place to the Son at the moment when the neophyte yields to the life and the Wisdom from on high by his renunciation of what was obscure and imperfect in the life lived by the simple faithful.

It is probable that a religious program of this nature must have encountered few obstacles to its acceptance. This must have been especially the case at Alexandria, for the very air of that city seems to have produced a thirst for esoteric knowledge. Valentinus himself was a native of Alexandria. The influence which this heresy was able to exert on the Academy and especially on Origen is obscure. It has been alleged that Origen owes to the gnostic protagonist his doctrines of the fall and of the restoration of souls. However, the documents on which this verdict is founded are few and have little historical importance in reference to the two great doctrines concerned.

The Extracts from Theodotus

It has recently been possible to apply to the Clementine book of *Extracts from Theodotus* a precise and methodical examination of its sources. It was hoped that some such research would enable us to understand fully the part played by the teachings of those Christian heretics in the great drama of dogmatic development. This hope was based on the assumption that a ready welcome had been given to their doctrines at the Academy of Alexandria. But this research was limited by the fact that the required documents are too few; and, on the other hand, the gnostic activities in the Church of Alexandria were far too great and much too important to be explained by the parallels which the critics discovered in two or three passages of the Clementine manuscript. Here, then, is the actual problem: the first impression given to us by the known facts lead us to believe that we have here a set of historical circumstances which may be classed as normal and that the Christians of Alexandria were as deeply imbued with gnosticism as were the rest of the citizens. But any such fancied resemblance vanishes under the searchlight of criticism. The only result of the analysis of the *Extracts from Theodotus* has been a few texts, a few expressions, nothing more than the dust of doctrines long forgotten, all of which is trifling compared with the vast development which we seek to explain.

CONFLICTING VIEWS ABOUT ORIGEN

The difficulty is further complicated by a problem of psychology. How could the Academy, despite its repugnance for the pseudo-learning of the heretics, share some of the heretical ideals and ambitions? Yet some scholars suppose that Origen was hostile to the gnostics and that at the same time he never ceased to imitate them. When the history of the Valentinian heresy is under discussion, we are told that Origen's opinions on that heresy were prejudiced and that therefore his testimony can be dismissed; but, on the other hand, we are told that his inner convictions on the value of the Valentinian doctrines were the fruit of his respect for the prestige of their founder. Origen had but a poor comprehension of his gnostic predecessors, it is said, but he was unconsciously influenced by them because their teachings were in the atmosphere in which he lived. The pervasive gnosticism of the day would have overcome every resistance. It was like one of those habits of childhood that do not react favorably to the discipline of early education. Some such repressed complex, the beginnings of which were buried in his early life, made its presence felt in the activities of Origen the scholar.

The answer to these assertions is readily found in Origen's work at the Academy. When he lectures there against the gnostics or composes his treatises in rebuttal of their doctrines, his references to them are almost entirely free from anything resembling the influence of a repressed complex. His treatment of quotations from their works is clear and lucid. There is no ambiguity or equivocation in his language when he accepts the opportunity to discuss their doctrines at length. Sometimes, however, he gives a diluted approval to some element of their teaching, but only because it starts within him some train of thought that carries him far beyond it. Origen availed himself of gnosticism but did not yield to it.

A form of Valentinianism was already, it has been said, a part of the academic atmosphere of Alexandria in the days when Clement and Origen were teaching there. We are told that, when inheriting the catechetical school from Pantaenus, they inherited also a legacy of gnosticism. But the difficulty is thus merely pushed farther back, for we have little knowledge about Pantaenus and his activities. Besides, the assumption that the strangest doctrines are always the oldest doctrines opens the door to many theories. It is not certain that the origins of a movement or a school are always crude and formless, or that the movement or the school is more sensitive to external influences at the outset than at later stages of its existence. History tells us of conflicts that are more clearly defined than the subsequent developments to which they gave rise. Clement, in fact, was much more faithful to orthodoxy than his successor was. All the evidence at hand leads us to believe that Origen himself began with the traditional teaching of the Church and proceeded later to the formulation of those features of his system which have been most subject to attack as being colored with gnosticism. Gnosis was not a natural part of the atmosphere of the Academy. It was something that was studied there.

However, the fact that it wielded a certain influence on Origen is part of a larger problem. Little difficulty would be encountered in explaining what the critics call the general resemblances and the literary borrowings which are alleged to indicate Origen's debt to gnosticism, if we assume that each epoch in the history of human thought has its own special philosophy, what is called the mentality of the period. This mentality is the product of man's effort to adjust himself to the difficulties of the period in which he lives. An adequate description of it is that it is a totality of mental attitudes, or a totality of ways of looking at the problems presented to us from without. Within any one period of man's history those attitudes and perspectives are repeated again and again, from the poorest efforts at reflection where every thought is the result of sensuous and confused impressions to philosophical systems which seem to take no account of the great emotions of the day although they are always at the mercy of them. It is the privilege of a thinker to understand the restlessness of his time. Thus the critic, in studying the philosophy and the gnosis of the second century, finds everywhere the same Platonism, everywhere the same Pythagoreanism. Origen's day was no different. It also had its own mentality, and the student of the history of Christian philosophy cannot ignore it.

The Valentinian gnosis, owing to its reliance on the Scriptures, presented this mentality under a religious aspect. Origen encountered the mentality of his day in his hours of study, and he retained something of it in the perspective of his philosophical system. Because he was a philosopher, he naturally borrowed from the writings of the contemporary gnostics; but he did so only in that measure in which gnosis was a cosmology and a philosophy of the soul. His doctrine has some of the weaknesses of Neoplatonism, but it contains none of the excesses that mark the theories of Valentinus or Heracleon. The *De principiis* and the first two books of his *Commentary on the Gospel of St. John* are full of his ideas. Although they show the influence of the gnostic movement, their general philosophy, whether it is to be approved or not, always shakes itself free from any connections with the system of Valentinus. Examples of this can easily be found. Let us take the doctrines common to Origen and to the fragments of the Valentinian gnosis which are preserved in the *Extracts from Theodotus*.

Heracleon taught that the world is a desert inhabited only by wild beasts. The soul has lost its way there and is covered with the filth it picked up from its contact with matter. Heracleon uses the episode of the Samaritan woman at Jacob's well as a symbol of this pessimism; he regards it as a ready-made fiction, the old fiction of the courtesan not yet devoid of the feeling of shame. Her feeling of sin is reduced to a confused and thinly veiled confession, and she asks Jesus where one must adore. Since she desires neither to lie nor to make open confession of her shame, she questions Him. By this ruse she allows Him to see the basis of her life of prostitution. That basis is her ignorance of God which has made her neglect the worship due to God as well as all the other obligations of her life. Thus she knows that she has fallen into sin; but she has just come forth from the earthly city, and her life is not utterly lost, even though she does not yet know where the true spouse of her soul dwells.

The Valentinian gnostics whom Clement knew had a perspective that was larger and less gloomy than this. They saw in the universe itself a number of hidden aspirations which were impregnated with something divine and which were, therefore, not without hope. Their ideals were akin to the dream of the lover rather than to the poetry of revived love. The demiurge of this low world is not evil, and it is his task to take care of the Church. The fact that his skill is unconscious, explains why his work has become the slave of his vanity. "He did not know the Wisdom which used him as its instrument, and therefore he attributed the work of creation to his own power." This was an echo of the *Epistle to the Romans*, interpreted in the way that was almost habitual with the gnostics. According to this interpretation, St. Paul wished to recall the fall of the world and to announce its restoration when he said: "For the creature was made subject to vanity, not willingly, but by reason of him that made it subject, in hope that also it would be delivered from the servitude of corruption."

THE FALL

The story of the Fall is found in Origen. In the first book of the *De principiis* he discusses these very words of St. Paul, using them in that part of his work which treats of defection or falling away. After considering the divine nature as the source of being and intelligence and holiness, he proceeds to inquire how reasonable beings share in that divine source and how the unity of the supreme intelligence is the principle of a universe composed of multiple and unequal beings. In God there is nothing that is subject to decay, and in the Word nothing that can be divided, and in reasonable beings nothing that is made for evil. Religious ignorance and the trouble of making moral decisions are a consequence of voluntary weakness. Sin does not inject into the soul the notion of something irrevocable, of an impurity that cannot be washed away, or of a shame that can never be overcome. There is no remedy for such results of sin. Besides, they generate in the soul the habit of easy indulgence as well as a pessimism that embraces everything. The soul is endowed with a power of self-restoration and self-healing. Hence the servitude of reasonable beings is remembered in the splendors of the liturgy with which they worship the author of their existence. The universe is a harmony of free wills, accomplishing order and perfection by their longings to return to the Wisdom which gives them life and to dwell in the Word which enlightens them diversely in its unique plan.[1]

Origen's interest was not confined to the works of the gnostics. His studies ranged also over the philosophical commentaries of the second century. His problems were to find their Christian solution in the Neoplatonism that was about to dawn.

ESCHATOLOGY

The complement of the gnostic myth of the fall of human souls was the myth of their ascent, a myth that belonged to the realm of eschatology. The various religious philosophies in vogue at Alexandria had no place for any theory of the periodic return of souls. They believed that there is a heavenward progress consisting of a number of different phases where initiators, in their moments of rest, transmit to others the secrets of the gnosis. This belief went through various forms, sometimes grossly material and sometimes highly intellectual. At first the faithful will glow in the sun itself, with the angels who are assigned to the duty of escorting that planet; then they will ascend to their first celestial home, leaving behind them a place for their disciples who will follow them, in an

[1] Cf. *De princip.*, I, vii, 5.

ascending series of homes, until the final state of perfection is reached. Or the angels will mingle with the faithful souls and instruct them for a thousand years. Having duly completed their task, those angels will allow the initiated to instruct newly arrived souls and they themselves will be promoted to the rank of archangels. Some of the schools taught that all this would take place at the end of time. Others held that the ascent of the faithful follower would begin at the end of his earthly life.

The Valentinian teachings, attributed to Theodotus and forming the central part of the *Extracts*, remained closer to the dogma of the Church, although they did not renounce the notions of progress through celestial phases or of instructions to be given by the angels. The doctrine outlined in this part of the Clementine manuscript took the glorified Christ as the main theme of its eschatology. His soul entered heaven, with the demiurge at His left hand. In His train there followed all the elect who form His body, the spiritual Church, which is the seed that has come from on high and is hidden in the world. All those chosen souls proceeded with the historic Christ across the seven heavens until finally they came to their place of rest. Then was completed the final restoration of those chosen ones, thus finishing the work begun by their individual restoration and being in this way the last phase of the process of their initiation. At the end of time those new spiritual beings must lay aside their souls, and the chosen of lesser rank would join them at the banquet of the heavenly spouse, beyond the lower heavens. This progress was illustrated by a concept taken from the Levitical ritual, from which Philo took a number of his most famous allegories: "Aaron will return into the tabernacle of the testimony and, putting off the vestments which he had on him before when he entered the sanctuary, will leave them there." Among the ornaments thus put aside was the gold phylactery, a symbol of the impressionable soul and of the heart wherein is written the sacred name.

This verse from Leviticus (16:23) was taken to represent the way the chosen soul progresses in the world of intelligences, after it has been helped by the sacrifice and the human prayers offered by the angels. Gradually divesting itself of the things of earth, and undergoing a number of changes that make it progressively more godlike, the soul is ultimately united with the Word and is assimilated into its substance. Then it receives from the Word the gift of perfect knowledge and becomes of itself a principle of movement and operation. The chosen soul is now a high priest of God and has entered into the kingdom of grace and power. The Alexandrians found this theory of a series of successive initiations easy to understand, for they had acquired a certain skill in describing the gradual unveiling of mystery and were alert to every new thought about the spiritual restoration of the world.

In his early years as a teacher, Origen was not uninfluenced by this notion of the ladder of paradise. There were times when he dwelt on the thought of the soul of Christ being transplanted into heaven or when he meditated on the progress of those chosen souls who approached nearer and nearer to God by the practice of contemplation. In his case, contemplation was the really important thing.[2] When it became necessary for him to consider the phases of the soul's ascent to God, he rejected the hieratical imaginings with which the Valentinians of his day used to amuse themselves. He had no love for such myths, for he resented their spongy mixture of Greek and Jewish expressions and considered them to be full of an intellectual vinegar, offered to Christ in derision. He was consumed by a hunger for knowledge rather than for purification or immutability, and he turned to the Pythagoreans when he wished to meditate on the meaning of the steps on the ladder of paradise. He pictured to himself the joy of associating with the chosen of God and of learning from them the inner reasons of particular things, the causes of the four lower spheres, and the principle that ruled the sphere of the fixed stars. The day would surely come when he would know the vast spaces surrounding the spheres. In that day he would comprehend the truth. It was all merely a scholar's dream, and its realization would come only when time should be no more. In his visions of his own mystical progress he welcomed the Pythagorean concepts of the harmony of numbers and of the music of

[2] *In Psalm.*, 1, 3; P.G., XII, 1088.

the spheres. But in the factual world of his everyday life he relied utterly on the practice of two essentials: intellectual keenness and purity of thought.[3]

II. SPIRITUAL PROGRESS

Let us put aside, then, the mystery of the ladder of paradise, for the stages of the interior progress of a soul are more important. For Origen this is the one great problem that emerged from his examination of gnosticism. What is spiritual progress? The followers of Valentinus understood this expression as meaning a higher initiation into esoteric knowledge. To the master of the Academy it meant Christian perfection.

SPIRITUAL TRANSFORMATION

The Valentinian was not interested in the problem; the practice of detachment was sufficient to effect the transformation of his soul; its inner power then became the instrument of the Savior. Clement had held that the continuity of intellectual activity created a kind of subsistent divine life, a state in which the soul is immovably fixed in the love of God. The religious philosophies of the day, being confronted with this problem of spiritual progress, sought a solution in the stability, the detachment, the general way of life of the gnostic initiate; they held that for a soul that has once been initiated into the ways of esoteric knowledge there is no longer possible anything but a perceptible and necessary progress.

Here we have the case of a gnostic Christian who has none of the simple assurance of a new convert. Born into Christianity, he has been educated by the trials of persecution and the stern discipline of personal mortification. He has known the risks of moments of weakness and has learned the danger that lurks in even the slightest apostasy, for he has seen how the downfall of even the most elevated souls can begin there. At the same time he is a master in a field of knowledge where no teacher guided his footsteps. Like all self-taught men, he insists on finding his own intellectual food and

[3] The two principal texts correspond. Always the second exposition is put forth more prudently and moderately. *De princip.*, II, xi, 6; *In Joan.*, XIII, 40–43.

takes a firm stand on his right to believe freely. Clement had halted on the threshold of a science of first principles, but this man has boldly crossed it, encouraged thereto by his study of the psalms, the Book of Genesis, and the Book of Proverbs. He has given himself his own initiation into the Wisdom of God and the Father of all things. According to his own expression, he has read the Bible as one who has not yet a full knowledge of what it means. He finds the gnosis a stimulant, an intellecutal discipline, the very stages of which are laden with trials: to know, then to penetrate, finally to see—this is the same as to understand. It thus becomes a preliminary to the task of contemplation. Only as a result of contemplation can the hoped-for union with God be finally achieved.

Origen's first revulsion against Valentinianism was caused less by its fantastic picturizations than by its claim that the initiate's soul finds repose in God so quickly and so easily. Progress meant, to him, a system of training, with individual liberty as an indispensable condition. There is in the human soul no hidden germ which of necessity produces the gnosis, nor any real knowledge which abounds in contemplation without a prolonged association with truth, nor even any religious life which is assured of salvation in advance. Liberty consists in the development of the means we have received of contemplating the Good, and for that development a sustained attention is necessary. Continuity of attention washes out sin, for sin is chiefly a negligence; it also increases within us the capacity to receive knowledge of the Good. To refine the spiritual sense, a transformation of the soul must take place. That transformation cannot be reduced to a mere divesting or to a sudden change.

Such a concept of spiritual progress is quite different from the hypothesis of the Valentinians with their notion of the hidden germ within the soul and of the evolution of a nature whose entire history up to its final development is already written in the germ. Nor has Origen's concept any resemblance to the Valentinian determination of a subject endowed with two contrary virtualities in equal measure, death and life. To this subject there comes a moment when it is at once drawn from this state of indifference by a sudden transformation that assimilates it to the spiritual world.[4] Origen held that the spiritual progress of a soul can only be restrained and voluntary, and because it is voluntary it must be continuous. Such a controlled and deliberate progress allows the intelligence to regain its pristine state and to become again as the Father made it at the beginning. Love of God, the unceasing search after truth, and the inner joy thus produced gradually restore it to its true home. The heretical sects always depicted spiritual progress as a process of detachment or of purification, and the final result of this process was assured as soon as the deeper self was stripped of the lower or superficial selves. Origen would be the first to attack the problem of the religious transformation of a soul.

THE SOUL'S DEVELOPMENT

The Academy of Alexandria was not the place where he would describe the most intimate stages of the soul's development unto holiness. In the De principiis, which he composed there, he desired only to build two obstacles to the gnostic infiltrations of Christianity, by making himself the defender of liberty and the champion of intellectual training. But he was still far from perceiving the possible applications of his doctrine, which were the progress of the Christian soul in mystical experience, in the practice of faith, in meditation of the Gospels, and in personal holiness.[5] Besides, he knew only his own school of thought and, like Clement, confused it with the Church. The religious life seemed to him to be especially a succession of studies, and he sought for himself the joy of comprehending it and the slaking of his burning curiosity about the loftiest thoughts that filled his mind. True progress meant for him, at that time, progress in knowledge. Thus we understand why his Alexandrian discussions of spiritual progress are concerned with its object rather than with the atmosphere in which it is possible or the source from which it derives its vigor. He held that there are

---

[4] In Joan., XIII, 59; P.G., XIV, 516. There is no transmutation that can give to a being a nature contrary to that which is received from its Creator. Cf. In Cant., II.

[5] Progress in the faith: In Joan., XX, 27. Progress in meditation of Jesus crucified: In Matt., XII, 17–20. Progress in the mystical life: In Joan., XIII, 3. Progress in sanctity and the virtues: In Matt., XVII, 8.

spiritual mysteries which the intellectual Christian can understand, but of which the simple are ignorant. There are higher teachings which are closed to the uneducated, and a more reasonable religion than that practiced by the main body of the faithful.

Thus Christian thought was divided into two compartments, a division that was in harmony with the spirit of the Academy rather than with the beliefs and usages of the Church. The same division was found among the Valentinians. Indeed, it was part of the mentality common to all the teachings of the time, for it reproduced the distinction which the contemporary Platonism succinctly expressed as that between the sensible and the intelligible. But the beliefs of Christianity were based upon sensible facts, the life and death of Jesus, and consequently the practical application of this Platonist dichotomy was a danger for the Church. For example, the Valentinians confined the only-begotten Son or the Truth in the plenitude of God's being and held the work of the historic Christ to be a separate thing. Although Origen had no desire to embrace the doctrines of gnosticism, he philosophized like the others of his day. Soon he was distinguishing a somatic Gospel and a spiritual Gospel. The elementary preaching which announced that Jesus was made man and was crucified unto death was not enough for the friend of Wisdom. That sort of Christian teaching belonged to the catechism of the Corinthians, a simple and illiterate people. But those who are perfect in the spirit need something more.

The gnostic divided divinity. At the Academy, however, the division was merely in the method which led to the knowledge of God. Origen thought he could institute such a division without danger by the expedient of proposing a hierarchy of theological concepts. He understood those theological concepts as the progressive views which Holy Scripture gives of the divine nature, its attributes and its powers. For instance, he could arrange in order the titles given to Christ by John or Paul or the prophets. Thus the divine names on which Philo, and afterward Clement, founded their systems of theology, became for Origen, under the new name of "concept," the stages of a progressive research. Starting from the multiple and contingent aspects of divine action, that research finally led to the consideration of God's eternal attributes. He proposed to make the research on two lines: first, he would study the various "concepts" of the Savior, and the "concepts" of the only-begotten Son. The former set of concepts was proper to the plan of salvation; the latter, to the divine nature.[6]

To the first group belong such names as light, propitiation, shepherd. If men had not been blinded by evil, the Savior would not have made Himself the Light that shineth in darkness. If Adam had not sinned and thus lost his incorruptibility, Christ would not have died in propitiation for our sins. On the other hand, such names as Truth and Wisdom, perhaps also Word, Justice, and Life, do not depend upon contingencies; they reside.[7]

By the mediation of the Word, the Logos, the High Priest whom Clement had already placed at the extreme summit of the world of visible things, the transition was made from the lower order of concepts to the higher. Origen regarded the Word, in a sense, as the reason which is shared by every man who has grown beyond the years of infancy. In another sense, he spoke of the Word-God, who is near the Father and whose glory John had witnessed, the only-begotten Son who in the supernatural order shares His perfection with the saints. His revelation and His sacrifice intercede between the imperfect reason which is in the world and the immutable reason of God. When the Lamb has removed our sins, we can be fed with eternal life.

These aspects of Christ are given only as views of Origen's thought, for assuredly they were far from representing the divine powers, as Philo understood them and as Clement, in one or two passages, suggested them to be. Yet it would be difficult to deny that several of these degrees had a concrete foundation. Is not the sensible really distinct from the intelligence, and the contingent

---

[6] In Joan., XIX, 1; P.G., XIV, 536.

[7] We find diverse enumerations of "theological concepts" in the Alexandrian commentary on the Fourth Gospel (books 1 and 2). In Joan., I, 11; Johannine list: life, light, truth, way, resurrection, door; Pauline list (I Cor. 1:20): justice, sanctification, redemption. In Joan., I, 22; absolute attributes: wisdom, word, life, absolute truth; contingent notions: shepherd, redemption, and so on. In Joan., II, 8; absolute attributes: truth, wisdom, light; participated attributes: life, light, containing wisdom and truth.

from the necessary? This, however, did not save Origen from an immediate criticism, for his contemporaries accused him of teaching the existence of two Christs and of holding the inevitable doctrinal consequence that Jesus of Nazareth finally disappeared behind the pre-existent Word. The cult of the intelligible absorbed the historic Christ, to the profit of the gnosis but not to the good of religion; it divorced religion from life and concealed it within the walls of the sanctuary.

The sensible was, in its way, an inconvenience for the intelligible. Origen placed in the same series such different concepts as the good shepherd, the light, and wisdom. Some of the concepts in a series were essences of the divine, others were historical aspects of the Savior. Origen was the more likely to fall into confusion on this matter because Alexandrian tradition considered all the divine attributes as manifestations that bind God to the world, so to speak, or as intermediaries between His divine transcendence and the imperfect beings here below. Thus, under the aspect of a multiplicity of powers, a lesser divinity was interposed between God and the world, whose function was to connect the soul to its divine principle. It was thus that the Alexandrians disposed of the mediation of the God-man who had come at a definite moment in history. They substituted the mediation of an inferior deity who was charged with the task of communicating being and truth to a hierarchy of chosen souls among whom it was itself the first and most perfect.[8]

Lastly, does it not follow from the logical order established between the more elevated concepts that there is in the world of intelligences a procession of essences? In his first writings on the subject Origen viewed life as seated at the right hand of wisdom. Life throws out its rays in the light of truth or in the light of what was called the only-begotten Son. The prologue of the Fourth Gospel was exposed to the risk of developing into a series of hypostases, to be later begotten as the entities of the Valentinian myths; with the reservation, however, that too much emphasis must not be laid on the lyrical character of this genealogy.

[8] This tendency appears in *In Joan.*, I, 42; *P.G.*, XIV, 104.

Alexandrian gnostics had always preferred another mode of emanation to the gross myth of successive yokes or pairs. They based the first procession on the act whereby intelligence knows itself, and they called this the act of reflection. God reflects on Himself, and from this ineffable knowledge of Himself there is derived a thought which, by expressing itself in different ways, is known as Son or Truth or Knowledge. Origen hesitated, however, to push the theory of the divine attributes to any such extremes. He recognized no procession other than that of the Word, and the way he viewed it was certainly not Valentinian. Among the divine names he saw differences of dignity but not a real hierarchy. All the necessary attributes have the same title to divinity. They belong to the Father absolutely, and to the Son in the measure in which He makes imperfect beings share in them. Life, light, and truth are so many aspects of the divine. We ought to study them in their order, but they do not form a vital chain between heaven and us.

To see all this and to state it clearly, Origen set himself the task of dissipating the confusion created by an idea so strange to Christianity. The spiritual progress of the soul was not from the sensible to the intelligible, or from the contingent to the necessary, as the religious philosophies and the heretical sects imagined. What was more sensible than the mediation of Jesus, this God whose sufferings made such an appeal to the human heart and who bore our miseries and died for us? When the Father revealed Himself through His only-begotten Son, was not that a contingent fact? When Jesus was born at Bethlehem in the reign of Tiberius, was there not a contingent fact there also, although it admitted us to the intimacy of God Himself?

ORIGEN'S VIEW OF SPIRITUAL PROGRESS

Origen would have none of this distinction of two orders. Spiritual progress is not to be confused with the methods that lead from the sensible to the intelligible. If Christianity is merely a myth like the Platonist fables, we can forget its history as soon as we grasp its meaning. But its entire life revolves about a Person. "To seek

Jesus is the same as to seek the Word, Wisdom, Justice, Truth, and the almighty power of God, as Christ is all these." [9] The various degrees of the so-called hierarchy, then, must follow one another in ways very different from that set forth in the Valentinian theory. They may be classified as items of knowledge varying in importance, or as subjects for meditation adapted to the progress of the contemplative, or as new ways of knowing the inexhaustible riches of the same divine object, or as more and more abundant currents pouring forth from the well of eternal life. Origen illustrated this thought by several suggestions: he spoke of the Lamb of God, of the bread that comes down from heaven, of the true vine. In the measure in which the soul becomes more capable, the knowledge it gains from such meditation becomes more direct and thus more real and more efficacious. "For the Word of God is adjusted to the needs of human souls and is to be measured by the desire of him who enjoys it. It is like the bread which does not change, but the taste of which depends on the hunger of him who eats it." Here was Origen's notion of the work of transformation, the labor of love, where the Christian soul measures its own spiritual progress.

III. CHRISTIAN GNOSTICISM AND ITS MEANING

Such were Origen's encounters with the Christian gnosis of Alexandria, which for nearly a century had been making its presence felt in the Church. Gnosticism was less a heresy than the deep-seated tendency of every heresy. It asserted the right to find in the bosom of the Church a religion more conformed to Hellenism, but more powerful and more esoteric than the philosophy of the Greeks. It worked within, but its interests and perspectives were all for the without. Christian commentaries on the Gospel must equal and even surpass the esoteric doctrines of the *Republic* and the *Timaeus*. Christian initiation must promise no less than the mysteries of Isis or Eleusis. The Alexandrians were ever comparing the two wines, without ever reaching a decision about their relative merits.

---

[9] *In Joan.*, XXXII, 19. We have in this doctrine one of the clearest examples of the way Origen corrected his theology.

ORIGEN'S METHOD

In meeting this set of conditions, Origen followed the method already indicated by Irenaeus. He held fast to the chief points of controversy and firmly refused to attack gnosticism under its diluted, fugitive or unintelligible forms. To the gnostic principles he opposed the foundations of the Christian faith, erecting bulwarks of Christian teaching wherever he discovered a poorly defended sector or a badly protected line where the infiltrations of heresy could break through. "It appears to me, therefore, to be necessary that one who is able to represent in a genuine manner the doctrine of the Church and to refute those dealers in knowledge falsely so called, should take his stand against historical fictions, and oppose to them the true and lofty evangelical message in which the agreement of the doctrines, found both in the so-called Old Testament and in the so-called New, appears so plainly and so fully." [10]

The fierce desire for knowledge which burned in the hearts of the educated Christians of the day inclined them toward gnosticism Origen decided to satisfy this thirst for knowledge by showing the emptiness of gnosticism rather than by directly refuting it. He was aware of its powerful appeal to cultured minds and remembered how his dear friend Ambrose had yielded to that temptation. Surely it was not good to stand idly by and let those men of good heart wait patiently for the truth. They must be given Christian teaching. "When we neglect study, the truths that we already know lose their appeal," as the psalmist warns us. But Origen knew the risks of any such enterprise. The task, however, was pressing, and, in a truly Christian spirit and with full trust in the Savior, he dedicated all his powers to it. In his *Commentary on the Psalms*, he wrote to Ambrose in these terms:

"Under the pretense of seeking the knowledge of God, the heretics rise against the Church, bringing forward their works composed of numerous books in which they claim to explain the Gospels and the apostolic writings. If I remain silent and fail to put forward the true and real doctrines of Christ, they will then proceed to conquer

[10] *Ibid.*, V, *Praef.*; P.G., XIV, 196.

the greedy souls who, in default of healthy food, grasp at the filthy and abominable foods that are forbidden. . . . With regard to you, this was indeed your own history. Unable to find masters capable of giving you the higher knowledge and captured by an unenlightened and ignorant form of belief, you sought the love of Christ in opinions you had formerly abandoned. But you subsequently renounced those opinions, by abjuring them as soon as you made use of the intelligence which has been given to you. I speak thus in order to defend those who know how to teach and to write. But if I must speak for myself, I will confess that I am not perhaps such a man as God renders capable of being His minister of the New Testament. I may be so according to the letter, but not according to the spirit. So I have been guilty of presumption in devoting myself to the work of scriptural exegesis."

INFLUENCE OF PHILOSOPHY

At the end of the Alexandrian period of his life, Origen thought his activities at the Academy had been anti-gnostic. Did he suffer from self-deception in any degree? There is always some self-delusion in the estimate which even the most sincere man forms of the value of his own labors. Origen, indeed, took little account of the indirect influences that must have affected him in the days of his tutelage, of the devious ways of many disputations in which he had to follow his opponent in order to refute him, of the unconscious habits of complaisance acquired by a professor who daily has to face an enthusiastic audience, or of other such imponderable forces that compose the mentality of a school. But he could lay one flattering unction to his soul: he never compromised with any adversary. Whatever rash speculation he might find in his work, he attributed to the limitations of his own mind, to the difficulty of making an analysis of mysteries that were lofty and sublime, and, above all, to the insufficiency of Greek philosophy to meet the demands of the Christian scholar who studies the doctrines and traditions of the Church. He expressed his own *mea culpa* later, when he said that he had been too much influenced by the teachers of his time and by the Greek philosophers.

A definite problem emerged from all such reminiscences. Those early encounters with gnosticism had taught him that the gnostic spirit of his time was a greater challenge to Christianity than the heretical teachings of Marcion or Valentinus. In controversy after controversy he had learned that when the champion of Christian beliefs pushes his argument to first principles he encounters difficulties that cannot be solved without the help of philosophy. Certainly the faith of Christianity throws light on the problems of man's origin, of the soul's destiny, and of interior growth in holiness. But no man can defend that faith with any degree of assurance unless he has been disciplined in the habits of sane and clear thinking. Could philosophy be the means of justifying the Church's message? Could it show the agreement of Christian beliefs with the best findings of human thought? Could it harmonize with human reason the doctrine of the Word made flesh?

Origen's activities against the gnosticism of Alexandria became the soil where this problem took root and grew to blossom. We are about to study the process of its germination and growth. "It left a certain mark upon Catholicism; and partly by shaking the older faiths, partly by preparing men's minds for a better belief, partly by compelling the leaders of the Church to ask what they believed and why they believed it, it aided not inconsiderably in the triumph of the Gospel and in the development of the Creed." [11]

[11] Bigg, *The Christian Platonists*, p. 62.

CHAPTER VIII

The New Philosophy

IN SEEKING definite and assured principles to guide him in the work of controversy, Origen employed all his philosophical skill. The origin of the world and of the evils that beset it must find its explanation in the way imperfect beings participate in the being of the supreme Good and the way their essences are realized there. In his analysis of the condition of dependence which is the lot of rational beings and in his meditations on the struggles and efforts in which they live, he began to have a better understanding of how salvation works, of what spiritual progress really is, and of what a return to God involves. The more he thought about these questions, the nearer he came to what emerged as the logical focus of all his philosophical inquiries. He found that, to safeguard the essentials of the Christian religion, he must make a profound analysis of the notion of participation. Only thus would it be possible to understand the relation between the spiritual world and its principle of being.

The outlines of the problem were clear and definite, and the eclectic philosophy that had satisfied Clement was of no help to Origen in his efforts to solve it. He discarded the eclecticism he had learned from Clement, because he discovered that even the adding of his own incomparable knowledge of the Bible to the opinions so elegantly and fittingly assembled by his early teacher was far from sufficient for his needs. Therefore he would turn to another source for his philosophical armor. We can recognize what that source was; his method, his ideas, and the order of his system indicate the philosophical school that gave him his principles. We know who his ancestors were. Philo was the head of his ancestral line. His own predecessors, Numenius and Ammonius, were in it, as were also Amelius and Plotinus, who had been his fellow stu-

dents. Every advance in our knowledge of early Neoplatonism casts
new light on certain parts of his doctrine. Besides all this, the entire
story of his life and works, even where it does not belong to the
domain of philosophy proper, indicates that the first half of the
third century was one of those intermediate periods in human history when great philosophies are being welded into shape under the
pressure of new, profound, and ardent convictions which are striving for their logical justification. This is particularly clear in his
writings of the Alexandrian period. Those writings give us a foundation on which to reconstruct the origins of Neoplatonism.

THE BOOK OF GENESIS

In the days when he was engaged in his work as a biblical exegete,
Origen perceived the uses of philosophy. One of his early studies
was concerned with the Mosaic account of creation as it is set forth
in the Book of Genesis. In the first volume of his *Commentary*,
which he composed even before the *De principiis*, he made an interpretation of the first two verses: "In the beginning God created
heaven and earth. And the earth was void and empty, and darkness
was upon the face of the deep; and the spirit of God moved over the
waters." He interpreted those verses as meaning that the world depends on God, who has created heaven and earth in all their entirety. He is a God of almighty power, superior to everything that is.
His action is subject to no condition. By His word He issues a decree, and in virtue of that decree things are made.

If Origen's pupils wished to express these conclusions in a form
suitable for philosophical reflection, they could enunciate two
propositions: first, God is transcendent in His relation to the world;
second, He created the world without drawing upon any pre-existent
matter. But the two propositions were far from enjoying an equal
popularity with the Hellenist philosophers who, at the end of the
second century, were beginning to react, in varying measure, to the
influences of biblical thought.

For a long time the interest of pagan scholars in the sixth book
of the *Republic* and in the *Timaeus* had been preparing men's

minds to accept the notion of an incorporeal God, a deity superior to the world and free of every taint of imperfection. Gradually there was established a definite resemblance between the God of the philosophers and the God of Abraham as He is described in the Bible. The rabbinical schools were not slow to see the value of this resemblance in the domain of Jewish apologetics. Thus it is logical for us to infer that the practice of reflecting on the teachings of the Bible was not unknown to the Platonist commentators who were attracted to the *Republic* and the *Timaeus*. Greek thinkers, in fact, became interested in natural theology.

While this interest was mounting, Stoicism was the prevailing philosophy. It owed its popularity to the prestige of its long experience in the field of ethics and to the technical superiority of its definitions and dictionaries. Men asked of it, however, only teachings that were of secondary importance: its theory of the Word, for example, its notion of the force which penetrates all parts of the universe and serves the purpose of maintaining the cohesion of the parts with the whole. But that venerable Greek philosophy had no answer that could satisfy the loftiest aspirations of humanity and no theory of a salutary providence to assuage the longings that vexed the hearts of men. But, by going farther than the most religious forms of Stoicism, the philosophers found an answer in a new version of Platonism, which was beginning to take shape and substance. In that new system philosophy learned how to pass from the physiology of man, so to speak, to a knowledge of the principle from which everything proceeds.

Armed with this new equipment, the philosophers faced the question of how the universe came into being. Naturally a number of schools arose, each treating the relations between God and nature in its own way. Certain Eastern schools were the strongest contributors to the new development. The most notable school of all was that taught by Numenius in the town of Apamaea, which flourished under the Antonines. "Speaking of those nations that have adopted the opinion that God is incorporeal, he enumerates the Jews also among those who hold this view; not showing any reluctance to use even the language of their prophets in his treatise and to give it a metaphorical meaning." [1] He did not hesitate to make use of the prophetical books and to interpret them in a figurative sense. He considered Plato a prophet and calls him the Moses of Attica. Adhering to the myths of the soul, he wrote a treatise on the secret doctrines of Plato as set forth in the *Phaedrus*, in the seventh book of the *Republic*, and perhaps also in the tenth book. Like all Pythagoreans he thought highly of symbols and instinctively discovered passages in the *Dialogues* which show Plato as being influenced by the teachings of Pythagoras.

THE THEOLOGY OF NUMENIUS

Numenius revived the ancient teaching by discovering its vestiges in the works of the most illustrious of its adherents. He brought new enthusiasm to the study of the mystery of the divine. His efforts to find the truth behind myths and fables were marked by a desire for ineffable revelations, a longing that went far beyond the allegorical tradition of the sect to which he professed allegiance. He never uttered the names of God without fear and reverence, and the invocation of the *Timaeus* found its echo in the Semitic piety which inspired him. The prophetic style of his writings later brought upon his name the charge of unduly violating the sanctity of the religious secret, the guardianship of which was a solemn obligation on all philosophers who had been initiated into the inner mysteries.

With such sentiments as these he wrote his treatise *On the Good*. He remembered that a Platonist theology was no new thing, for Plato himself had founded it, probably in the course of his oral instructions. The Greeks had identified the Good, presented in the sixth book of the *Republic* as the source of being and intelligence, with the One of Parmenides and also with the absolute Living Being which the demiurge of the *Timaeus* takes for the model of his work. Numenius studied the names of this ineffable, admirable, and eternal God whom Plato sometimes calls the Father and at other times simply He who is.

[1] Origen, *Contra Cels.*, I, 15. Cf. Bigg, *The Christian Platonists*, p. 229: "The real source of its doctrine is undoubtedly Jewish."

Numenius could not bring himself to believe that the God of all created the world. He held that the creator was the Son or demiurge, who imposed the necessity of order on the universal mass because order is a good. To achieve this purpose the Son or demiurge duplicated himself, as it were, or engaged in one or other of two mutually exclusive activities: sometimes being intent on the study of his model, and at other times turning aside in order to move the celestial sphere.

The Platonism in vogue at Alexandria was far less impressed by the cosmogony of the *Timaeus*. Numenius took care to subordinate his entire theological system to the primary monad and to insist on the union of the first and second God, "who are one only thing." This did not save his theory from the charge of polytheism, a doctrine that was most repugnant to all who had been in any way affected either by Judaism or by Christianity. We know that at this period a number of Marcionites, led by Apelles who had taught at Alexandria, renounced all notions of divine plurality. Even in the inner circles of the Platonist schools the theology of Numenius was soon being confused with the genealogical romances of the gnostics. Thus the Syrian philosopher is an isolated figure, one of those thinkers who appeared out of due time and who stimulated others in the direction of philosophical research even though they guarded themselves against the doctrines he taught.

ALEXANDRIAN STUDY OF CREATION

At Alexandria the emphasis was on a different element of the problem. Instead of considering a secondary deity as being engaged in imitating a model which he contemplates, the Alexandrians wondered how the wisdom of the unique Intelligence and His ideas could enter into the reality of the spiritual life of the world. Take the order which Numenius held to have been imposed by the demiurge. Is it not easier to understand what that order is if we remember that all created things are governed by the supreme Reason which is, at the same time, the foundation of their being? Can we not see the birth of existences as an essential participation, a new relation, whereby words are united to the Word and whereby the rational beings with whom the world is peopled are united to the ultimate Reason of all things? If it is true, as the Book of Proverbs (8: 22) says, that God established wisdom "in the beginning of His ways," would not the Word exercise its office of demiurge? And would it not do so, in virtue of the Wisdom of God, as the representative and the spokesman of intelligible objects assembled around the primary unity? This was the prevalent philosophy in the circles where Origen moved. "All who hold that Providence intervenes in the affairs of men affirm that the qualities of things have no existence proper to themselves, but that God, according to His will for the organization of the universe, makes them subsist by His Word, in virtue of the ineffable resources of His power and His wisdom." [2]

This theory approached the biblical teaching but could never harmonize with it. The road that it followed led nowhere. Although it professed to solve the problem of the creation of the world, it taught that matter was not created by God. Besides, it held fast to the Platonist idea of the demiurge as the artisan who brought the whole universe into being. Thus the divine will seems here to be less the act of a Creator than the act of an artisan; it organizes and rules but it does not produce, and it operates within a set of conditions which limit its action. We should note that this serious reservation affects something else besides the notion of creation; it makes it difficult to understand how God's providential action corrects, heals, and saves the Christian soul.

These consequences of the Alexandrian beliefs on the problem of creation were brought out in harsher lines by the doctrine of Numenius when it reached Alexandria in the middle of the gnostic crisis. Indeed, no sect could have avoided them. The gnostics portrayed matter, as distinct from the divine work of creation, under the darkest colors to be found in the pages of Plato. This harsh view of matter was further aggravated by the pessimism prevailing at the time. The philosophers held that what changes in the act of creation is the mass, for the demiurge of the *Timaeus* reduces it to order. They regarded the universe as a turbulent and infinite sea, where providence rules and sees only the Good: that infinity of matter has

[2] *In Gen.*, I; P.G., XII, 48.

its own nature, is limited by the blind necessity of the *Timaeus*, and possesses within itself the rebellious soul of the *Laws*. It is the breeding ground of misfortunes and evil passions of every kind. To the tyranny of destiny and of the stars they opposed a Providence which controlled the blind forces, and for fatalism they substituted a divine decree. This was the problem that vexed all the philosophical religions of the day, the very problem that we have already encountered in our study of Alexandrian Marcionism: two empires are established in the world, and God has accepted the collaboration of fate.

THE ORIGIN OF MATTER

Origen undertook an analysis of the difficulty. He concentrated his efforts on two problems: the problem of the origin of matter and the problem of the foreknowledge of God. His entire criticism was directed to the exposure of an ambiguity by which the philosophers of his day were misled.

His adjustment was based on a classical doctrine of philosophy. Matter was always considered an unbegotten substance as old as the divine ideas themselves. It is the receptacle of qualities. It is quite undetermined and quite without form, if considered simply in itself. Actually, of course, it cannot be separated from the modes of being which give it existence. In itself, it always lacks determination, yet it always receives some determination.[3] Posidonius had taught that matter possesses a certain predisposition. The Posidonian hypothesis led to the notion that there is an anterior providence or nature which furnishes God with material for His action "in order that the skill subsisting in Him should not be without its proper effect, which it would be if deprived of the necessary substance." Unless non-being is fully and completely indeterminable, there must be an organizer for it, a first demiurge whose function it will be to make it plastic for the hands of the artisan of the world. This primary demiurge is necessary to the solution of the problem. Destiny fails to explain the actual order of created things and has

[3] *Ibid.*; P.G., XII, 48.

had no greater success in affording an explanation of the adaptation of matter.

This supposition appears at first to help us little in solving the difficulty. But let us assume that this primary demiurge is the Creator Himself. He has created matter by giving to it the quantity and the quality necessary to enable it to receive the divine ideas. This much simpler hypothesis explains also the plasticity of things in the hands of the artisan of the universe. Why, then, should we have need of imagining a different worker in the process of creation? Is it not more logical to think of matter as being predisposed to order because this predisposition has been given to it by the almighty power which originally created it?

Besides, the hypothesis of unbegotten matter is not only useless but even disastrous to any man who believes in divine transcendence. Are we to offer our congratulations to the Creator for having found the special set of circumstances, lack of which would have prevented Him from being the demiurge, the Father, the benefactor, the God of justice and mercy? He has no need of destiny or chance or even of an anterior nature to set Him to work. His governance cannot be dependent on a preliminary condition. If the adversary admits this, it follows that his entire argument of a hierarchy of creative spirits falls to the ground and he loses the right to defend his system of thought. Moreover, he has already injured his own case by admitting that matter could of itself be in harmony with the divine thought.

This line of argument receives confirmation when we reflect that the result of an inferior and obscure necessity would in no way lend itself to the construction of such a work as the creation of the universe. Nor could it lead to such a display of divine power as is now evident in all its magnificence. Certain divine ideas might probably be realized. But the general lines of the creative plan which we call the universal system could not have been realized by any such necessity. We must not forget that the world, in its creation, received the totality of the ideas formed by the divine Wisdom.[4]

[4] *De princip.*, II, i, 4.

The Greek system of cosmology, as it was known at the Academy, was laden with other philosophical handicaps, all arising from the same cause: it failed to realize what the notion of creation implies, it failed to understand the utter dependence of the world, and it did not admit that God can foresee acts of free will. Its concept of God's foreknowledge made Him an eternal overseer who presses a button in order to initiate a series of free acts but who has not within himself the source of each of the acts that follow. To such a spiritual being the future is a chain of necessary events, and his knowledge, like the mysteries that manifest it, is conditioned by fatalism.

Seen from this viewpoint, the God of the Bible presides at the unfolding of the Stoic's universe where events are woven, in advance, to the smallest details of the circumstances in which they are to occur. The Platonism of the day was still holding fast to the old concepts; and Origen, even before Plotinus, denounces the timidity of his Platonist adversaries. "In their excessive fear, certain of the Greeks are of the opinion that future events are determined by necessity and that, if God foresees the future, there is no free will. In fear of excluding from the divine attributes what they call the divine magnificence, they have dared to put forward this impious teaching." [5] By their vaunted reverence for the dignity of God they sought to justify their assumption that His knowledge determines the future. They were acquainted, of course, with the Bible, where the word "magnificence" is one of the titles of providence and is employed in the text of the Septuagint as a reminder of the marvelous benefits that God showered upon the people of Israel.

Plotinus was not far behind Origen in his attack. He, too, recalled that a number of the disciples of Philo had been misled by the notion of destiny. "Starting with the principle of the universe, they deduce everything from that principle and make it the cause of all things, teaching that it is not only a mover but also a creator of all beings; for them that principle is both destiny and supreme cause." At one and the same time they professed an interest in the Bible and remained fixed in the lines of their Platonism. Claiming

[5] *In Gen.*, III; P.G., XII, 61.

to safeguard the majesty of the Creator but desiring to justify the incantations and horoscopes of the pagans, their only success lay in the production of a number of discordant hypotheses, as indeed usually happens at the beginning of most of the great movements of human thought. However, their disregard of the rules of logic had a very salutary effect: it forced upon their successors the unavoidable responsibility of making a thorough study of the problems which for so many centuries had been exercising men's minds.

The gnosticism of Alexandria, ever responsive to the restlessness of contemporary philosophy, was not slow to put forward its own theory. Its notion of the origin of matter, set forth in the form of a dramatic and mystical hypothesis, is to be found in the central part of the *Extracts from Theodotus*. Although the text itself is obscure, we can perceive the confusion inherent in a theory that represents matter as depending on the demiurge and as being, at the same time, the explanation of the existence of ignorance, imperfections, and evils. There is a jerkiness in the exposition of the theory, and the reader is likely to be disturbed from time to time by the sudden emergence of some new argument that takes his mind off the main issue. Here, in brief, is the theory.

Two essences, light and darkness, were originally created by the demiurge. From the essence of light the demiurge creates the heavenly spirits. Then the curtain rises on the situation described in the Bible: "and the spirit of God moved over the waters." As a result of this, the spirit of light now impregnates matter. Plato calls matter a gross, inert, and heavy thing, but the Bible calls it invisible in order to signify that it is incorporeal. The words "Be light made" mean that God, in imparting the essence of light to inert matter, introduced distinction into chaos and thus gave causes and order to the world. This having been done, the demiurge proceeds to the creation of inferior spirits and of the three material elements; and all this latter creation has its basis in matter, the primary source of terror and want.

THE PROBLEM OF EVIL

The main idea of this theory is, it would seem, the avoidance of anything that might suggest dualism. Matter is created by the demiurge and is, of itself, incorporeal. Whatever enters into its essence is the product of a spiritual life which has fallen from its first estate, and this fall ultimately manifests itself as suffering and pain. Further, matter contains within its own essence a power of inner resistance inseparable from the work of the Creator. This inner resistance is reinforced over and over again, progressively gaining new accesses of strength as it meets challenge after challenge of whatever restraints or controls are exercised on it from without. In a bold effort to express this theory in its own terms, Plotinus interprets it as saying that the soul produces matter by its inclination to matter. But his desire to make a sympathetic statement of it dies almost at birth. Is it possible to explain how, if matter does not already exist, the soul makes its first inclination to it? "The darkness still existed. There was no occasion for the soul to incline itself, unless the cause of the inclination is in the very nature of the soul rather than in the darkness." But this means the introduction of duality into the intelligible world and the attribution of evil to the first principle of things.

However weak and clumsy such theories as this might be, they indicate for us the line of thought pursued by the religious philosophies of the period under review. It became an axiom that the totality of things owed its creation to the first principle, and equally axiomatic that evil has an accidental cause. With these two axioms to start with, the philosophers soon found that the old notion of matter was nothing less than an embarrassment to them and that the new values which they were trying to formulate were quite different from the values employed by philosophers over a period of several centuries. That this was the case is quite obvious in any study of the Platonist gnosis. For example, the *Extracts from Theodotus* seemed to admit, as Plotinus observed, that the source of the soul's inclination is to be found in the soul's own activity. This was one of the new values which the Platonist gnostics allowed to go unchallenged although they rejected it in their hearts. Their concept of the divine magnificence debarred them from admitting any theory that involved a derogation of the majesty of God, and at the same time they failed to understand how the creature could be utterly dependent upon God without being entirely determined by Him. In addition, they believed that rational beings were created by some sort of higher fatalism or by some spirit less than God, the imperfections of whose work somehow involved God. Torn between the old and the new values, they became the authors of the crude theory set forth in the *Extracts*. By what cause they could not imagine, the blessings that came to the world in the moment of creation became somehow degraded and their further diffusion among men became the source of misery and pain.

Origen, on the contrary, had no difficulty in admitting that the cause of evil is within the soul. In his view, the soul might not have come into being at all, and even in this created state it does not necessarily possess all its being or all its good. Seeing that it can weaken without involving the Creator in the responsibility for such weakness, he recognized sin as the sole cause of evil. Thus, matter will no longer be the force of rebellion but the most imperfect of the things created by God, an occasion of trouble and annoyance for the souls that dwell above it on the levels where the spirits move and live. With regard to primeval matter and the elements with which the Creator performed His work, Origen will find them in the divine thought itself, in the wisdom established "in the beginning of His ways."

But the great thoughts that found expression in the De principiis could not have been coordinated if their author had not had the support of a genuine philosophy of God, of the soul, and of the world. The Platonism of the day gave proof of its inability to find a place for matter in the Creator's work. So great was the confusion that a modern critic has described the period as one wherein God and the world were torn to pieces, the unity of the human being was crushed, and the cultured Hellenism of the day was spending its best efforts in vain. Origen saw the need for the formulation of a philosophy that would re-establish the unity of the divine thought of the creation by subordinating the world of bodies to the world of spirits and by clarifying the unity and the hierarchy that exist among rational beings. He felt, too, that any such philosophy must address itself to the study of the dynamism of the soul if it would explain how the soul achieves union with the body. Thus he would open to himself the long perspective of a genuine spiritual progress, a progress personal to himself as well as continuous for the universality of men. However obscure may be the historical conditions of the development of this philosophy, it is certain that Origen acquired its first principles by his own study of the problems with which the minds of men were wrestling in Alexandria at the time.

CHAPTER IX

Ammonius Saccas

Ammonius Saccas

WE HAVE just considered some of the tenets of Alexandrian Platonism. It was soon outmoded by the philosophical activities of Ammonius Saccas, a remarkable figure who had risen from obscurity. He was said to have earned his living as a porter and to have been at one time employed in that capacity at the docks of Alexandria. Born of Christian parents, he turned to the study of philosophy at some unknown date during the reign of Emperor Commodus. However, he retained a reminder of his former occupation, for he was generally known by the name Saccas ("Sack"). Although the school where he seems to have taught was a state institution, his disciples were a philosophical brotherhood rather than a body of students; they wore the philosopher's cloak and were under the philosopher's obligation to keep secret the teachings imparted to them by the head of the school. Furthermore, they refrained from publishing any philosophical works. In this connection it is to be remembered that both Origen and Plotinus preferred the spoken word to any other method of teaching; the treatises they left to posterity are merely echoes of the doctrines they taught by word of mouth.

PHILOSOPHER AND DISCIPLES

In the third century of the Christian era the philosopher's design for living was the community life, lived with a chosen few where the master devoted himself entirely to the pupil and really formed him, teaching him everything he needed to know; to speak in public, to discuss a philosophical theme, to prepare the minds of his audience and to gain their attention by a gradual process of persuasion and effective argument. This had been the pattern of the philosophical life from the days of antiquity. Plato, for example, considered the resources of oral methods of teaching to be far above those of writing and, for this reason, felt a distrust of his outstanding works. The argument was that a book can be stripped of its persuasive power but that a speech is never open to such a form of attack. Although this was the conviction of all the great masters of Greek thought, the literary generations to which they lectured never took kindly to the notion. The Athenians in particular, with their powers of sane and clear vision, were far from partial to the supremacy of any special system of philosophical beliefs or to the glorification of any one object of scientific enthusiasm. The acceptance of an acknowledged leader of contemporary thought required a less sophisticated public and an enthusiasm under a less rigid intellectual control than existed at Athens.

It was otherwise at Alexandria in those first decades of the third century of our era, for the conditions required to ensure the personal ascendancy of an outstanding thinker were present in abundance. Greek learning still flourished there in undiminished glory, but men's reverence for it was about to be warmed by all the fervor of religious enthusiasm. It would be difficult to reproduce in other intellectual centers of the period the situation indicated by Origen when he says: "It is when we turn away from the life which is life in appearance only, not in truth, and when we yearn to be filled with the true life, that we are made partakers of it; and when it has arisen in us, it becomes the foundation of the light of the higher knowledge (gnosis) ." [1]

DOCTRINES OF AMMONIUS

Although Ammonius was not responsible for any published works and although his disciples were bound by an obligation to the secret of the school, several doctrines were being diffused under his name toward the end of antiquity. We find references to them in the works of authors of diverse schools of thought, both at Alexandria and throughout Syria. For example, Hierocles, a Neoplatonist who flourished during the first decades of the fifth century, wrote a treatise On Providence and Destiny. In the seventh

[1] In Joan., II, 19; P.G., XIV, 157.

book of that work he recalls a Platonist theory held by Ammonius. At the end of the preceding book he had asserted that, owing to some forged copies of the *Dialogues*, quarrels had arisen between the Platonists and the Aristotelians. In the beginning of the seventh book, which has its own introduction, we find the eulogy of Ammonius: he is described as one inspired by God and as a man who showed the thorough agreement of the two great philosophers "in the principal and more necessary doctrines" on providence, the immortality of the soul, and the order of heaven. Then, following the general plan of the work, Hierocles proceeds to discuss the school of Ammonius and its two most famous pupils, Plotinus and Origen. In the compilation of the works of Hierocles by Photius, the latter makes a brief synopsis of the seventh book, repeating two passages where the doctrine is preceded by the name of Ammonius and reproducing the original text almost in the same words as those used by Hierocles. In the second passage the quotation is shorter, but its brevity does not prevent Photius from preserving the eulogy of the Alexandrian philosopher.

Some few years earlier but in the same century as Hierocles, we find another reference to Ammonius. Toward the end of the fifth century, Nemesius, bishop of Emesa, published a treatise On the Nature of Man. In two passages of this work the author refers to Ammonius. In the second chapter, where he argues generally against those who teach that the soul is corporeal, he expresses his satisfaction "with the opinions of Ammonius, the master of Plotinus, and with those of Numenius." In the succeeding chapter he discusses the union of soul and body, explaining to his readers "how Ammonius solved this difficulty." Ammonius' argument is carefully expounded up to the point where the author himself arrives at a certain deduction from it that was to be of aid to him in the theological discussions of the period about the two natures in Christ.

The authenticity of these different opinions attributed to Ammonius has been strongly challenged. How could it happen that the teachings of a philosopher who left no written work behind him could reappear two centuries after his death? In the study of complicated arguments so difficult to preserve in the tradition of a school that lacked any written work published by its founder, is it scientific to attribute to them a date so remote? Thus the principal objection of critics rested on the absence of an intermediate document. At what center of learning did Hierocles and Nemesius acquire their philosophical training? A philosophical school, it was pointed out, would naturally make its founder the oracle of everything it believed to be true. Hierocles could easily have discovered some traces of Plotinus in the works of Porphyry and would readily attribute to Ammonius this sweetened Neoplatonism, and then the mistake would have crept into the treatise written by Nemesius. But a further study of the dates proved that Nemesius could not have borrowed from an author whose date was subsequent to his own.

Other hypotheses were then put forward. Nemesius alone might have been misled by some writer of the long interval between the third century and the period when he wrote his *De natura humana*. Or Hierocles would have been quite satisfied to pronounce a eulogy on Ammonius; he would not have quoted from him, but would have proceeded to his own interpretation of Plato and to the elaboration of his own philosophical beliefs. Even a confusion of names might be the cause of the whole difficulty; another Ammonius, the son of Hermias, flourished at Alexandria during the fourth century.

Soon, however, the difficulty that had given rise to all those learned guesses was satisfactorily solved. H. von Arnim proved that the doctrine referred to by Hierocles was to be found, sometimes in exactly the same words, in the *Reply to Chosroes* by Priscian. In that work the sources of the doctrine are indicated as follows: first, the *Notes of Ammonius* compiled by one Theodotus or Theodosius; secondly, the *Miscellaneous Questions* by Porphyry. One of the two modes of transmission suggested the existence of a direct witness, probably a writer of Alexandrian origin. The other indicated a compiler of a later collection which was composed of notes made at lectures given by Plotinus. Thus some teachings of the master— a synopsis of his public lectures or an account of an unusually brilliant discourse—had been salvaged from the notebooks of some of his hearers, a practice of which the period furnishes other examples. The philosophers of the fourth century, at a time when a tendency toward eclecticism was in the air, became acquainted with one or other of these two links with Ammonius, if not with both at the same time.

The Notes of Ammonius

Recently a confirmation of these results was furnished by Heinemann's success in comparing the *Notes of Ammonius* with the theories that are known to have been prevalent in Alexandria in the early days of Neoplatonism. Heinemann was able to reconstruct from the fragments enough of the original to establish its date. Further, the context of the reconstructed original has meaning only within the limits of the period when Ammonius studied and taught at Alexandria, and the ideas transmitted by Nemesius and Hierocles under his name correspond to a philosophical situation that existed at no point in history except a brief period at the beginning of the third century. Heinemann's demonstration is guilty of only one fault: it takes no account of Origen, whose teachings afford decisive evidence in favor of the antiquity of the Ammonian fragments.

In our analysis of the elements of this problem we are less concerned with stimulating the study of the Alexandrian thinker than in clarifying what is known about Origen's development as a philosopher. Our interest will extend neither to the scope nor to the literal accuracy of all the texts, and our efforts will be concentrated exclusively on the opinions most obviously connected with the name of Ammonius. So we shall not delay over the second chapter of the treatise written by the good Bishop of Emesa, where we might find it necessary to distinguish the doctrine of Numenius from that of his Platonist successor. His third chapter, however, proves to be of interest, for in its first part we find the union of soul and body explained by a theory which is identical, often even literally so, with the *Notes of Ammonius* quoted by Priscian. The very form of words used by Nemesius indicates an Alexandrian origin of the passage.

The two documents, the one furnished by Theodotus and the other by Porphyry, are sufficient to indicate for us the founder of Neoplatonism. The posthumous history of Ammonius does not show, as many of the critics were prone to believe, the birth of a historical fable; on the contrary, it testifies to the survival of a tradition. Nothing remains unforgotten so long as a secret, and particularly the secret of a philosophical school; sooner or later the secret doctrine will be committed to writing, for a man loves to ensure the preservation of the goods he has acquired rather than to dally with the fleeting things of his own thought.

ORIGEN'S ATTITUDE

When we study Origen in relation to Ammonius, it is less important to investigate the totality of the ideas he received than to know his attitude toward this new philosophy, the nearest approach to Christianity that the world had seen up to that time. On some points he appears to be a disciple. Yet he stands forth as a disciple who is himself a master, a theologian who can follow an argument to its utmost consequences in order to apply them in his own inimitable way to the problem of the soul and its salvation. We shall be content to accept him in this role, without concerning ourselves about the conditions in which it was possible. Ammonius' influence on Origen may have been simply that of the philosophical environment. It may have been exercised in lecture halls. It may even have been the result of a personal friendship. With any such surmise we are not concerned.

THE PROBLEM OF CREATION

The relations between providence and the act of creation constitute the principal problem. Ammonius solved it by a theory of origins which he considered in conformity with Platonism. "Things are sustained in being by God, who is the demiurge of all organization, apparent or hidden. The artisan of the universe has given it existence without drawing it forth from any matter. An act of his will is enough to cause beings to subsist." Origen meets the problem in the same way and solves it with the same words: "When

God decides that a thing shall subsist, He can cause it to subsist
as He wills, since there is no obstacle to His will and since He does
not change it." [2] In other words, the world is altogether a contingent effect, the result of a free act of an all-powerful will. Origen
does not hesitate to dispose of the objection that every artisan needs
matter from which to produce his work. He says that the comparison is not valid and that any such simple view of the act of creation
needs enlightenment: "Providence supplies the artisan with the
material on which to work, for the material comes from a preceding
skill, due either to man or to God." [3] Thus disappeared the chief
difficulty which had confronted the thinkers of preceding generations: the artificial division of the Creator and matter, between
providence and necessity, between the Word and inferior influences. The unity of the world thus became an effect of a creative
power that was infinite and illimitable.

QUESTIONS OF COSMOLOGY

When we come to the study of the comparative cosmology of
the two thinkers we find ourselves on firmer ground, especially in
the matter of the dates, for in the history of philosophy each period
has its own understanding of the universe. In the principal elements of the problem before us we find all the familiar notions, all
the special viewpoints common to the philosophical circles or
schools with which we have been dealing: first, a hierarchy of
reasonable beings; secondly, a wisdom which rules over them and
distinguishes them one from another; and thirdly, the idea of providence and of destiny.

The emerging Neoplatonism of the early decades of the third
century constructed its view of the organization of the universe on
two definite principles. The first of those principles was that bodies
are subordinated to spirits: "the realization of the incorporeal essence is part of the incorporeal workmanship of creation so that the
finished work, which is at one and the same time simple and complex, is composed of two orders of beings." The second principle is

[2] *In Gen.*, I; *P.G.*, XII, 48.
[3] *Ibid.*

that the creative wisdom establishes a hierarachy of beings according to the degree of spirituality which they severally enjoy and that those beings, through the interplay of the relations between them, are maintained on the spiritual level on which they are created: "the lower beings are guided by those that are immediately above them."

Nature thus tends to fall into the pattern of a community of intelligences. At the summit there is a spiritual life, with a special function to regulate the entire system of intelligences; they called this Wisdom. Below this ruling spirit there are diverse spiritual beings that are regulated, and the totality of these beings composes the universe. Each of the intelligences constituting the universe is itself a consciousness, clear or obscure, of the contemplation which Wisdom eternally possesses of its own ideas. Natural laws are therefore moral laws, because they are the reflection of a divine order as seen in the mirror of a universe composed of intelligences which are in varying degrees of enlightenment. Those laws conserve and ensure the harmony of the universe of intelligences. Thus "providence is nothing but the paternal regime of the Creator, and what men call destiny is the order of justice which is a consequence of that regime." The universe is thus seen and heard as a magnificent song of praise which is to inspire the Christian philosophy of nature.

No view of the universe could differ from the cosmology of antiquity more than this does. Instead of a determined series of events such as was envisaged in the notion of a seed which goes through its due process of development, we have here a paternal providence. Instead of a generic nature, we have now a universe of individual natures, each with its own rank and its own manner of realizing the divine plan of creation. Instead of destiny, we have the notion of spiritual progress. In such a universe, justice is the one element that is predetermined and necessary, and this justice is the supreme law that places each intelligence in the rank to which it is entitled by merit. Here we have the primary axiom of the Neoplatonist cosmology. "Destiny is neither the irrational fatalism of the readers of horoscopes, nor the inner force of the Stoics, nor the fate which Alexander of Aphrodisias identified with what Plato called the nature of different bodies, nor the behavior of things which charlatans claim to control by incantations and sacrifices. . . . Destiny is an activity of justice exercised upon created things by the decree of providence. It restores our conditions of soul, bringing them into their due order and alignment by relating them to the deliberate principles of free acts."

In this Neoplatonist view of the universe we have Origen's entire cosmology: the contingency of creatures identified with free will, the natural law interpreted as a moral law and as immanent justice, a providence watching over the sequence of human events in order to evoke from us salutary decisions and holy choices, thereby training or healing our wills: here is Origen's teaching, but presented in a form more technical and more personal than is found among his works. Certain elements of Plotinism are also to be found in the theory, for it portrays the interior life as being in a fair way to dominate the physical life. As a matter of fact, these two concepts, free will and contemplation, are found, in varying degrees, in all the philosophical systems of the third century.

ORIGEN'S COSMOLOGY

Now let us return to Origen himself. The second book of the *De principiis* opens with a similar discussion of the world and the creatures who are part of it. The treatment is philosophical rather than theological, and Origen here gives the stamp of his approval to several opinions that had been vigorously challenged at the Academy. Among such opinions we must take account of the theory attributing material substance to all spirits, on the ground that "material substance . . . appears to have been formed for them (rational natures) or after them." [4] New influences, hitherto unknown to Christian tradition, make their presence felt here, and it becomes obvious that Origen is reacting to the Neoplatonism in the atmosphere around him.

"It is one power that grasps and holds together all the diversity of the world and leads the different movements toward one work, lest so immense an undertaking as that of the world should be dissolved by the dissensions of souls. And for this reason we think that

[4] *De princip.*, II, ii, 2.

God, the Father of all things, in order to ensure the salvation of all His creatures through the ineffable plan of His word and wisdom, so arranged each of these that every spirit, whether soul or rational existence, however called, should not be compelled by force, against the liberty of his own will, to any other course than that to which the motives of his own mind led him (lest by so doing the power of exercising free will should seem to be taken away, which certainly would produce a change in the nature of the being itself). And He so arranged that the varying purposes of these would be suitably and usefully adapted to the harmony of one world, by some of them requiring help, and others being able to give it, and others again being the cause of struggle and contest to those who are making progress. Among these their diligence would be deemed more worthy of approval, and the place of rank obtained after victory be held with greater certainty, which should be established by the difficulties of the contest." [5]

The simplest comparative study of the texts is enough to make it obvious that a profound kinship exists between the two systems of thought. Suppose that we put aside, for the moment, the reference to Ammonius in the fragments of Hierocles or even erase it from the text altogether. Then the most natural explanation of the similarity of thought is to say that the fifth-century Neoplatonist was well versed in Origen's system of philosophy and shared with the great Alexandrian the general beliefs that marked the Christian catechist as an heir of the Platonist tradition. This hypothesis would not be wholly untenable, for, just as Origen's activities went far beyond the limits of Christian literature, it is not astonishing to find everywhere references to his work.

However probable this interpretation of the facts may seem at first sight, it meets grave difficulties when submitted to examination. Although the two sets of concepts are allied, each of the two authors has his own method of presenting them. The ideas mentioned by Photius in his compilation of the teachings of Hierocles are found in Origen; not, however, in a neat recapitulation but at different points and sometimes even incidentally. In the former the unprej-

[5] *Ibid.*

udiced reader may discern a plan for one or more philosophical discussions, but in the latter he finds a number of spiritual applications of the doctrine to the purposes of theology. The cosmology of the *De principiis* illustrates in many ways the theory of a universe peopled with beings created by God; the world is a proving-ground where providence raises up the stronger for the help of the weaker in the struggle for perfection, and thus the communion of saints is adjusted to the harmony of nature. All such excursions into the field of theology presuppose a knowledge of the philosophy expounded in the compilation by Photius.

But this latter work possesses a definite feature which indicates that it is not to be regarded as a mere compilation, for it contains, in addition to references to the third-century controversies on destiny, a number of philosophical elements strange to the doctrine of Hierocles and even to that of Origen. Their presence in Photius' work definitely confirms the impression of archaism which our literary analysis of the text has already given. Rational natures are there divided into three classes: heavenly beings or gods, ethereal beings or good spirits, and human souls. Each such class is exclusive, and no being ever passes from one class into another.

No such hierarchy of classes is found in Origen's concept of the spiritual universe. For him, the universe consists of a multitude of dwellings, as it were, peopled by souls that are ever in process of either rise or fall. Above men are the spirits of the stars and of the angels, and below them are the demons, plunged in the deepest degradation. At the beginning those spiritual powers were all intelligences, and they can still return to their pristine condition. Their original unity and equality render possible the restoration of the world. To save someone, it is necessary not only to help him, but to raise him to himself.

No opinion of Origen's was more challenged than this and none became more famous; indeed it is impossible to study his cosmology without being affected by it, if only with the desire to correct it. Yet Photius ignores it. In fact, he expounds quite a different hierarchy of beings, the hierarchy which was accepted at Alexandria in the generation to which the teachers of Origen belonged. It is found in the fragments of Ammonius and in the seventh book of Clement's *Stromata*. It is not too much to assume that Clement was engaged in setting this theory down on paper at the moment when Origen was beginning the study of philosophy.

According to this teaching, the organization of the world is subject to no essential variation. The Word or providence received the divine plan and accepted the task of superintending the organization of the world. In the exercise of its power it had the assistance of a host of angels and of lesser deities. Since it was carrying out the Father's decision, every created thing fell into its due place. Three classes of beings are suspended from one sole government like the rings of a chain from a magnet. The fortunate institution of the angels is at the higher limit of the visible world and has the task of guiding and helping the weaker souls of men who still hesitate in the path of perfection. The plan of providence is to lead to salvation and to contemplation those souls who choose the ways of virtue.

This is the sole Alexandrian cosmology in agreement with the cosmology suggested in the fragments of Hierocles. It is found in one of the last chapters Clement wrote. Must we say, then, that Hierocles borrowed from Clement? If we do so, we lay ourselves open to far more serious objections than can be leveled against the hypothesis that he knew the writings of Origen, because the work compiled by Photius has nothing to suggest that it is a recapitulation of the *Stromata*. Besides, if Origen's influence on Hierocles was unlikely, it would be even more difficult to admit that the profane Neoplatonism of the fifth century revived the antiquated and little known theory of a Christian thinker who lacked the prestige of his great successor. All the evidence compels us to believe that Clement's cosmology and the cosmology expounded in the dissertation by Photius are related, because they belong to one and the same period. In the fifth century, Hierocles reproduced this Alexandrian cosmology, although it was then two hundred years old, and his purpose in doing so was to salvage something from the works of an illustrious thinker, one who followed in the ways of Pythagoras as he himself did, and who was, besides, the founder of two of the

greatest philosophical schools of the third century. In the eyes of
more than one philosopher, Ammonius was held to have been enlightened by God when he rediscovered, beneath the debris of the
recurrent rivalries of the various schools of thought, a genuine
philosophy.

SOUL AND BODY

We have just seen that his notion of providence testifies to his
anxiety to derive the order of the universe from the relation between
the creature and the almighty and fatherly will of God. From this
he is led to give a privileged place in his system to the life of the
soul, to its struggles, and to its salvation. The divine government
already described appeals to free beings or to beings on the way to
be free. Such beings avail themselves of matter and are able to lift
themselves above it. A thoroughgoing harmony unites the spiritual
essence and the corporeal essence, permitting the free action of the
forces of direction and perfection. The ensemble of these forces
trains and molds the soul. The psychology proclaiming this idea of
the world is found in the treatise *De natura humana*, in the chapters
where Nemesius quotes from Ammonius.

The *Notes of Ammonius* definitely teach that the nature of the
soul is unchanged by its union with the body. Intelligences can
descend into matter without being likened to it and neither lose
their own properties nor are subjected to any substantial alteration.
The soul is of itself incorporeal and remains imperishable, without
matter, without quantity, and without mass. Without any shadow
of doubt it is said to be a prisoner in the body, but we must understand this expression to take account of the fact that the soul is
prepared for the body by a sort of inclination to it. It is present in
the body and operates in it by an influence analogous to that which
God exercises in the world. A mutual sympathy can be observed
between soul and body, which explains why such a spiritual principle can enter several human bodies in succession. It cannot enter
the bodies of animals, because it has no predisposition to a union of
that kind. In formulating this philosophy of the soul, Ammonius
believed he was reproducing the thought of Plato, a belief quite in

harmony with the philosophical temper of a day when scholars were leaving the *Phaedo* to the elementary classes and were concentrating on the *Phaedrus*, the *Republic*, and the *Timaeus* for their studies in the history of the soul. The psychology of Ammonius was, therefore, a diluted Platonism. It preserved the dogma of the Fall by liberating it from the pessimistic consequences with which the majority of the gnostic sects remained content. This was precisely what Alexandrian orthodoxy was trying to do at the beginning of the third century.

ORIGEN'S PSYCHOLOGY

Origen adopted this new psychology. It allowed him to seek the salvation of the soul, not in any escape of the soul from matter but in its progressive adaptation to matter. In place of separating the spiritual element from the body, he was bold enough to unite it more closely to the body, believing that to be the best means of safeguarding its dignity. With the sole exception of God, no being is without a body. The soul is not lost in the body, for the body is made for it. It is always distinct from the body, in the sense that it is always indivisible and uncircumscribed by place. It possesses a life of its own; "what is superior to the body feeds itself upon incorporeal thoughts." Thus the old Alexandrian metaphor of spiritual nourishment acquires its full meaning. Although immortal natures are in no need to preserve themselves from corruption, they must seek the mystical food that renews their vigor. It follows that our life here on earth is less a place of imprisonment than a time of testing and trial. No defilement can befall us except the neglect of contemplation. In that neglect we allow the irrational elements within us to gain the upper hand, and it is not to be forgotten that this evil never comes upon us from without. Origen also admits, in accordance with the principles he held in common with the *Notes of Ammonius*, that there is a transmigration of souls or a succession of bodies for one and the same soul, but he distinguished it clearly from the metempsychosis of his day.[6]

In these ways Platonism was preparing the instrument that would

[6] Cf. *De oratione*, XXVII, 8.

be needed by the mystical theology which was about to come into being. No longer was the life of the spirit defined as a nature. It was now a force in quest of achievement, a set of conditions out of which it was possible to pass. The soul within us was indeed no longer what it had originally been, but it had the power to become again all that it had been in the beginning. "As it is itself when it reflects, so it is in its intelligence when it thinks." [7]

As we shall see, Origen would revive the functions of the soul. The directive part of the soul became, in his hands, the power of contemplating the Good. Judgment was an unstable activity needing to be grounded in divine wisdom that it might resist its manifold temptations. The imagination was the mistress of error, prone to culpable distractions, and ever ready to seek occasions of trouble from without. But when prayer envelops the man of serious mind, "the soul raises itself and turns to follow the leading of the spirit by separating itself entirely from the body; and indeed it not only follows the spirit but immerses itself in the spirit, according to the text: Toward Thee I have lifted up my soul. Is it not true that it lays aside its nature, then, in order to become spiritual?" [8] This inner aspiration, the one great feature that makes Origen's meditations the beautiful prayers they are, could be justified only in a new version of Platonism, a Platonism stripped of all the somber dreams which a restless generation had permitted to gather around the classical doctrines of the soul.

In Plato, as in all great sources of enthusiasm, there is to be found a certain temptation, and it was never more powerful than in the period under review. In the higher reaches of Platonist speculation, where men's minds were affected by the rarefied air, their philosophical enthusiasm became a sort of delirium, a madness that peopled their mental world with fables, myths, and obscurities of various kinds. However vague and mysterious such concepts might be, they were real enough to the dreamer to enable him to see them in the brightest and most attractive colors. His soul seemed to be borne upward to the highest levels of human thought without ever

[7] P.G., CIV, 80.
[8] *De oratione*, ix, 2.

being satisfied in its desire for truth, and at the same time his imagination reeled under the impact of what seemed to be beauty. The garments of loveliness in which Platonism clothed its myths and fables had more appeal for Origen's contemporaries than any other part of Platonist philosophy; men asked more and more mysteries from the philosopher and were content to leave him in peace with his arguments and reasons as long as he gave them what they sought.

It is conceivable that even Plato might have yielded to the fatal beauty of his own concepts if he had not been so fortunate as to have Aristotle for his pupil. The great Stagirite appears on the scene in all the dramatic crises of Platonism, sometimes as an adversary but more often as a friendly critic who kept his master's theories within the bounds of common sense. The Platonist myth of the soul was corrected by the psychology of Aristotle, by his analysis of the will, and by his doctrine of the human *compositum*. Thus it happened that Ammonius, out of his sympathetic knowledge of the close association of the two Greek thinkers, proposed to "reduce the two philosophies to a common mentality." In this project he drew encouragement from the fact that Aristotle was formulating the basic principles of one of his earliest works, the treatise on the ideas, during the period when he was teaching at the Lyceum and the further fact that he wrote it while he was still under the spell of Plato's teaching. Ammonius was not alone in his plan to reconcile the two great philosophies. Earnest and sincere men everywhere were filled with the desire to adjust the divisions that separated the various schools and to restore the unity of Greek thought.

Thus it happened that Origen became acquainted with Aristotelianism and was influenced by it when he was building the groundwork of his own great system. He based his theory of evil on the convertibility of good and being. He studied the ethical teachings of the Peripatetics, their notion of the three fundamental goods and of the just mean which had been elaborated by their later disciples. Those researches gave him a vast number of useful definitions and also a new viewpoint which tempered his Platonism, diluted the concentrated dualism of his philosophical environment, and enabled him to reconcile nature and free will. On this title alone he is a worthy disciple of Ammonius, the philosopher who was able to reconcile Plato and Aristotle.

Perhaps Ammonius and Origen and their fellow Alexandrians were betrayed into a form of self-deception, for the reconciliation of Platonism and Aristotelianism would soon be vigorously challenged. But in the eyes of all those earnest men, philosophy rested on two principles and on two principles alone: the doctrine of providence and the soul's free will. On these two points, which Ammonius counted as the basis of the reconciliation, his adjustment of the two Greek philosophies achieved solutions that were free from every trace of fable or myth and were therefore truly philosophical. The Alexandrians asked nothing more.

CHAPTER X

Origen and Plotinus

TRADITION has preserved for us, under the name of Ammonius, nothing more than a plan for a certain course of university lectures and some notes on psychology. A comparative study, however, of the teachings common to several thinkers of the period enables us to acquire more definite knowledge of the first Neoplatonist of Alexandria. In this connection two names come readily to the mind: Origen and Plotinus. Each of these two men founded a great philosophical system, and the two systems would soon be in opposition to each other. Each man became a professor; Origen of a Christian mysticism, the saner parts of which would later be absorbed into the mentality of the Church, and Plotinus of the last philosophy of Hellenism. Yet we cannot fail to perceive a definite relationship between them, a kinship that sometimes manifests itself in very lively resemblances in their methods, in the problems which they discussed, and in the prefaces and style of their various writings.

PLOTINUS AT ALEXANDRIA

The comparison of these two writers shows that they sat at the feet of the same master. For several years before he left Alexandria, about A.D. 200, Origen attended the lectures of Ammonius. Plotinus spent a much longer time with Ammonius, eleven years, during the period when Origen was already settled in Caesarea. The consensus of critical opinion is that "if they seem to agree occasionally or to solve certain problems in a similar way, the explanation is to be found in the fact that they had learned those solutions from the same master."

The hypothesis that Plotinus had absorbed, at least in part, some of the lectures that Origen gave at Alexandria has been summarily dismissed by the critics as being contrary to the evidence at hand. For example, everywhere in the *Enneads* passages occur which are direct contradictions of theories known to have been held by Origen. Furthermore, in the cases where the two authors agree, the agreement is always on certain special problems brought forth by the revival of Platonism. As critical research on this period brought more evidence to the surface, historians were gradually forced to discard the notion that the Hellenism of the third century was Greek philosophy pure and undefiled. Undoubtedly there had been a preliminary period of no short duration during which Platonist philosophy had been subjected to the influence of Judaeo-Christian thought. Is it not logical to believe that, in any such preliminary period, philosophical doctrines acquire what we might call their behavior-patterns, if not their whole viewpoint, as human beings do in the formative years of childhood? Neoplatonism was born in Syria, but the years of its adolescence belong to Alexandria where the philosophy of the Bible was reinforced by the strength of a Christian tradition that was two centuries old.

In this study we are under no obligation to make a new appraisal of Plotinus, for our research is concerned with the task of throwing light on certain problems to which he fell heir rather than with the spirit that informed his philosophy. Nor is it within our scope to make a complete analysis of his teachings. We seek merely to reconstruct to better advantage the set of conditions that nurtured the philosophy which claimed his allegiance from his earliest years. Alexandrian Neoplatonism contained its own view of destiny, its theory of productive intelligence, and its idea of the history of the soul.

I. THE TRADITIONS HELD IN COMMON

THE VIEW OF DESTINY COMMON TO ORIGEN AND PLOTINUS

When ethics began to be limited to an art of personal happiness, the problem of destiny became one of the most insistent questions in philosophy. The question acquired a new sharpness at a later date when philosophers developed the notion of a higher Providence on whom the destiny of each individual depends. In the philosophical environment in which Origen labored, men were asking themselves how prediction, prophecy, and foreknowledge under all their forms could be brought into harmony with the work of salvation. The genuine Christian believed in prophecies but put no credence in astrologers. The problem was, therefore, how to safeguard the notion of Providence and how to show the absurdity of fatalism. The first phase of the battle had already been waged in Syria. Christian writers there had used against the vendors of horoscopes the arguments of Carneades, who borrowed his weapons from the resources of Jewish apologetic. The impostures of the charlatans who claimed to read the lessons of the stars were strenuously attacked. The Christian leaders accused the charlatans of hiding their ignorance of the divine mysteries under a mass of specious words. At the same time they were prepared to admit that there are men to whom God communicates His foreknowledge by means which He himself chooses and which surpass the normal powers of men.

Origen was acquainted with those Syrian refutations and did not hesitate to use them to confirm his own teaching. He preferred, however, a more learned theory. This theory was more in harmony with the Alexandrian cosmology of the time, intent on discovering the hidden relations between things and in establishing the degrees of knowledge on which the invisible hierarchy of spirits was founded. In the third book of his *Commentary on Genesis* he reproduced a brief treatise on foreknowledge and astrology, which dealt with four problems: how God's eternal foreknowledge is in harmony with the creature's free will; how the stars are not causes but only signs of events here below; how men can have no exact knowledge of those signs which are under the influence of the higher powers; and for what reasons God instructs men by means of those signs. After giving his own brief outline of the question, Origen proposed to make as concise a synopsis as possible of the treatise in question.[1] When Plotinus turned to a criticism of astrology, he took exactly the same line of argument, reproducing the treatises of his predecessors. These writings included a dissertation

[1] *In Gen.*, III; P.G., XII, 61. Later on Origen was accused as a heretic for this dissertation on foreknowledge.

of the cynic Oenomaus and a more accurate analysis which furnished him with a multitude of proofs. The conclusion of his argument was that the stars do not cause human happenings but merely announce them.

INFLUENCE OF THE STARS

This teaching, which was unknown to classical philosophy, relies on the same arguments and is expounded with the same logical sequence in Origen's little treatise and in the considerations put forward by Plotinus. Dealing with the claims of the astrologers to be able to tell the conditions in which a man's relatives are living from a simple study of his birth chart, Origen asks: "How can the arrangement of the stars today have caused events that happened years ago?" In the same strain Plotinus asks: "How is it possible to say that the stars are the cause of the nobility of a man's relatives, since those relatives already possessed their nobility before the stars fell into the position on which the astrologer makes his prediction?" Besides, on what will the astrologer base the connection of several destinies? Origen remarks that, if a man is due to be killed by robbers, "those people claim to know that fact from the records of his birth; and if he has several brothers, from the horoscope of each one of them." Plotinus uses the same example: "They announce a man's death according to the horoscope of his brothers." It is worth noticing that this monograph on Genesis, the fragments of which have thus come down to us, is not the work of either of these two authors. Yet, on the one hand, the treatise supports the Christian apologetic, which normally denies the possibility of an astrological prediction; on the other hand, it goes beyond the criticism leveled against the astrologers by Plotinus.

Plotinus attacks the astrologers' prejudices rather than their trade. He is willing to admit that the stars may exercise an influence if this influence may be included in the system of mysterious energies that constitute the harmony of the universe and if such an influence does not imply that we attribute to those divine beings "our wills and our passions, our impulses and our vices." But the very notion of a sign, when he stops to reflect on it, seems to be infected with anthropomorphism. Evidence of reservations and revisions appears in a later study of the same subject; an analysis of those works shows a growing desire to exclude from his cosmology any action that might be construed as that of a free and personal intelligence. The same desire is manifested in other parts of his philosophy. It was his act of defiance against an interpretation that approached too closely to the traditions of Alexandria. It seemed as if there were moments when his philosophy resisted every such temptation, whipped up its energies, and gathered itself together in an effort to maintain in undiminished strength the perfect ways of Greek thought.

In his first analysis of the claims of the astrologers, Plotinus associates prediction with allegory, thereby coming very close to the Platonism of Origen. Two readings of the heavens are possible: a purely matter-of-fact reading and a scientific reading. The latter reading gives us a knowledge of the eternal Thinker whose handwriting we see in the skies. Prophecy and symbol are thus joined together. "In reading the stars as he would read a written page, he who knows the language of the heavens reads the future from the words or figures he sees in the sky by using the method of analogy to interpret their meaning: for example, a bird flying high is an indication of lofty actions." This symbolic method was quite well known to the followers of Plotinus, and he refers to it briefly as a man might do in regard to something admitted and acknowledged by everybody.

ASTROLOGY

In the course of one of his subsequent studies he expresses his thought with a greater degree of accuracy, thereby enabling us to see how his researches are carrying him away from his early philosophical moorings. Astrology is a science based upon the spiritual solidarity of the different parts of the universe. "No part is treated as if it stood by itself; it is considered only in relation to the function it has in the life of the whole." Thence he proceeds to the conclusion that "the art of the soothsayer consists in interpreting the characters written by nature, and those characters unveil a plan of order in which no suggestion of disorder is ever found; or rather, that art consists in evaluating the evidence given us by the movements of the heavenly bodies, which tell us of certain qualities before such qualities are manifested in this or that particular man."

Plotinus' final effort to solve the problem led him to justify the practice of soothsaying because of his idea of the world. But the stars must not be considered a plurality of independent powers. He wishes that the stars should be called self-moving letters if their power to signify is a consequence of their other functions. They are a realization of the order of the universe. But everything that happens is a part of one sole harmony, and the future can be foretold as a present which is not yet directly perceptible; we know it in some such way as we know one part of an animal from another part.

Thus Neoplatonism would try to discover a rational justification for astrology, as it would try to justify the practice of incantation. Origen, however, would have no share in any such compromise. He would reveal himself more and more as the vigorous foe of every effort to limit the empire of free will and of every attempt to curtail the activity of the providence which respects that free will, elevates it, and heals it. Here, more than in the case of any other element of the problem, the divergence of the two great thinkers is made manifest. To criticize a science where neither of them was competent, they had recourse to the teachings of Ammonius. In those teachings everything hinged on the role of the demiurge. God's intelligence surveys the future of every being from the beginning of the creation of the world. No earthly being exists whose entire history is not told in the book of the heavens, where He has written it. Above us and beyond us there ceaselessly unrolls, from eternity to the hour when the divine plan is consummated, a Bible truly worthy of the mighty design containing within itself the infinity of events.[2]

Origen did indeed accept these lofty speculations of Alexandrian Platonism, but he grafted upon them more than one idea borrowed from the contemporary Aristotelianism. In the brief treatise found in the third volume of the *Commentary on Genesis* he explained,

[2] *Ibid.*, III; *P.G.*, XII, 64.

somewhat as Alexander of Aphrodisias did, that contingent happenings, and especially the decisions of the free will of human beings, are not undetermined from the viewpoint of a spectator who sees everything. God's providence, the divine foreknowledge, is a knowledge of everything, of the possible as well as of the real; and therefore this knowledge applies to the possibles that shall become real.[3] With this argument Origen was able to perceive why the heavenly spirits or powers duly accept the missions entrusted to them; they are ministers charged with a round of beneficent duties, designed and planned as helps to man's slightest movements in the direction of good.

This concept of a universe in which the design of providence is realized with the cooperation of free creatures is precisely what is described in the fragments attributed to Ammonius Saccas. In Origen's treatment of the question we find the same hostility toward the mechanical view of creation favored by the Stoics, the same suspicion of the diluted determinism, the undigested mixture of fatalism and free choice, which the Platonist schools had been advocating up to that time. The truth is that a new notion of causality was beginning to appear. The relations of beings were moving out of the realm of material fact and were about to be studied on a suprasensible level. Origen saw the need of seeking the primary foundation of free will in the divine intelligence, which prepares the succession of events and forms them in advance of their actual occurrence. The divine intelligence conceives them as they will be, either necessary or free, and it sees them both in themselves and in the circumstances in which they happen. In this view wisdom becomes the force that guarantees the order of the universe.

THE DYNAMISM OF THE DIVINE INTELLIGENCE

In such a philosophy everything comes back to the theory of the divine intelligence: creation, the organization of the world, and prediction. Creation, because beings must, from the very first, subsist in the thought which at once distinguishes them and unites them. The organization of the world, because order consists of a hierarchy

[3] *Ibid.; P.G.,* XII, 64, 68.

of rational substances which are docile to wisdom. Prediction, since the soothsayer interprets the signs given to him by a foreknowledge, which is higher than nature and which contains or embraces all individual facts. This divine intelligence is then an emanation from God, the demiurge, the unity of the world. It is a thought that comes forth from the divine will to give life to the ideas, to arrange them in their distinction and their order, and to allow them to express themselves in the manifold harmony of creation.

The influence of this doctrine on Origen and Plotinus is quite clear. In each system it occurs often, even where the context is directly concerned with other problems. Origen makes use of the doctrine to complete the theology of the Logos, which he had found among his predecessors. It produces a number of important adjustments in the Plotinist doctrine of the three hypostases. For example, the divine intelligence, considered as the demiurge, sometimes seems to hold the place usually given by the Neoplatonists to the soul; or the Logos seems to step into this role, in the third rank of the triad. Why Plotinus shifts the concepts to and fro is not always clear.

When Origen realized that the success of any theological research is based upon the philosophical equipment of the inquirer, he began to study philosophy. From his earliest years he had been taught that the Word was born before every creature. He loved to contemplate the Logos in Christ, the Word sent by the Father and preached by the Apostles. But to meditate adequately on his belief in the Logos, he had to have a help that would enable him to define with more rigor the mode of the Son's eternal generation from the Father. All his knowledge of the labors of his predecessors, from the earliest Christian apologists to Hippolytus, stimulated him in this effort. And many others were to try it after him.

St. Augustine would illustrate the dogma of the Trinity by comparing the triune God to the immanent operations of a soul contemplating itself and reflecting on itself. St. Thomas would establish his theology on the substantial relation of perfect being. Origen, borrowing from the earliest developments of Neoplatonism, started with the notion of active contemplation. He conceived the procession of the Son as the dynamism of an intelligence, which filled the twofold role of subject and object. Divine wisdom safeguards the basic unity by its faithful correspondence with the being, which it receives in its thought under manifold aspects and to which it gives subsistence. The entire role of the demiurge is reducible, then, to an immanent operation of the supreme Intellect or to a divine intuition which becomes pregnant, as it were, by the simple act of reflecting upon itself.

This divine intuition contains within its unique unity all intelligible beings, and it sees them directly in the creator-power proper to the first principle of things. It is an intuition of omnipotence itself, a ray or an image of it, but an image utterly and completely representative of the original. When the supreme intelligence contemplates itself, intelligence subsists; and in the act of subsistence it gives form and limit to the essences contained within its unity. To this act of divine self-contemplation was given the title of demiurge.

The notion of the Logos remains subordinate to the notion of intelligence. Logos here means the movement and activity of an intelligence which, in the very act of self-contemplation, produces or creates its own proper object. Thus, the Logos manifests the primary principle, but it also tends to share with the physical world the diversity of essences it contains.

This doctrine is the inner core of the Neoplatonic teachings, so frequent in the works of Origen. Before he considers the Logos, he treats of wisdom. This is something subsistent, like a distinct reality. More accurately, it is the subsistence of the objects that it sees in the Father. "The wisdom of the God and Father of all things does not apprehend His substance in mere visions, like the phantasms of human thought. Whoever is able to conceive a bodiless existence of manifold speculations, extending to the rationale of all existing things, living and, as it were, ensouled, will see how well the wisdom of God is above every creature." [4]

---

[4] De princip., I, ii, 2: "Let no one imagine that we mean anything impersonal when we call Him the wisdom of God. . . . The only-begotten Son of God is His wisdom hypostatically."

ORIGEN'S NOTION OF WISDOM

Interpreted thus as subsistence, wisdom is maintained by a conversion, a turning back, which attaches it to the principle from which it is derived. The being that thus emanates from the Father acts by the force of its union with the Father. Wisdom, the daughter of God, subsists and thinks and operates solely by the contemplation that animates it in the sight of the primal power. Of itself it has no relation to beings, but it is bound up with the divine skill because every creature comes into the sphere of the real and of subsistence in conformity with wisdom. Wisdom surveys things by its foreknowledge and allows them to be made by the Word.[5] This is the sense in which wisdom speaks of herself, as she says in Proverbs: "The Lord possessed me in the beginning of His ways." The Word, to which is given the role of the demiurge, is not different from wisdom, but it expresses the perfect agreement between a thought and its creative ideas, the tacit consent, the decisive acquiescence of the Son agreeing and cooperating in the plan of the creation of the world. The union of the Word with the Father rests on the same reality of God, on the substance of the ideas that it possesses in wisdom.

Hence the work of the divine artisan is manifested in its becoming an eternal and immanent act. The Word is the principle, solely because of its being wisdom and not because of any mission or property that would arise at the origin of angels or of other rational beings. It contains the genera and species, and perhaps also the ideas, of individual things. It analyzes the richness of the plans it carries within itself. In this way the Word acquires a relation to beings because they share in it and are a part of the system formed by the divine archetypes.

Here we have the greatest effort ever made to refine the metaphor borrowed from human ways in a description of the ineffable act of creation. We start with the notion of a workman. According to Origen this workman must find within his own thought the matter of his creation. He produces or creates by the simple voluntary re-

---

[5] *Ibid.* In this treatise is first found the exposition of the theory of intelligence, the One is in Himself the object of vision.

flection with which he sees the creative power contained in the being which he perceives. To understand adequately what happens in this operation, we should be able to represent to ourselves all the efficacy of a perfect intelligence.

In following this manner of study according to the degree of perfection that we are capable of perceiving in the divine plan of creation, we can consider the demiurge under several aspects. The notion of wisdom, for example, is nearer the primal unity. "The demiurge, considered in relation to the structure of contemplation and thoughts about the whole of things, is regarded as wisdom; but in relation to that side of the objects of thought, in which reasonable beings apprehend them, it is considered as the Word." [6] Interpreting the demiurge in this second way, we have, in the Only-begotten, the fully intelligible expression of the relation of every being to its principle. "The Only-begotten is the truth because He embraces in Himself according to the Father's will the whole reason of all things with perfect clearness; and being the truth, He communicates to each creature in proportion to its worthiness." [7]

Wisdom it is which gives itself, a living water, a source of life and of truth. Hence we are accustomed to give it the role of the supreme interpreter. "In the same way in which we have understood that wisdom was the beginning of the ways of God, and is said to be created, forming beforehand and containing within herself the species and beginnings of all creatures, must we understand her to be the Word of God, because of her disclosing to all other beings, i.e., to universal creation, the nature of the mysteries and secrets which are contained within the divine wisdom." [8]

Knowledge of the principle would be obtained by a process of thought which could reduce to unity, as far as we are able to do so, the different notions by which the same intelligence is manifested. This concentration and persistence of thought was a method peculiar to the Neoplatonists, for they considered the world to be the logical development of an intelligible reality. "If one considers

[6] *In Joan.*, I, 22; P.G., XIV, 56.
[7] *Ibid.*, 27; P.G., XIV, 73.
[8] *De princip.*, I, ii, 3.

the multitude of speculation and knowledge about God, beyond the power of human nature to take in, beyond the power, perhaps, of all originated beings except Christ and the Holy Ghost, then one may know how God is surrounded with darkness."

DIVINE EMANATION

This would be Origen's metaphysical system if, in his studies of the mystery of the Trinity, he had been content to be merely a philosopher. But even in this domain of intellectual speculation the resemblances that exist between him and Plotinus serve only to throw into greater relief the differences which separate them. The procession from the divine intelligence leads the Neoplatonist to the universal soul with which each of the individual souls in the world identifies itself in its own particular manner; and the emanation proceeds, without any interruption, to the different beings that are in the world. On the contrary, the God whom the Christian adores in the Father, the Son, and the Holy Ghost, is separate and transcendent. He is also personal. Origen's manner of explaining the eternal emanation of the divine intelligence takes account of the conscious activity of the Father. The Father is eternally capable of possessing the good, which He loves, and His perfection knows no obstacle. Plotinus, in an effort to explain the act of divine contemplation, employs a metaphor taken from nature, with which the Academy of Alexandria had little sympathy: he compares it to the superabundance and necessary bursting-forth of a pod that is heavy with seed or to the beneficent shining of a sun that sends forth no warmth.

Moreover, when the Alexandrian philosophy is thus adjusted to the teaching of the Church, its shortcomings show forth the original character of Christian tradition. In adopting the method of considering creatures as thoughts of the eternal wisdom, it dilutes the notion of existence. According to the Bible created things are something apart from their Creator. They must be considered as a completely produced work; and God, as their author, stands apart from His own work. The Neoplatonists of Alexandria believed that they were conferring an independent reality on created things by regarding them as having been conceived by an animated thought that was at once active and personal. They held that the notion of subsistence was safeguarded if created things are delimited and definite, and they taught that things possess being in the measure in which they are capable of becoming objects of intelligence. Things come into existence as an achievement of the essence. Only on a secondary title, if we are to consider the actual world, is there any place for the notion of existence, properly so called. The Word, to whom is given the role of the demiurge, wills things to exist and gives to each individual thing its rationale and its principle. Seen from this viewpoint, the procession of the Word appears as one stage of the development by which essences move into the field of reality and by which multiple beings are produced from one single thought. Idea of ideas and Virtue of virtues, this single thought must embrace several objects if it is to communicate itself to the diversity of the real, which it wills and organizes. Since it is a phase in the emanation of a world of multiple beings, it is a plurality, and therefore is opposed to the One.

Understood in this manner the original thought, or whatever is conceived of as filling the role of the demiurge, is subordinate to the Father and comprehends Him without exhausting Him, as a sculptor comprehends his own ideal but does not exhaust it when he reproduces it in stone. The demiurge, or the Son in the role of demiurge, sees the finished effect of divine power. But the Father, the source of the creative will, alone comprehends everything and sees everything as dependent on Him in its being. The Father's knowledge is therefore greater than the Son's knowledge. The Son does not know all that is in the principle, who is above truth itself.

THE TRINITY

Because of this philosophical conception of the Logos, Origen applied to the Word, considered as the demiurge,[9] the expression, "the Father is greater than I." He did not, however, regard this procession as signifying an inferiority of essence. Without any compromise of the equality of persons in the Trinity, he could teach

[9] *In Joan.*, I, 40; P.G., XIV, 93.

that the Father is the principle of all being and all good, and that the Son is the reflected knowledge of the supreme intelligence. But if the role of demiurge imposes on the Son the contemplation that makes Him the Son and truth and wisdom, it makes Him an intermediary. Origen recognized this fact and therefore made the Son subordinate, not inasmuch as He proceeds but inasmuch as created things proceed from Him.

The best-informed theologians of the day thus found their studies of the Trinity complicated by this problem of the mode of creation. Origen, however, was more sensitive than the others to the common faith of Christendom, and thus was much more aware than they were to the dangers indicated by this difficulty. He therefore subordinated the Word, not as an agent of the Father, but as a divine thought that is realized. He knew well that his proposed solution was rash, and that Christian tradition was opposed to every suggestion that the Son was inferior to the Father. This attitude on the part of the strictly orthodox is easy to understand. But if it was true that the dependence of the universe on God did not mean a correlative dependence of God on the universe, and if the relation between Him and created things is not reciprocal, any search for intermediaries between the Creator and His work would merely prolong the life of a problem that was henceforth of no value. The notion of divine transcendence would be safeguarded without any loss to the notion of creation itself because the reality of every created being was still a contingent effect. But the subordinationist theory stopped short at the mere suggestion that creation emanated. It admitted that the world was not created from pre-existing matter, but claimed at the same time that created beings were produced from a second thought, which was nothing else than intelligible matter.

Thus it becomes obvious where Origen failed in his attempt to apply this theory of subordinationism to the dogma of the Trinity. But his study of the act of intelligence was not in vain. It would lead him to a clearer understanding and a more accurate expression of the eternity of the Word, begotten before every creature by an eternal act of the divine intelligence. By following this method of research, Origen would later gradually repudiate the inequalities he at first maintained in his studies of the Trinity. Furthermore, his theological genius drove him to the task of building the generation of the Word on a relation existing within the divine intelligence itself. Thus theological interest in this dogma adopted a method of research, which remained the principal method of studying the Trinity.

THE FALL OF THE SOUL

The Alexandrian philosophers tried to apply the same method to the problem of the origin of souls. They regarded souls as thoughts of God, assembled about the Word in a certain unity, which was at least formal. An act of dispersion caused them to pass into a distinct existence. Thus they tried to explain the multitude of rational beings that inhabit the world.

But when the philosophers tried to study the degree of emanation at which this supposed act of dispersion occurred, the method previously followed met with resistance. The genesis of souls must take account of something more than a fall or a dispersion from their first principle. Furthermore, the problem of the soul in general is far greater than the problem of the individual soul. This became especially obvious at Alexandria where the contemporary Platonism had built up a theory of universal animism. Certain metals were considered living beings. At a later date Numenius gathered all souls, even the souls of plants, into a special quarter of the heavenly city and from there launched them into the world. Material essences depended on the movement of spiritual beings, and the only universe that mattered was the universe formed by them.

In describing the origin of souls, the Alexandrians were concerned only with this lower world, with its sin, its misery, its beings that die, and its general inconstancy and restlessness. Such a world could not come from the first principle. There was a lack of equilibrium, and its cause lay in the soul itself. Thus the old doctrine of the pre-existence and the fall of souls reappeared at Alexandria. It was a myth that had been long forgotten at Alexandria, and was revived when the question arose of assigning to the creation of an imperfect world a Creator who was not the actual maker of the world.

But the Alexandrians were unwilling to go so far as to assert that this departure from the primal unity indicated the existence of a second principle of the world, a principle of evil that disturbed the due development of the divine plan. They felt that the rebellious movement of the soul would have to be minimized as much as possible and reduced to an infinitesimally slight disturbance of equilibrium. Something like this natural diminution of equilibrium occurs in the spiritual life when it flows from the Word to imperfect words, from the supreme Reason to reasonable beings.

Confronted with this problem, both Origen and Plotinus sought at first to solve it in the same way, by the application of the principles of Platonism. Souls were united to God, equal to one another in essence, in power and activity. How could they be other than equal since there was no element of inequality in the intelligence that engendered them? But they opposed their principle, as weakness opposes strength, as fatigue opposes perseverance, as inertia opposes activity. They wished to be free. The result of this primary resistance followed gradually, but it came as inexorably as the result of an infringement of a natural law. It was as if a physician were to retire from the practice of his profession. "By his neglect, at first a few things will gradually escape him, then more and more, until in course of time everything will be forgotten, and be completely effaced from the memory." Then the corrupting influence of his negligence begins to make itself felt. "At first, the loss is very slight." But it leads the being who has yielded to it to obscurity and death. Thus the angels fell away, some more and some less, and each received in the world of bodies the place which he had merited.[10]

This account of the fall, in which are harmonized a scorn of the sensible world and an optimistic conception of the universe, proved to be of little importance to either Origen or Plotinus. Origen indeed found it utterly useless. When he rejected the story of the fall in order to study the existence "of the things which God made

[10] *De princip.*, I, iv, 1.

when they were not," he had no need to assume any such thing as an initial diminution of equilibrium, for he held that it is the very condition of a reasonable creature to be free and to be capable of sin. What purpose was to be served by extenuating the beginnings of sin? Every sin consists in a turning away from God. Every sin means that the creature, by neglecting the practice of good, establishes himself in evil.[11] Plotinus, however, was somewhat less successful in dealing with the question of the fall. When he explained the original loss of equilibrium as resulting from the attraction of matter, he gave a new version of the fall. The soul bends over, as it were, to illuminate what is below it, and there is no disorder. Thus Plotinus held that it is not proper to talk of a sin or a fall, because there is merely a defilement.

In those two different ways there was avoided the excessive valuation which the Alexandrian Platonists placed on their own commentary on the *Phaedrus*. The Christian philosopher refused to admit an original degradation. The Greek thinker did not recognize the existence of sin.

II. THE EARLIEST NEOPLATONISM AT ALEXANDRIA

Thus a common tradition was interpreted in different senses. But it remains reasonable, and we can summarize the principal elements of that Neoplatonism of Alexandria. Instead of a divine artisan who fashioned his work in eternal matter, the Neoplatonists posited at the beginning of things a power in which they saw the total cause of being. To explain the harmony of the universe and the subordination of bodies, they had recourse to their concept of an intelligence which draws its ideas from its contemplation of God and which distinguishes rational beings according to the rank they must keep. They had no belief in fatalism, and they regarded the universe as a society composed of three classes or grades of beings: gods, powers or demons, and men. A fatherly providence watches over the world by educating the souls that dwell in it. In the order of the celestial bodies there are signs of His knowledge, because wisdom knows how to dwell in the sensible world even while its

11 *Ibid.*, II, ix, 2. Cf. *In Joan.*, II, 7; *P.G.*, XIV, 136.

own proper abode is in the bosom of God. The origin of evil is an error prior to this life. Evil itself is a carelessness, slight and trifling at first, which has betrayed souls into a wickedness in which they forget the lessons of holiness. But the nature of the soul is in no way changed by its imprisonment within the body. The soul always has the power to think and to meditate. In this salutary practice it can regain the dignity of an intellectual being.

ALEXANDRIAN PHILOSOPHY

Such was the great Alexandrian philosophy in which the Bible and the riches of classical antiquity, the Gospel of St. John and the teachings of Plato, seemed to be merged into one harmonious whole. But another day would soon dawn, a day when it becomes impossible for men to understand that brief moment of common scholarship. The very traces of that united effort disappeared and men forgot that it had ever been. The fateful day came in the second half of that third century, during the lifetime of Porphyry and during the period of the great persecutions when Greek thought gathered all its resources in its endeavor to destroy Christianity. Neoplatonism seized the occasion as an opportune moment for claiming an exclusive right to the Greek tradition of Alexandria and thenceforth passed as its legal heir. And in our own time a historian has asserted that it is almost unnecessary to mention the name of Ammonius because that thinker's system passed whole and entire into the possession of his pupil Plotinus and is to be found in the writings of that philosopher.

Who would have ventured to challenge this claim? The pressure of Christian opinion had forced Origen to a reorganization of his theological system, and this task compelled him to discard a large measure of the philosophy on which he had relied. So we find Porphyry reproaching Origen for having betrayed Plotinus, his classmate of earlier days. The charge was not without foundation, from the viewpoint of a critic examining the situation from without. For the greater part of his life Origen remained under the powerful influence of this early Neoplatonism, not only when he was striving to escape from it but even when he believed he had already done so.

The same influence continued to affect him after he realized that
the Word and truth are the same thing, and therefore turned aside
from the mixture of truth and fallacy which the philosophies gave
forth. Only toward the end of his life, when preaching in Caesarea,
did he recall those elements of Greek learning that had formerly
stimulated his appetite for knowledge. Reminding his hearers that
the Greeks taught that God, Father of all and King of all, created
the universe and continued to reign over it and that some of them
even knew that He had created everything by the Word, he said:
"Some of their philosophers strove for purity of heart, and with
all their soul and all their strength sought the light of divine power
. . . but this grace must come to pagans only through Christ." [12]

In spite of his rapid estrangement from Neoplatonism, the great
theologian of the Academy of Alexandria is perhaps our most credible witness on the subject of that philosophy. Because he was not
professionally a philosopher, he was immune from the temptation
to innovate, but he was sufficiently familiar with Neoplationist
teachings to understand their implications. We can be assured that
in certain Platonist pages of the *Commentary on Genesis* and of the
De principiis we have what is undoubtedly the least imperfect record of the system of cosmology taught by the master of Plotinus.

GREEK HUMANISM

What is certain is that Origen was imbued with Greek humanism more deeply than any of his contemporaries. He believed that
the intelligence, in order to know God, was in no need of annihilat-
ing itself but only of rising above itself. He was confident that the
idea could ultimately reach its appointed goal, which he held to be
vision rather than ecstasy. By making the free will of man the foundation of his psychological system, he subordinated natural energies
to the realm of ends, the primacy of which Socrates endeavored to
prove by his acceptance of death. He reminded the pessimists that
no part of nature is contemptible and that the least of living things
is worthy of the universe. In these matters as well as in several

[12] *Hom. in Gen.*, XIV, 3; P.G., XII, 237.

others he was a Greek because his Christianity confirmed the wisdom of the ancients.

A century later, Christian philosophy, now sure of its footing, could return to Plotinus and yield without fear to the charm of that great genius who had known the appeal of transcendent reality. Men forgot the fragile enterprise of his Neoplatonism and remembered only his philosophy of the spirit. Without being conscious of it, the mysticism of St. Augustine found again the Plotinist good, the God of Abraham and of Jesus, in a Platonism that had never wearied of studying the relations between God and the world He made. Without thinking of it, the Christian turned back to the period, that had passed all too rapidly, when Alexandrian theology and Alexandrian Neoplatonism, each following its own road, were united against a common enemy: the fatalists, the soothsayers, the astrologers, and all those others who challenged the primacy of the soul. The collaboration of those two movements opened a window, as it were, on the contemplation of God, a window that had been too tightly closed to admit the healing breezes of spiritual life. Then the work was taken up again, with the illumination and the grace with which the Bible had touched Plotinus without reaching the degree where it might have influenced him to accept the truth of Christian belief.

CHAPTER XI

Origen the Pagan

THE comparative study of the two systems of thought justifies us in the assertion that the Platonism which Origen acquired at Alexandria in the beginning of the third century was the decisive factor in the development of his philosophy. Thirsting for its teachings on the origin of the soul, the hierarchy of spirits, the role of providence, and the genesis of created things, he sought from it far more than the ordinary student who was content to find in it a sufficient number of commonplaces for his religious studies. In arriving at this conclusion about the source of his system of thought, we deliberately exclude all problems of biography. Even if he had never attended the classes of Ammonius, we should still have to find a place for him in this preliminary period of the history of Neoplatonism. But then would arise the difficulty of explaining how he became so steeped in this particular version of Platonism. It is revealed in his writings as a doctrine acquired, mastered, and retained for the help he drew from it in his studies of the soul and of God.

PORPHYRY'S TESTIMONY

A contemporary witness asserts that the young Origen followed the lectures of Ammonius Saccas over a period of years. The record is found in the *Treatise against the Christians* which Porphyry wrote in the year 274. "This man, having been a hearer of Ammonius, who had made the greatest proficiency in philosophy among those of our day, with regard to knowledge, derived great benefit from his master." Eusebius does not deny the influence of Ammonius although it lessens the stature of his hero. On the contrary he confirms Porphyry's statement by quoting a letter written by Origen in the days of his exile. In that letter the great Alexandrian scholar acknowledged his debt to Greek learning. He says that he became a pupil of one whom he calls a master of philosophical sciences. He was then older than the ordinary student, for he informs us that he followed the example of Heraclas, his colleague, "who I have found persevered five years with a teacher of philosophy before I began to attend to these studies." This enables us to fix the year 210 as the earliest date when Origen could have joined the classes of Ammonius. At that date Origen was more than twenty-five years old. It is true that Ammonius is not mentioned in this letter, but it is obvious from the context that the school of Ammonius is the locale of the studies which Origen refers to.

A more serious difficulty is created by the fact that the critics have discovered a number of errors in Porphyry's testimony. Porphyry seems to imply that Origen was reared in Greek paganism and was a convert to Christianity. Eusebius is not alone in this interpretation of Porphyry's text, and the conclusion would therefore be inevitable that Porphyry was guilty of confusing two different writers. But the fact is that Porphyry was concerned with nothing more than Origen's ideas and with the sources of the allegorical method of exegesis that made his teachings so well known. He accuses Origen of taking from the Greeks, as an excellent instrument for use in making his commentaries on the Bible, a method of interpretation to which his first years at the catechetical school had introduced him. Of a conversion, properly so called, from Greek paganism to Christianity, there is no question in the quotation given by Eusebius: "But Origen, having been educated as a Greek in Greek literature, went over to the barbarian recklessness. And carrying over the learning which he had obtained, he hawked it about, in his life conducting himself as a Christian and contrary to the laws, but, in his opinions of material things and of the Deity, being like a Greek, and mingling Grecian teachings with foreign fables." It was an appraisal which Origen's history must readily have suggested to a non-Christian writer.

There is nothing in Porphyry's testimony to allow us to accuse him of error or of falsehood in what concerns the personal life of the great Alexandrian. Further, he is correct in implying that Origen was not a member of the brotherhood formed by the disciples of Ammonius, as Heraclas undoubtedly was. Origen was merely a

hearer, with the purpose of acquiring a method, a philosophical attitude, and a familiarity with certain problems rather than a definite
set of doctrines. There was nothing astonishing in the fact that the
Christian catechist should follow the lectures of a philosopher of
Christian birth whose spiritual tendencies were well known. Besides, the time had not yet come, as a modern writer remarks, when
Neoplatonist philosophy enrolled under the banner of Greek polytheism. If it is desirable to distribute Porphyry's observations
among more than one person instead of applying them exclusively
to Origen, the head of the Academy at Alexandria, it is not because
there are errors in the text, but because other texts seem to indicate
that this is the course to be pursued.

Contemporary documents, among which are numbered other
references by Porphyry, seem to offer, on this subject of Origen, a
number of statements which are in contradiction to what is in-
dubitably certain in our knowledge of his history. In point of date,
the earliest passage where we find his name associated with that of
Ammonius is a fragment of the treatise *On the End* written by
Longinus the rhetorician before the year 268. This author gives us
a list of leading scholars whom he had known when he was a young
man. The list, covering the years from 230 to 235, includes the
Platonists Ammonius and Origen. "I attended their classes for a
long time. They were far more intelligent than any of their contemporaries." This man, with the name of Origen, was not considered a genuine writer. He was one of those authorities who did
not take the trouble to leave books to posterity or to polish a treatise,
but who regarded the writing of books as a matter of secondary importance. He did, however, write one book, a treatise on the demons.
Porphyry's testimony confirms this item of information; the reference is found in his biography of Plotinus, written after the year
298 to serve as an introduction to an edition of the *Enneads*. We
would have to suppose that Origen received from Ammonius the
same grounding in philosophy which had been given to the founder
of Neoplatonism, and that he violated the philosophical secret by
publishing, in addition to the tract already mentioned by Longinus,

a second work, *That the King Alone Is a Poet*, during the reign of Emperor Galienus.

Farther on in Porphyry's biography of Plotinus we read that one day the great man was filled with confusion when he found that Origen was in his audience. The incident took place at Rome, where Plotinus is known to have conducted a philosophical school at some period after the year 244. As Porphyry describes the scene, it is quite in harmony with the sentiments of those Platonists of Alexandria who regarded the lectures of a master as a sort of condescension on the part of the philosophical mind, a diffusion of light in the darkness of less gifted minds: "One day the master blushed and wished to rise from his seat when he perceived that Origen was in the audience. When Origen besought him to proceed with the lecture, he replied that he no longer had a mind to do so since he was sure of addressing people who already understood what he was about to say. After a few brief observations the master rose from his chair and left the gathering."

With regard to this evidence from Longinus and Porphyry, neither the greater part of the alleged facts nor the dates nor the titles of the works mentioned can be brought into agreement with what we know of Origen, the head of the Academy at Alexandria. One way to explain these data is to suppose that they refer to another man of the same name, whether the two authors had such a man in view or merely confused him with the Christian catechist. In any case, the confusion gave birth to the hypothesis of a second Origen, often called Origen the pagan, a hypothesis which is today accepted almost universally by the critics.

The humanists of the Renaissance, however, seem to have been ignorant of any such theory.[1] But the authority of Valesius, editor of the *Historia ecclesiastica*, gave it a certain credibility in the seventeenth century, a period when scholarship, welcoming all kinds of distinctions, was quite ready to accept every notion by which sacred history and profane literature could be kept in watertight compartments. Valesius considered that the treatise written in the reign

[1] Baronius, *Annales*, ann. 248.

of Emperor Galienus was a work of flattery addressed to the Emperor, who is known to have composed a number of poems. This, however, was attributing to the Neoplatonists an interest in politics, an alien activity in which they had never shown the slightest concern. Another critic thought that the treatise might have been written in jest, if not in downright irony. It is beyond question that the name of Origen was borne by a well-known contemporary of the Alexandrian catechist, like him an Egyptian, a Platonist, and a rival of Plotinus; it is also unquestionable that Porphyry was acquainted with this second Origen. Huet and Redepenning concur in this opinion. The Tübingen school, however, has rejected it, but for reasons that carry little weight.

CONFUSION OF NAMES

Even as late as the nineteenth century, Origen the pagan was being allowed to usurp the place of honor which history has always given to Origen Adamantius, and this in spite of the fact that Porphyry's statements in the treatise against the Christians apply only to the former. "Porphyry, who was an excellent man, no doubt spoke in good faith, but he has confused the heathen Origen whom he once knew with the Christian Origen whom he can never have known, and therefore no weight at all can be attached to what he says. The teacher may well have been Ammonius, but this fact is by no means certain." [2] On the basis of evidence gathered from a number of different sources, we know, on the contrary, that Porphyry became acquainted with Origen the pagan at Tyre or at Caesarea, probably at each of those towns. Yet he attacks Origen the Christian. He attacks him on the basis of his faith, which was built on a foundation of Alexandrian Platonism and on a number of philosophical works of which his attacker finds it possible to give a list.

It is difficult to understand how a confusion of names can complicate a matter of personal polemics, but in this case an ill-founded hypothesis blotted out evidence of the strongest kind. How such a flimsy hypothesis could have been conceived in the first instance baffles comprehension. In historical fact, its sole support is the

[2] Bigg, *The Christian Platonists*, p. 156.

mention of the name of Origen, made incidentally by some Neo-platonists. That any such man existed at all is nothing more than a mere inference. The inference has been woven into the history of the life and works of the great Alexandrian. It occurs in no other problem of the period, and no confirmation of it has ever been produced by any independent source.

The Praedestinatus

The temptation arises to recall a similar ancient tradition. The same solution, which historical difficulties suggested to the moderns, had been already offered to the theologians in their concern with difficulties of doctrine. A number of sects, for their own purposes, made use of Origen's name. The noisiest of them was a group of Palestinian ascetics who upheld the reading of the apocryphal books, attacked the administration of the bishops, and even accused them of immoral practices. Discussing this group in his work *Contra haereticos*, St. Epiphanius does not go quite so far as to link them with the great Alexandrian. "They call themselves Origenists, but I do not know because of what author. I have no means of finding out whether they come from Origen Adamantius, who is also called Syntacus, or from any other. The name is all that I have." [3] This was, in itself, a small thing, but we find St. Augustine repeating the remark of St. Epiphanius in a more positive form. The anonymous compiler of the *Praedestinatus* acquired new information about the matter and discovered an additional heresy, if not two heresies, with which to enrich his catalogue. "The forty-second heresy had for its founders the Origenists, called after a certain Origen, not the Origen who is known to almost all of us, but a miserable Syrian of whom St. Epiphanius says that he taught such shameful doctrines that they must not be preserved for posterity."

The inquiry becomes better as it goes along. Although nothing is known of this first doctrine beyond the fact that it was heretical, we find that there were other Origenists who denied the resurrection from the dead and held that the Holy Ghost was a created being. This heretical sect had been founded by a third Origen. At

[3] Epiphanius, *Haer.*, 63; P.G., XLI, 1062.

this stage of his inquiry the author of the *Praedestinatus* encounters the objection that a mere reading of the works of Adamantius, and especially of the four books of the *De principiis*, is sufficient to show the presence therein of the majority of the errors of those different heretics. The objection causes him no dismay. His acquaintance with the *Apology of Origen*, which he had studied probably in the Rufinus translation, furnishes him with a reply. Origen's works have been tampered with, he says, and rags have been sewn on the cloth of gold, as the holy martyr Pamphylius has shown. In this solution the two or three heretical Origens fall into their proper places. The most heterodox passages in the Alexandrian's writings come from those men who bore Origen's name but lacked the Christian faith that inspired him. A manuscript transmits only words and ideas; but if it were possible to see the faces of the writers, the imposture would be unmasked.

Under the sponsorship of St. Epiphanius and of the author of the *Praedestinatus*, Origen the pagan thus makes his entry on the stage of ecclesiastical history, all decked out with a collection of heresies. Nevertheless it is well to note that his existence is, from the very beginning, a matter of mere hypothesis in the mind of St. Epiphanius, a fact that considerably weakens the value of the tradition about him. Certainly we find in Christian antiquity no fact or writing that could be attributed to this hypothetical personage whose history would have been intimately joined with the destinies of Origenism. The tolerant manner of his admission to the franchise of the philosophy of Christian antiquity is, we confess, a definite warning to us to be unusually careful in his regard.

I. THE WORKS

THE COMMENTARIES ON PLATO

All recent study of Neoplatonism establishes the fact that a special trait of its adherents was their care and fidelity in conserving all notes and manuscripts pertaining to their doctrines. From this fact the belief has arisen that Neoplatonist tradition was less careful than usual in the case of this Origen, for he certainly would have been one of its own. Proclus, in his *Commentary on the Timaeus*, quotes a number of Origen's interpretations: modern critics, for the most part, attribute them to a Platonist philosopher of the same name.

Like all his contemporaries, Origen the pagan showed a preference for the myths of Plato. Being an enemy of literalism, he found in them an esoteric doctrine. Those mysterious fables were intended to test the student's mental caliber, to stimulate his thoughts, and finally to flood his soul with an inner experience the beauty of which baffles description. He says of Plato that "assuredly he is not indifferent to beauties of literary style, but the goal he seeks is not the mere entertainment of the reader." This was not the critical verdict of Longinus, who regarded the myths as pretty ornaments. In regard to the other Platonists, such as Numenius and his disciples, they saw everywhere in Plato veils and secrets and interdicts at the threshold of divinity.

The Timaeus

In the work by Proclus, Origen follows his own principles in his interpretation of the perfect city, the great lines of which are drawn in the opening pages of the *Timaeus*. In that outline Plato prepares the reader for the contemplation of the divine plan. "He used this image to produce a harmonious condition of the soul to which his doctrine was about to be presented." [4] Origen no longer believed the myths of Atlantis, a matter in which he agreed with Numenius. He regarded the account of the Egyptian soothsayer as a fiction which contained a hidden doctrine, because "Plato was not solicitous about beautiful metaphors but wished that his fictions could persuade spontaneously, with frankness and accuracy. He resorted to this method of expression as befitting one who was a great scholar." [5]

Symbolism such as this was no common theory, for it was compounded of the accuracy of the learned and the wisdom of the holy. The myth was the touchstone of delicate souls. It put them in a

[4] Proclus, *In Plat. Tim. Comment.*, Diehl, p. 60.
[5] *Ibid.*, p. 86.

state of grace before giving them a passport to wisdom. Clement had recommended this method in his *Stromata*. He says that the seed must be allowed to germinate "after preparing in this careful way those who are worthy of it." Instead of a truth being at once presented in its austerity, it was at first introduced by a scholarly metaphor that rendered the doctrines more attractive and their possession more agreeable.

The Republic

Origen, being Clement's pupil, had a preference for this method of spiritual instruction, and we know that his opinion of its value was confirmed by his reading of Plato. In the sixth book of his *Stromata*, commenting on the third book of the *Republic*, probably with reference to the *Timaeus*, he makes this observation: "for the benefit of souls it is often necessary to employ a ruse." Like many modern critics but with more success, Origen wished to explain the myths of Plato by the application of this principle. Certain methods of deception are a useful kind of therapeutic knowingly employed by those who govern. But it is illicit to invent a religion for the people or to employ crude and gross descriptions to render a doctrine acceptable to the illiterate and uneducated. Truth lowers itself to the comprehension of the simple for no other purpose than to lift their hearts to God. In the twilight zone of their belief, allegory excites and stimulates them to further inquiry, myth assumes the semblance of truth, and the entire fiction is adjusted to the temperament of him who hears it. Thus allegory introduces the souls of the simple to a truth too mysterious for them to understand directly. "But if the condition of the hearer demands it, the teacher uses ambiguous words, and brings forth his meaning by way of enigmas, both in order to maintain the dignity of the truth and to ensure that what might be harmful if it were candidly spoken to the illiterate should be uttered in words that conceal something of its full meaning. But let the teacher on whom this necessity falls be careful that, when he uses a fiction in this way, he employs it as a sort of condiment or medicament. Thus he will preserve the right order of things." [6] Understatement and exaggeration are equally alien to a sane method of instruction, and neither technique is ever permitted, even where it seems desirable for the spiritual progress of a beginner.

Outside the most scholarly circles of modern criticism it would not be possible to find as comprehensive a theory of the myths of Plato. Even yet a number of our moderns have much to gain from a study of the ingenuity of Alexandrian methods of interpretation. Origen was wrong on only one point: he desired to apply his method to all myths, especially to those which are called genetic myths, such as those telling of the wars in Atlantis. If he had taken better care to distinguish between fable, which Plato calls mythology, and traditions which are half-didactic and half-historical, his spiritual commentaries would have been more prudent. He especially failed to understand that a recorded fact is not a symbol; the method of interpretation which was suitable to explain certain passages in Plato could not be applied at all, even at the cost of many reservations and of multiple changes, to the historical books of the Bible. The history of the dealings of providence with the affairs of men is the direct opposite of a myth, since the value of that history is to be found primarily in the events themselves.

THE THREE CITIES

By use of this method Origen constructed, in the manner of the Timaeus, his threefold plan of the order of the universe. There are three cities: that of God, that of souls, and that of natural forces. From what city does Socrates wish to speak when he describes the highest form of government? From the first, where gods and angels live the life of contemplation? From the second, where the angels are drawn up in battle array on the frontiers of the visible world, attracting to themselves the best of souls? Certainly not the third, that of the passions, because it is excluded. Origen chose the first, the intellectual city, "because it is there that the sciences are entrusted to the guardians," to those of whom the *Republic* speaks.

[6] *Strom.*, VI; *P.G.*, XI, 101.

This heavenly abode is described in Platonist language in the first book of the *De principiis*, Origen's nearest approach to the commentaries of the Greeks. "Certain races of souls are set apart in a city of a special character. . . . On that lofty level types of vice and of virtue are presented to them." [7] The contemplation uniting all those souls to one another surpasses every other knowledge. Even when they leave the higher city to constitute the angelic army, they can still instruct fallen beings by salutary lessons drawn from their own knowledge.

The second city, that of the warlike life, is represented in the account of Atlantis. On this point Proclus writes: "Several commentators interpret it as indicating the rivalry of certain demons or powers, the good demons against the bad demons, the former superior in numbers and the others superior in force, as Origen supposed." The power of the angels is more clearly expressed in a fragment from the *Commentary on Genesis* and is discussed at far greater length in that part of the *De principiis* from the fifth to the eighth chapter of the first book; this entire section is a thorough study of spiritual beings. The angels clarify our powers of decision and help us to vanquish the enemy. Their influence is especially powerful in the city of those souls which occupy an intermediate place between good and evil powers and as yet are placed in a state of struggle and trial. [8] With regard to the heavenly movements, those movements exercise their influence within the bounds of the higher city. Souls conserve there "the delicacy and the blessed movement of their nature because of the whirling of the universe which surrounds them and draws them along in its rotation." [9]

We must now consider some aspects of the scholastic regime at the school of Ammonius. Although it was known as a philosophical school, its curriculum did not give equal value to each of the philosophical sciences. Astronomy, geometry, and even logic were excluded in favor of metaphysics, the reason being that this last-named science alone led to knowledge of the soul and therefore to

---

[7] The authenticity of this fragment is doubtful. It is inserted by Koetschau in the *De princip.*, I, viii, 4.

[8] *In Gen.*, III; P.G., XII, 84; *De princip.*, I, v, 1.

[9] Proclus, *Tim. Comm.*; Diehl, p. 162. Cf. *De princip.*, I, viii, 4; III, ii, 5.

the study of intelligences. The different parts of philosophy were merely so many different aspects of metaphysics as the supreme necessity. Besides, the method followed in the classes forbade any dallying with topics not immediately connected with metaphysics. The usual analysis of a passage from Plato was as follows: observations based on the science of physics led to a discussion about the history of souls in the world; a kind of transcendent ethics was then applied to the hidden forces involved in the struggle in which the rational conscience is ever engaged; finally, Alexandrian mysticism, which was far removed from magic and the occult sciences, was brought into play to show how the activity of contemplation may become greater or less in the spiritual beings that are charged with the administration of the divine plan. In addition to this, the text sometimes called for a philological analysis.

The first part of the *Timaeus* was the text usually employed for those commentaries. Advanced students also made use of the *Republic* and especially of the *Phaedrus*, in the study of which they began their researches into a philosophy of the universe, although the destiny of individual souls, a problem more akin to religious ideals, continued during this period to hold the place of primary importance. The *Phaedo* and the *Banquet* were less in evidence in the activities of the school. Belief in immortality was a topic discussed in the elementary classes on Platonism. The question of the ascent of the individual soul belonged preferably to the general cycle of the fall and the re-establishment of souls. Such were the ordinary exercises of the student at the school of Ammonius. Origen spoke of them as the clearly defined highway to knowledge.

Thus far we have found that our Origen bears a striking resemblance to his fellow pupil, Origen the pagan. Indeed, they might be almost mistaken for each other. Origen the pagan breathes the air of the school of Numenius during his early studies but does not adhere to its teachings. He accepts the hierarchy of beings in the form expounded by Clement and Ammonius, but he does so with the reservation that the angelic beings are not far removed from the level of men. His vision of paradise takes note of the signs of combat, a new element unseen by the philosophy of impassibility sponsored by his predecessors. His thought is that even in the world of intelligences virtue is not a natural attribute but rather an acquirement or an attainment that stands midway between merit and sin. He has found in Holy Scripture a number of descriptions of battles, with their alternations of victors and vanquished, and has taken them as the key to certain ineffable mysteries.[10]

Origen the pagan is our best guide for an approach to the first book of the *De principiis*. He not only uses its ideas and expresses them in its phraseology but he also manifests its general tendencies. But his thought is more akin to that of the fragments belonging to the *Stromata* of Origen Adamantius.

The Stromata

Origen's mind was steeped in Greek learning. Greek scholarship never lost its attraction for him. He had a special admiration for the work of Greek philosophers on certain matters of science and morals. The notion came to him to compare Christian teachings with the theories of the Greeks on those points. For this work of comparison the most suitable form appeared to him to be the literary style of Clement's *Stromata*; it was a method eminently fitted for his plan of eclecticism, and Clement's former pupil recognized its value. Its flexibility and its adaptability to varying shades of thought permitted of its being reserved for the outstanding pupils of the Academy. They were capable of deriving profit from it by their own labors without intruding in any appreciable degree on Origen's own researches.

Adopting Clement's conviction that sacred and profane learning ought to blend, Origen quoted, among other authors, Plato and his principal commentator Numenius. Nor did he exclude the Stoics; two representatives of the final phase of that Greek system of thought found a place in his work. These two were Cornutus, the master of the poet Persius, and Cheremon, the librarian of Alexandria. It is probable that he also borrowed from the Neo-Pythagoreans. This great effort to weave into the texture of Christian belief so many different strands of Greek learning was rendered the easier

10 Cf. *De princip.*, IV, ii, 8.

by Origen's fondness for the allegorical method of biblical interpretations. Following the example of Hippolytus, he preferred to
apply it to the deuterocanonical books of the Old Testament, in
which history was of less importance than doctrine. He used it especially for the elucidation of a number of passages from the Book
of Daniel.

The work was completed at Alexandria about the year 221, not
long after the accession of Emperor Alexander Severus. Like Clement's similarly named work, it was the fruit of several years' labors,
and the young professor made use of it as a way to dispose of the
surplus of his progressively increasing store of learning. Its literary
form enabled him to discuss all manner of subjects, as long as he
maintained a certain unity of tone. Hitherto unused notes found a
place in it, especially the commentaries on St. Paul which he had
written during his controversy with the Marcionites. Its third book,
for example, explained a number of passages from the Epistle to the
Romans; and in its fourth book, where he discussed the First Epistle
to the Corinthians, he presented virginity as a virtue of the heart,
far surpassing the simple purity of the body. Farther on, another
commentary on this same Epistle asserted the continual role of
Christ in the life of the people of Israel. This same fourth book reminded its readers that superior souls, such as the soul of St. Paul,
are not of a different essence from those of the common run of men;
they share the weakness of ordinary human beings; as other men are
weak, so also are they.

Everywhere throughout this work we find the somewhat bookish
scholar of the early commentaries, reaping now with ease and certainty the plenteous harvest of his years of contemplation. Beyond
the other benefits with which God had showered him, he feels now
that he has been granted, in his possession of the secret of truth,
the highest reward, the feeling of physical and mental integrity
which a rational being finds in the due exercise of his intelligence.
Prayer is an elevation of the soul rather than a petition. In the great
cry of the innocent Susanna are heard again the voices of the pure
souls of whom he had already written in the *Commentary on the
Psalms*. God hearkens to the cries of His holy ones. Their appeal

becomes clearer and stronger on account of the love that glows in their hearts, the uprightness that prevails in their minds, the acknowledgment of the divine greatness which their intelligence offers to God. The temptation of the two elders is described in the manner of the psychology which would later become habitual with Origen. At first a passion is born; or, to speak more accurately, a disturbance. This yields to the weakness of the flesh, and the power of right judgment is blinded. Then there follow the deformation and the denial which are the preliminary to every act of sin: the moral sense is ruined, and the eyes of the intelligence are so utterly blinded that the sinner no longer sees the things of heaven, no longer remembers either God or man or the primal tendency which urges every being in the direction of the Good.

St. Jerome's translation of the section dealing with the Book of Daniel reproduces, in vigorous Latin, those traits of Origen. The accuracy of the translator and his deep love of souls could not fail to preserve the sweet odor of Origen's thoughts and perhaps to add to it, so that those lofty concepts become, as it were, hothouse flowers transplanted into a richer soil. Yet it is still possible to recognize here and there the Alexandrian elegance of the Origen of the *Commentary on the Psalms*, his skill in the choice of words, and his technique of the balanced phrase.

But Origen's great effort was doomed to failure. In all the literature of Christian antiquity we find not a single quotation from it. It meets the fate of all the other efforts of reconcile sacred and profane knowledge. Every such work succeeds only in drawing down upon its author the thunderbolts of both parties. The philosophers, on the one hand, always accuse such a writer of misusing their teachings and of selling them off at second hand. This was, in fact, the charge leveled against Origen by Porphyry, who probably read the work. The Christian theologians, on the other hand, resent the degradation of their doctrines to the level of the profane and feel a sense of outrage at the sight of the dogmas of the Church being compared with the teachings of pagan thinkers like Cornutus and Numenius. The great dogma of the resurrection is unrecognizable to them if Origen declares that it is to be explained simply as a vivifying effect produced in a rational being by a mysterious revelation. Thus, under assaults from both sides, the work falls apart. Each body of critics interprets it with praise for one half of it and blame for the other. Because of this divided reception, the work soon becomes quite unintelligible for posterity. Is this not the entire history of Origen the pagan?

THE PLATONIST TREATISES

We must now consider the two treatises mentioned in Porphyry's biography of Plotinus as having been written by Origen the pagan. Here, in its very cradle, the hypothesis of a second Origen is far from impressing us as being a vigorous and sturdy infant, for the titles of the works in question reflect the philosophical activities with which Origen was preoccupied at that time. In his hands the Alexandrian system of teaching was becoming more dramatic and more ample. The order of the universe was to be realized not only by a system of mutual help and prudent education of souls, but by a warfare. The war was a struggle between righteous spirits and evil spirits, and above all between favorable powers and adverse powers. The purpose of providence in presiding at this combat was to restore fallen intelligences to the angelic state. If the Alexandrian catechist was to complete his philosophical theory of the divine plan, such as he understood it to be taught by the spiritually minded philosophers of his day, it was necessary for him to write a *Treatise on the Demons* or on the powers, as those beings were named at the Academy.

The other great Alexandrian problem of the period was how to unite in one comprehensive theory the doctrine of providence and that of what was called the production of the world; of those two doctrines, one was intellectualist and the other voluntarist. The Ammonius fragment lets us understand what the difficulty was: the will of God is the cause of the subsistence of the universe, and wisdom has the subordinate role of an organizer that establishes the hierarchy of beings by the exercise of a certain discrimination. Origen solved the problem by reconciling the two notions. He argued that an act of will is an act of a spiritual being. For him, intelligence was the primal unity from which all beings proceed. With this tenet Neoplatonism assumed the role it would hold until the emergence of Plotinism, half a century later. The divine intelligence governs all things. It is likewise the principle of all things. And it manifests its operation simultaneously by the demiurge and by providence. Whether He creates or presides at the course of events, "through wisdom, God has power over all things." [11] This doctrine of the intelligence-demiurge, or at least some trace of it, is found in all the representatives of the first period of Neoplatonism, in the writings of Longinus as well as in the early works of Porphyry.

From this philosophy, Origen derived the equipment that enabled him to give a decisive reply to the heterodox. The King is a Creator, he said with the Platonists. Then, turning toward the habitual foes of the Academy, he added: "He is the one and only Creator." In thus giving him assured principles in his controversies with the heretics, the new philosophy did not deceive his hopes. Since the intelligence of God has created the world, it was impossible to see the universe as the half-spoiled work of a poorly equipped artisan or of a worker not adequately conscious of his own idea. It was equally impossible to set limits to the work of providence. The King of intellectual nature, in guiding rational beings, guides also their corporeal nature. The three great cities of the Cosmos proclaim the almighty power of Him who is at once their Creator and their Ruler. Looking at the matter from another angle, is not this the teaching of Scripture when it proclaims the kingship of Christ? [12]

To say that the King is the one and only Creator was an adaptation of early Neoplatonism to the theological studies with which the Academy was engaged. It was the first step in the construction of a philosophical weapon for the defense of orthodoxy. The form in which Origen expressed his great principle was taken from the paradoxes of the Stoics. In such a case he had no objection to incur this small debt.

There is no impossibility in the supposition that the head of the

---

[11] *Ibid.*, I, ii, 10: "Through wisdom, which is Christ, God has power over all things." Cf. *ibid.*, II, ix, 7: "All things were created by the word of God and by His wisdom, and were set in order by His justice."
[12] *In Joan.*, I, 30; *P.G.*, XIV, 77.

Academy was the author of the two treatises attributed to Origen the pagan. On the contrary, the probabilities for the truth of such a supposition are very strong. It is not impossible that each of these treatises came from a collection of independent essays found somewhere among his works. The supposition is reinforced if we remember that Longinus and Porphyry could have known or quoted from dissertations which originally belonged to the *Stromata* or to other Origenist writings. As a matter of fact, the first book of the *De principiis* contains in the first two chapters a dissertation on intelligence considered as a principle. From chapter five to chapter eight the same book contains a complete essay on the heavenly powers. Further, Origen himself called one of the books of the *De principiis* a treatise. Thus would be explained the failure of Eusebius to include in his catalogue of the writings of Origen the two essays mentioned by Porphyry and Longinus. Those two essays would have been inserted or partially used in Origen's subsequent writings.

Longinus does not say, as has so often been assumed, that the philosopher Origen did not publish any other works. Longinus was a Greek philologist, fastidious in his use of language and ceaselessly urging his pupils to have a care for the susceptibilities of posterity. It was his severe judgment that whatever works Origen may have written outside this particular treatise did not deserve the name of literary productions. Even the paradox treating of the creative intelligence did not seem to him to be worthy of mention. In thus neglecting the contributions of the Alexandrian thinker to the history of philosophical literature, the Athenian philologist ranged himself naturally on the side of the Hellenists. "Origen lacks what makes masterpieces. His writings are improvisations that should have been condensed or subjected to further and more careful study. In the history of Greek literature he belongs only to the second rank." We may add that a great part of the exegesis, some echoes of which could have reached Longinus, was an esoteric doctrine at the Academy of Alexandria and that students were admitted to the study of it only after a long period of probation.

II. THE FACTS

THE MEETING OF ORIGEN AND PLOTINUS

The real difficulty is not in the titles of the two essays mentioned, but in the alleged facts adduced by Porphyry. In his biography of Plotinus he gives an account of a meeting supposed to have taken place between Origen and Plotinus in Rome at some date after the year 254 while the latter was conducting a philosophical school there. There is no evidence for this second visit of Origen to Rome. Porphyry also asserts that the second of the tracts in dispute, *The King Alone Is a Poet*, was published during the reign of Galienus. This emperor came to the throne in the year 254. Now, no historian would admit that Origen lived very long after the Decian persecution, and the general opinion is that he died about the year 252, at the beginning of the reign of Gallus.[13]

He may have been in Rome at some time during the pontificate of Fabian, for he had tried to justify himself with that Pope by means of a letter addressed to the Bishop and the Church of Rome. His apology was fruitless. If a journey to Rome was made subsequently to the sending of the letter, probably it had a humiliating result, and perhaps Eusebius in his biographical sketch of Origen preferred to pass the whole thing over in silence. If the visit occurred, Origen might have attended one of the lectures of Plotinus. The theories of that great thinker had not yet crystallized into a system, and their only effect on Origen would have been to remind him that he and Plotinus had sat at the feet of the same master.

Quite different is the importance of the second difficulty, which is concerned with the date of the treatise. This alleged fact, and this alone, is in contradiction with the history of Origen Adamantius; and it agrees very little better with the biography of Plotinus. The following is what Porphyry says: "Herennius, Origen, and Plotinus made a joint agreement to keep the teachings of Ammonius secret, as they had heard them expounded with uniform clarity in the lectures delivered to them by their master. Plotinus kept the promise.

[13] Bigg, *op. cit.* Valesius places the death of Origen at 252; Redepenning at 254; Baronius at 256.

. . . Herenius was the first to break the agreement, and Origen followed him. . . . For a long time Plotinus continued to abstain from writing anything, but he gave his lectures in accordance with the teaching he had received from Ammonius. This was his practice for ten whole years." We know from Porphyry that Plotinus began to write about the year 255. This is the earliest date that can be assigned to the essay written by Origen. If the two philosophers were publishing at the same time, Porphyry's anecdote loses all its meaning. It is impossible to believe that Plotinus waited very long to follow the example of his former classmate.

This text, confused and obscure from whatever angle it is examined, was the work of an elderly man who wrote fifty years after the alleged incidents were supposed to have happened. In regard to its references to Origen, does such a text require the creation of a second personage whose sole destiny was to be present at the date vaguely mentioned by Porphyry? Reduced to its elements, this is the problem of Origen the pagan. To reach a simpler solution of the difficulty, is it good historical technique to invent an Origen on whom everybody must agree? Recent historians certainly agree, for they ignore him altogether, except for the document which the hypothesis of his existence is supposed to justify without ever quite succeeding. Are there no possibilities except the clumsiest and costliest hypothesis of all, the gratuitous addition of a name to history?

The critics might feel obliged to accept the hypothesis as long as an imperfect knowledge of the origins of Neoplatonism rendered it impossible to clarify the relations of Origen and Plotinus. But the invention of a hypothetical personage was so easy that a number of critics began to be suspicious of it. Was it necessary to invent even a third Origen because the philosopher Eunapius, confused in his recollections of Porphyry's biography of Plotinus, called Origen one of the outstanding classmates of Porphyry? The scholarly Huet is hesitant before this new element of the problem: "If Eunapius is right, two Origens lived in Rome at the same time and were familiar with Plotinus. One of them was his former classmate, and the other was his pupil." In addition to the danger of this swarming of identities, those doubles, so like the great man that they are almost his second self and, besides having no right whatever to a place in history, they are furnished with documents bearing the surest marks of authenticity. Origen the pagan, whose existence is gratuitously assumed as proved, ends by usurping in the school of Ammonius the place occupied, according to the clearest evidence of the texts, by the one Origen whose history we know.

The one insoluble difficulty seems to be the mention of the name of Emperor Galienus. But the supposition of some mistake in the name or of a slip on the part of a copyist would resolve it. Then these phantoms would disappear, with all the dangers they imply. Origen the pagan would rejoin his contemporary, the second Africanus who was another invention of the infancy of historical criticism, in the realm of shadows, in that dim region where the myths of history sleep in a silence from which they never return. In that repose he would join Seneca the tragedian and a number of other such fabulous beings.

In a problem like this, which has been the subject of discussion from the beginning of historical criticism and which has persisted in its obscurity in spite of the fact that its limits are quite definite, it would be presumptuous to hold that we have finally reached a solution. But, for the history of Origen, it is important that a hypothesis should be debarred from entering the domain of certainty. It is equally important to remember that, when we encounter in that history matters we are not certain of, other conjectures, even mediocre ones, are preferable to the hypothesis which the critics have been in the habit of proposing.

Origen was a pupil of Ammonius. This is a point beyond doubt. It is upheld by two quite distinct traditions, that of the Christians and that of the Neoplatonists. It is known to have been accepted without question by his contemporaries and it was the universal belief up to the end of the period of Christian antiquity. A pupil already mature in years and in learning, he sought in the teachings of Ammonius the confirmation of the doctrine he himself had drawn from his Christian faith. His expectations were richly fulfilled. In this Alexandrian philosophy, with its vigorous ingredients of Judaism and Christianity, he discovered, in a form that was even more logical than his own, the conjectures that he himself had already scattered throughout his commentaries. His notion of a total creation, of no pre-existing matter, of an omnipotent providence that disposes the course of events for the education of souls, and that is a divine idea considered as the cause and guardian of the universe, all found their confirmation in the philosophy of Ammonius.

NEED OF A CHRISTIAN SYSTEM

Under the direction of Ammonius he, in his turn, began a comprehensive study of Plato's works. Parallels flooded in his mind. The King of all things, as Plato sketches Him in the *Philebus* and in the *Laws*, recalled to him the kingship of Christ which he had already found in the Epistles of St. Paul. The parallels were committed to his notes. Some of his discoveries were shared with his classmates, even with the unbelievers among them, for they listened to his account of Er the Armenian and to his analysis of the cosmogony of the *Timaeus*. Among them were found perhaps the Platonists Euclid and Democrites, and probably Herennius. In this association Origen undoubtedly passed three or four years, more time than he could have afforded at a later date. Whenever his labors at the Academy permitted, he would be found in the school of Ammonius Saccas. The *Stromata* was the principal result, but he found time also for the composition of two little works that were his first steps in the direction of the *De principiis*.

By acquiring the philosophy of Ammonius he strengthened his own views, which now began to fall into a more systematic form. His spiritual life, stimulated in his youth by his desire for martyrdom, was about to justify itself in a theoretical martyrdom by his sufferings from the imperfections that press heavily upon free souls like his. His theology would express the inner bond that holds creatures to the divine thought from which they came. He would lead human reason back to that supreme wisdom in which God is pleased to assemble His perfect ideas. Instead of shutting himself in the dusty cell of the Commentaries, the young head of the Academy would create his own philosophy and develop his own system of thought; but it would be a philosophy founded on the word of

God, a body of Christian teaching against which the heretics would hurl themselves in vain. Let us permit Origen the pagan to build up his great work and to use his memories of Platonism. Can he do anything else but develop the message of the Church, the one and only truth which Origen the Christian never ceased to carry within his heart?

The result justified only in part the optimism that inspired the vague and generous plan. In the life of Adamantius these two men were sometimes in opposition to each other, until posterity, startled at the complexity of such a soul, made of him two different persons.

CHAPTER XII

The Treatise *De Principiis*

AT LAST the hour struck for the systematization of the manifold ideas, the numerous lectures, and the entire series of philosophical activities to which the *Commentaries* had given rise. Origen now determined to weld them into a complete doctrine. This was the purpose of the *Tractatus de principiis*, his most important work. It stands out above his other publications, less by reason of the new theories it expressed than because it represents the coherent form into which his philosophy finally crystallized.

As we approach the study of this great work, our first obligation is to decide upon the method of criticism to be employed. Most of the original work has been lost. With the exception of certain extracts from it that are found in the *Philocalia* of St. Basil and St. Gregory Nazianzen, the chief source of our knowledge of it is in the Latin translation by Rufinus and in a collection of propositions or opinions taken from the work itself. Thus the relevant documents fall into two classes. The first class contains what amounts to evidence in favor of the famous treatise. The second, however, would lead to its rejection. The result is that the critical historian is unable to accept without question any of the evidence.

RUFINUS' TRANSLATION

The suggestion has been made that the critics should reject the Latin version left by Rufinus and rely exclusively on the Greek sources. But in this matter a hasty condemnation would be no less unfortunate than an excess of confidence. Whenever the due process of research can be followed, the wise critic will not abandon his customary technique. Paul Koetschau, in his masterly edition of the treatise, establishes a method of comparing the Latin version with the Greek fragments, whatever may be the context in which they are found, and this method must be employed if the critic is to achieve results. So far its application has produced conclusions that are the reverse of favorable, and Koetschau himself accuses Rufinus of having falsified the original text. Bardy, however, tries to rehabilitate the Latin translator and to prove that the principal features of Origen's work have been faithfully preserved. Despite their differences the two learned critics concur in the verdict that the Latin version shows a number of gaps, some of which are of great importance, and that there are also obvious additions, consisting chiefly of glosses or paraphrases, besides a large number of inaccuracies.

It has not been proved, however, that Rufinus ever substituted his own theories for the doctrine of Origen. His main preoccupation seems to have been the watering-down of the more rash expressions or theories, either by the simple process of passing them over in silence or by an effort to forestall possible objections. Wherever a passage was unlikely to offend the Christian reader, the translation is as exact as was permitted by the usage of his contemporaries, who were far from observing the stricter standards of modern criticism. Thus he reproduced the less coherent of the theories, regarding them as old and of secondary importance. Other parts of the work were too well known, too daring or too important, to justify any temptation he may have had to suppress them; and since Origen himself had taken care to present them as conjectures, Rufinus preserved them in their original setting. The one exception to this method of procedure was Origen's doctrine on the Trinity, for it might have given an advantage to the Arians of the time. The prudent and comprehensive way those speculations were advanced makes their authenticity the more certain, for this was always Origen's method of discussing free questions, as can be seen from the study of his other works. Rufinus is not to be held responsible for the mingled irresoluteness and subtlety of all such passages, for he usually considered it simpler to suppress what puzzled him. On the contrary, they were natural to a theologian whose rashness in speculation was always tempered by his respect for the foundations of Christian belief.

The researches conducted by modern critics on the authenticity of Rufinus' version establish the fact that it is marked by serious deficiencies, to use Koetschau's expression, rather than by any downright effort to tamper with the original. Taking this verdict as our basic principle, we can lay down certain rules to guide us in our own analysis of the treatise. In the first place, we will be on our guard against the temptation to endow St. Jerome's translations with unlimited authority, for his versions of Origen's text betray a tendency to force the thoughts of an author whose many-sided genius was so different from his own. In the second place, the propositions condemned under Emperor Justinian constitute a body of evidence that is still less trustworthy, because a number of them are quoted from other works of Origen and several of them are taken from glosses added to the original by students who suffered from an excess of zeal or enthusiasm. This must be kept in view, in spite of the fact that there is not one of those documents, whether of St. Jerome or of Emperor Justinian, which does not bear the impress of Origen's thought.

Origen's own works, then, will be the chief source of our standards of critical examination, especially the Greek parts of the *De principiis*, the *Commentary on the Psalms*, and the first books of the *Commentary on the Gospel of St. John*, all of which were written in the same period as the *De principiis*, and each of which can be used from time to time to verify passages in Rufinus' version. Furthermore, it must be remembered that a number of the doctrines proposed in the Latin translation had their *raison d'être* and their meaning for Origen's day and for Origen's system exclusively. They correspond to the controversies, the general philosophy, the dreams of a period not to be readily confused with the fourth century. That being the case, it follows that if the Latin version gives us the method, the style, or the favorite expressions that we know belong to Origen, and if we find there the outlines or the development of opinions he is known to have held, we must admit that each of the passages in question is authentic, at least in substance.

Rash theories, and even theories that run directly counter to the tradition of the Church, are not lacking to Rufinus' version. The timidity of the man's own theology and his loyalty to Origen's memory are a sufficient guaranty that he did not invent them. Indeed he is not even suspected of having done the slightest violence to them. Therefore the Latin translation by Rufinus shall remain in the foreground, but under suspicion, so to speak, and shall be open to challenge by all the techniques of comparison or reconciliation by which we hope to reconstruct the real Origenism, not the Origenism of the great man's over-zealous defenders or the Origenism of the bills of indictment.

CHARACTER OF THE WORK

The *Tractatus de principiis* is no longer an enigma as soon as it is considered part of Origen's life. Considered apart from that life, it was a cause of scandal from the hour when critics fell into the easy habit of regarding it as merely a part of the general philosophy of Alexandria during the first three decades of the third century. It is the manifesto of the head of a school who has gathered together the teachings of a number of years in order to give formal expression to a system of theology at the behest of his followers. Before undertaking the work, he had already begun and probably completed his commentary on the first twenty-five psalms; he had published the first volume of his *Commentary on Genesis* and probably the second; also included in his works was the *Treatise on the Resurrection*, which not only upheld Christian traditions and Christian apologetic but treated the relations between the body and the soul; in all probability his *Stromata* and several of his Platonist essays had already been written, since he claimed, as author of the *Tractatus de principiis*, to be emancipated from the philosophy of the Greeks. But he did not renounce any of the wealth of learning he had amassed in his studies of the Greek authors.

THE DATE

As Origen did not begin to publish before his journey to Rome and as he was finally persuaded to do so only by the persistent en-

treaties of his friend Ambrose, these different works are all of a
date later than the year 211 or 212. In the order of their publication they must have been distributed over several years. Since the
De principiis appeared when they had already been undertaken or
finished, the most probable date to be assigned to the publication
of the famous treatise is, according to the majority of the critics,
between the year 220 and the year 225. Because of the sweep and
maturity of its philosophy, it falls into place beside the *Commentary on the Gospel of St. John* and therefore belongs to the final
years of his professorial career at the Academy of Alexandria.

THE RULE OF FAITH

It is quite distinct from all his preceding works. Since it derives
its authority "from no other source than from the very words and
teaching of Christ," [1] it definitely belongs to theology. Neither
Plato nor any other of the pagan philosophers is mentioned in it,
nor is there any reference to the parallels admitted in the *Stromata*.
This does not prevent it from having a ready solution for each of
the great religious problems of the day, in dealing with which it
often advances a philosophical analysis before presenting the conclusive argument from Scripture. The author, like the Israelites in
the Book of Exodus, has left a strange country and has passed
through the midst of a dried-up sea, bearing with him the spoils
of the Egyptians, the vast treasures of pagan learning. Sometimes
the burden delays his progress, for between the *De principiis* and
his Platonist writings there is not as great a difference as he himself
is inclined to suppose. He has yet to learn what later becomes a
conviction with him: no Christian theologian can borrow from
the resources of Greek thought without being affected in some degree by its pagan spirit.

Nor is the form of its theology any less new. There is nothing here
to recall the argumentative methods of St. Irenaeus, the charm of
Clement's easy flow of language, the scholarly commentaries written by the youthful Origen and illuminated, time and time again as

---

[1] *De princip.*, I, *Praef.*

the occasion demanded, by his interpretation of the Bible. Henceforth he will devote himself to the project of composing a body of doctrine based on the Church's teaching, a theological system, the first great scientific effort with which Christian thought will endeavor to give rational proofs of the affirmations on which the faith is built.[2]

Starting from the principle that Christian knowledge has no other foundation than the common faith of all Christians, he considers it necessary to establish a connection betwen the elementary catechism and the knowledge with which he has been enlightened by his study of the Sacred Scriptures, by the learning he has acquired in the course of his controversies, and by the scholarship that has come to him as a result of his acquaintance with the problems of the various philosophical schools. The common faith of Christians contains some things that are clear and some that are obscure. Although it does not, of itself, endow the Christian thinker with all religious knowledge, it lays down the conditions with which such a man ought prudently to conduct his inquiry. Hence it is the norm or canon of every such study. Speaking generally, it can be said that the faith establishes the existence of supernatural realities and that it is the duty of theologians, or of those who have received the grace of wisdom, to investigate the essence or the origin of such supernatural realities.[3]

This ecclesiastical canon is not expressed as a formula. In its widest meaning, it is the sum-total of the beliefs held by the mass of the faithful. Here we have the rule of true religion as opposed to the ungodliness of the heretics. It is considered in its most perfect expression, as a working principle of the spiritual Church, of which the ordinary Church is eminently a part. But it is also the traditional method which guides the spiritual Christian in his contemplation on the mysteries of his faith and furnishes him with the means of interpreting all the enigmas of Holy Scripture, because

[2] *Ibid.*, I, 9: "and form, as we have said, one body of doctrine, by means of illustrations and arguments—either those which he has discovered in Holy Scripture or those which he has deduced by closely tracing out the consequences and following a correct method."

[3] *Ibid.*, I, *Praef.*, 3.

the canon of the Christian faith contains within itself the principles of symbolism.[4]

The Church's message, the apostolical traditions, whether understood by the illiterate or held only by the learned, the preaching of their successors: all are reducible to some fundamental points. Writing in his preface to the *De principiis*, Origen draws the first of these particular points from a baptismal formula. The catechumen, after renouncing Satan, gives his pledge to Christ and makes a short profession of faith, declaring his belief in one God, in His Son, and in the Holy Ghost. This public declaration of his most important beliefs places him under a solemn obligation toward the clergy and the faithful of the Christian community into which he is being received.

The second of the particular points is found by Origen in the traditional formulas pertaining to the Incarnation of the Word, whether they are part of the baptismal formula or not: that Jesus Christ was born of the Virgin Mary and of the Holy Ghost, that He was crucified under Pontius Pilate, and that He rose from the dead. Of these three articles, the second refers to the life of Christ on earth; and, according to the usage already established at the time, the third article is concerned with the inspiration of the prophets, the resurrection of the dead, and the judgment.

Origen's purpose in this preface is obviously to expound the canon of faith and to avoid textual analyses. Although he adheres to this general plan, he works it out in a manner that is variable, employing his own peculiar methods and adapting the general plan to his immediate need. For example, when the Alexandrians wrote about ecclesiastical institutions, they wrote as philosophers, using scholarly paraphrases. Origen's exposition of the canon of faith is marked by the same repugnance for literalism. Instead of stating simply that Jesus Christ suffered under Pontius Pilate, he elaborates the article into an affirmation that Jesus Christ did truly suffer and did not endure this death common to man in appearance only, but did truly die. Thus he manifests an ever-present eagerness to be

[4] Cf. *In Joan.*, XIII, 16; *P.G.*, XIV, 421; *De princip.*, IV, ii, 1.

ready for the heretics or to adjust his position to the needs of a
theory which he is about to propose. His general attitude is a blend
of what we might call a faith that is passive and a vigorously active
spirit of inquiry, an intelligence held under control and a boldness
of speculation. In this mental amalgam we have one of the marks
of the Academy of Alexandria. It is, therefore, incorrect to believe
that he ignores the simple rule of faith, and it is no less incorrect to
assert that he endeavors to reproduce it without the amplifications
to which his training had accustomed him.

A number of truths flow from the ecclesiastical canon by way
of corollaries, so much so that, although they are not articles, properly so called, they are presented as points that have been clarified
in the teaching of the Church. For instance, free will is not expressly included in the catechumen's baptismal formula; but Origen considers that it is implied in the dogma of the last judgment.[5]
The argument for this deduction is to be found in the fact that the
Church calls men to the practice of virtue and thereby assumes that
they are capable of a free determination of their own actions. The
entire plan of salvation, as it is understood or implied in the general
beliefs of Christians, separates the faithful Christian from the
heretic, just as the dogma of the Incarnation has separated him
from the unbeliever.

But it is also necessary to clarify the points which Christian tradition has left obscure, and to oppose to the false explanations proposed by private interpreters opinions that are endowed with greater
authority and are more in harmony with the mind of the Church.
For this purpose Origen will proceed to propose a number of hypotheses which he will check by comparing them with appropriate
texts of Holy Scripture. He will make this test with such care that
each such hypothesis gives a total explanation of the biblical text
with which it is associated, a happy result to which the proponents
of heretical doctrines cannot lay claim. Since many of the points in
question do not involve any definition of faith, he is not guilty of
temerity in proposing conjectures that appear to be novel or out of
the ordinary.

[5] *De princip.*, I, *Praef.*, 5: "This also is clearly defined in the teaching of the Church,
that every rational soul is possessed of free will and volition."

A PHILOSOPHICAL STUDY

The *De principiis* was, therefore, a philosophical study of Christian dogmas rather than a work of biblical interpretation. The authority of the Bible was usually invoked to confirm the author's deductions, a technique which led Origen to compose a sort of appendix to show that Scripture is inspired and contains the revelations of the doctrines professed in the body of the work. It was his belief that neither the ordinary efforts of human reason nor the higher evidence acquired by the enlightened consciousness of the spiritually trained offered sufficient ground for their acceptance. A firm foundation for every such doctrine must be sought in the inspired writings themselves. Those writings are divine because they lead to Jesus, to the evangelization of the world, and to the power wielded by the holy apostles.

Returning then to the traditional argument, Origen proved the existence of prophecy by the divinity of Christ. The power which accomplished those miracles henceforth proven to be true is also the "Lord," whose coming they announce. Now, divine books speak only of divine things. Are they not the revelation of the Logos, who is substantially united to the mysterious designs of Wisdom? Are they not addressed to souls who, in their striving to become perfect, have a definite need to know and to understand, according to their capacity, the operations of the Word-made-man and the way those operations affect their progress? Is it not true that those operations must finally teach men their role in the world and equip them with the knowledge of the helps or obstacles they will encounter there? Origen saw the wisdom of providence, the spiritual life, and the moral struggle as three enclosed cities. There was but one road along which each of those cities might be entered: the spiritual interpretation of Holy Scripture. From the necessity of being interpreted spiritually he did not exempt any part of the Bible, not even the accounts it gives of historical occurrences.

From that hour Alexandrian symbolism was placed at the service of a theological system. Origen felt that it was incumbent on him to employ it, even at the risk of conceiving ideas that might be false or gross or impious. His drastic criticism of the "impossibilities" to be found in Holy Writ if it is interpreted by the methods of literalism must, he believed, drive the unspiritual man into this leap into the divine, however much it frightens him. So we find him complacently gathering together, in a final chapter, a number of biblical passages whose meaning was obscure to him. He presents them as a proof of an obligation to go beyond the letter of the historical records contained in the Bible and beyond the face value of the precepts, and even beyond the findings of the moral sense which delivers men from unholy and carnal thoughts. Only by leaving all these behind is it possible, he thought, to discover the higher revelation that is reserved for purified intelligences. Holy Scripture makes known the destiny of souls, as it were, in the thought of God, in the same Spirit that illuminated the prophets and the apostles. The *De principiis* is nothing more than the rough draft of this profound research, the final results of which are not, perhaps, to be expected here upon earth.

Origen's purpose was less to augment the number of religious truths than to clarify the teachings of the Church by an exposition that would be at once coherent, true to Scripture, and scholarly enough to win the attention of the philosophers. In the pursuit of this plan, he endeavored to make secondary matters of Christian belief even more solid than the dogmas. By numerous adjustments he succeeded in his efforts, reducing the number of free questions little by little. In the end there remained but one free question of any importance: Is the soul transmitted to the body at the instant of generation, or is it inserted in the body from without?

Speaking generally, we believe that it is a mistake to try to seek in this preface to the *De principiis* a serious statement of the evolution of the rule of faith. Two dogmas that would be defined in subsequent centuries are here presented in the clearest terms. Origen acknowledges no freedom of belief in the articles wherein he teaches the eternal procession of the Son and the union of the two natures in Christ. Nor is there anything here to remind us of the mists of primitive religion, from which the magic of certain historians makes dogmas appear in process of formation. Any such hypothesis would necessarily be composed of credible elements and of guesses that might promise well but would only succeed in leaving the entire question still undecided. But here the case is quite different, for the firmness of Christian tradition can be easily recognized, even though Origen expresses the doctrines under an archaic form of words.

On the other hand, most of the questions discussed in the preface were general postulates of Christian philosophy or matters of simple curiosity, and neither class of questions includes any proposition that has been the subject of a conciliar definition. Concerning the soul of the stars or the planetary transformations that will take place at the end of time, the Church has nothing to say, and probably never will have anything to say. Such matters do not naturally come within the scope of the Church's definitions. These problems are ephemeral and cannot be regarded as marking a phase of dogmatic evolution. If we keep this in view, it is not difficult to see that the passages where the treatise formally offends against the traditions of Christianity are by no means as numerous as might be supposed, however disconcerting the impression left on the reader's mind by a hasty examination of the text.

ALLEGORICAL INTERPRETATION

Origen's rashness does not lie precisely in an espousal of heresy, and there is no longer any disposition on the part of the critics to accuse him of introducing new or strange doctrines. But in every phase of his research he is an individualist; yet, while claiming his right to be such, he remains always the theologian. His error is to be found in the particular method he employs, for that method was based upon an imperfect notion of spiritual progress. He violently rejects literalism in favor of the allegorical meaning. Although he admits all the ordinary standards of Christian thought, more than once he interprets Christian tradition according to the method by which he was accustomed to interpret Scripture. A modern critic hears him say, in his moments of rashness: "The whole problem consists in my duty to discover what God has hidden from me." But the Church makes no such distinction between faith and the-

ology. They are two different degrees of religious knowledge, but
they have the same object. The words of the Creed and the deposit
of tradition give the Christian something more than affirmations of
existence. Further, if it is true that theology is the intensive study
of the truths implicitly contained in the deposit of faith held by
Christians, it follows that it is the function of theology to explain
the nature of the supernatural realities proposed for the consideration of every Christian. Whether the faith of Christians is simple
or learned, whether it is crude or elaborated into a thing of beauty,
it carries the message of the Savior; and it carries that message according to its own mode, the mode of a knowledge that is always
obscure, always hidden, from learned and ignorant alike.

By his disdain for the value of the religion of ordinary Christians
and by his exaggeration of the importance of intellectual research,
Origen gave countenance to the tendencies of the gnostics. As a result, his contemporaries did not hesitate to charge him, not with
self-deception but with having raised problems that were superfluous and that tended to disturb the balance of Christian speculation. When he had more experience he endeavored to bridge the
gap between the two degrees of Christian belief. In the end he
sought the knowledge of God nowhere but in the progress of the
faith held by ordinary Christians.

TITLE AND SCOPE OF THE WORK

The title of the work reveals its scope. According to Redpenning,
whose opinion on this point is accepted by most critics, the word
"principles" means the fundamental truths on which Origen
founded his theological system. But we can hardly believe that
the title, *Tractatus de dogmatibus*, preceded a preface in which the
author's whole effort is to make a precise distinction between the
fundamental points and the purpose of his inquiry. In Origen's use
of the word, the connotation of "principle" involves two ideas:
cause and beginning. We find it in this twofold sense in those early
pages where he enumerates the meanings of wisdom, which contains the rationale and the species of every creature. One of the
Latin equivalents proposed by Rufinus confirms this twofold mean-

ing, and Origen himself tells us that principle is opposed to end. When he gives the list of the different meanings assigned to the word in the dictionaries, he pauses to say: "There is a beginning of action, inasmuch as we observe there a succession and an end." [6] He never separates the study of beginnings from that of the final consummation, for the correspondence of the restoration and the fall, of the recapitulation and the primal unity, are for him a primordial notion on which he builds his entire philosophy of the history of the soul.

The *De principiis* has for its scope the explanation of the origins and the nature of spiritual life. It expounds the providential dispositions which guide the soul, their vicissitudes and their different results. This exposition is founded on Origen's understanding of those dispositions as they are implicitly professed in the dogmas of Christianity, and especially in the final articles of the traditional formula. Philosophy rather than theology is the groundwork of this exposition in view of the fact that the conditions of a logical belief in providence was what gnosticism threatened above everything else. Origen studies what we may call the blueprint of salvation. He derives his teachings on the spiritual life from the final dogmas, the last judgment and the resurrection from the dead. His preface testifies to his great care on this point, for he desires to conduct his entire inquiry within the framework of the profession of faith.

USE OF FREE WILL

In comparison with this purpose all other aspects of the treatise are of secondary importance. Undoubtedly it would be possible to consider the *De principiis* as one of those philosophical systems of Christian inspiration which flourish in historical periods when reason and sentiment seem to go hand in hand. Origen anticipated Rousseau in the discovery of man's primitive state, but he ennobled it by the lofty thoughts with which he studied it. Man is born free; if he is everywhere in chains, the cause of the enslavement is traceable to that very freedom. In that primary freedom is to be found

[6] Cf. *ibid.*, I, iv, 3; *In Joan.*, I, 21; P.G., XIV, 56; *In Joan.*, XIII, 39; P.G., XIV, 466.

the origin of the inequality in Origen's city of free wills where the
misuse of freedom is a fault common to one and all. Rousseau studies this freedom on the plane of sociology. Origen, on the other
hand, assigns it to the heavenly city where the spirits who are to
become human souls conspire for their common fall by a turning
away from the Good and by the progressive corruption that follows.
In recent years the critics, losing sight of the theology of the treatise,
have produced a number of special monographs which reduce the
De principiis to this discourse on liberty. In doing so, they have forgotten that several writers of note have studied the treatise, not in
separate parts, but as a whole. The modern efforts to represent Origen's great work as a philosophy colored by Christianity, reduce it
to some affirmations that are not worthy to be called philosophy.
The critics have now reached the point where they regard the work
as nothing more than an effort to explain human morality by natural causes and to assign human modes of behavior to the life of animals and plants.

A "DIVINE COMEDY"

The more those monographs persisted in diluting the substance
of the treatise, the more Origen's history of souls, called by the
critics his transcendent myths, assumed the appearance of a mon-
ster. No wonder the historians could no longer establish any link
between those absurdities and the rest of his system. They called
them idle phantasies and even dull and uncouth ramblings. The
puzzle was to explain how this uncalled-for romancing could be
part of a system of thought which their first examination had pronounced to be of the highest value. In a number of passages, they
say, the De principiis is almost a Divine Comedy, with a symbolism
not unlike that of Dante's great work. Certainly, all the movements
of a vast poem are to be found in the treatise. The era of sin has
its beginning in Satan's pride. Pride is a metaphysical falsehood
leading to the destruction of the creature who believes he possesses
in his own essence the goods he has received in trust. Satan is the
prince of Tyre over whose fall the prophet weeps. He was not evil at
the time of his creation, for the Creator gave him a share of the

glory that illuminated all the holy ones of God. But he is fallen, he who is described as having been adorned with a crown of comeliness and beauty, and as having walked stainless in the paradise of God.[7]

POEM OF THE SOULS

Then there comes the poem of the souls. In their state of pre-existence they also turned away from the Good. Inclining toward matter, they received bodies, lighter or heavier according to their deserts. Those of them whose fall has been less than that of the others raise themselves, and in the measure in which their knowledge grows they move forward in their spiritual progress. The ladder of paradise, which the patriarch Jacob saw, is being traversed by those spirits that fall away or by those other spirits that are restored, in the course of several lives, to the dignity they had at the beginning. The poem of heaven unrolls according to the same law. Heaven is peopled by souls that have fallen away but are more docile than the others to wisdom, and they take part in the splendid liturgy of the celestial city. Moreover, a more perfect universe, in which rational beings were still perfectly united to the Word, has preceded this present universe. Another universe is to come, in which matter, having become pure and ethereal, will form the new world.[8]

This is the *Tractatus de principiis*, as indulgent critics see it. On the one hand, it is a philosophy of rational liberty and of the reign of natural enlightenment; on the other hand, it is an optimistic vision of the universe, a vision in which dreams predominate. Is this enough to explain the attraction of Origen's great work for the greatest theologians of Christian antiquity, in spite of the suspicion with which they viewed it? The gnostics of Rome are dead and have left no posterity. Origen's work lives, and another spiritual substance than theirs is hidden within its pages.

The truth is that the notions of pre-existence, of successive lives, and of the series of universes were merely conjectures subordinated to Origen's doctrine of the inner life. Despite all appearances to

[7] *De princip.*, I, vii.
[8] *Ibid.*

the contrary, this doctrine was Christian, as its later development proved. The notion of pre-existence, which was nothing but the theory of a philosophical school derived from Neoplatonism and from the Jewish apocrypha, left untouched the question of present responsibility. It was merely a sort of ornament. It had no place in prayer, in the examination of conscience, and in the redemption. The falling away and the migration of souls did not go so far as a changing of bodies, for the system rejected metempsychosis. The perspective of future ages did not reach the point of depriving holiness of a positive value. St. Paul's conversion was always regarded as an irrevocable gift. Despite the succession of universes, matter was not eternal. The present universe, the limits of which were the fall and the restoration of souls, had been conceived and created by a definite plan of providence.

Thus is explained why the spirit of the treatise remained traditional while its program failed to do so. The conjectures were soon forgotten. They were merely exaggerations prompted by Origen's intense desire to illustrate his teaching, an attitude of anti-gnosis which he assumed in the course of his polemic. His first intention would have been more obvious and his doctrine would have avoided the ambiguities and equivocations with which his critics charged him if he had adopted another method of controversy. He met the gnostic myths with contrary myths of his own devising. A better plan would have been to meet them by an immediate application of the principle of his own doctrine.

One of his great axioms was that God is not the author of evil. Light is refused to no man. Sin always has its beginning in a neglect of the gifts of providence. The Word abandons no man except one who already has turned away from it. Another such axiom was that the salvation or the loss of souls is not a matter dependent on fate. It is within the power of every rational being to re-establish himself in God's love and to return to the enjoyment of its primal dignity. There is never need to despair of conversion or pardon or final restoration. God's mercy has countless means of reprieve which we cannot foresee. Such was the spiritual government of the universe, as Origen saw it. He soon put it aside in order to look for causes in the origin of the world. This latter inquiry was of greater promise to him when he contemplated the mystery of creation in the simplicity of the Christian life.

CHAPTER XIII

The Three Worlds

RECOGNIZABLE at first glance, the principal divisions of the treatise are God, the world, man, and Scripture. Each is the main subject of a book, the entire work being composed of four books. In all probability this method of division was employed by Origen himself, and the general belief of the critics is that he was also responsible for the various subdivisions in each book. The titles of the chapters, which are the same in the *Philocalia* and in the edition known to Photius, seem to go back to the fourth century. Origen used various means of indicating the subdivisions of his subject. A few of the titles are to be attributed to the Latin translator.

The plan adheres to the order of the questions indicated in the Preface, but the system requires a new grouping of them. The management of the spiritual life depends upon an act of providence. This act of providence comes into reality as another aspect of the act of creation. Its operation may be recognized in the three stages represented by the three cities. First, there is the supreme city, where God appears as the origin of the intelligences that contemplate Him and go forth from Him. Secondly, there is the spiritual city. This city is part of the order of the created universe. Within it God manifests to Himself the providential design to which souls conform, thanks to the mediation of the Word-made-man. Thirdly, there is the natural city, the place of temptations and of trials to which man's free will is subjected in a series of salutary ordeals. The first three books discuss the questions of man's liberty, of evil, of the fall and the restoration of souls. These questions are considered on different levels, so to speak: first, on the level of the interior contemplation of God, then on the stage of the universe and of man's history, and finally in the moral life. A fourth part is devoted to the educational training which the spiritual Christian must undergo and to the allegorical interpretation of Scripture. What Origen called the spiritual sense of Scripture, as distinguished from the moral application of the text, henceforth confines the inquiry of the initiate to meditations on the truths hidden in the divine word.

I. THE WORLD OF THE INTELLECT

THE TRINITY THE SOURCE OF BEING

The treatise considers the Trinity as a principle. It does not affirm either the distinctions of persons for itself or the unity of persons for itself. The divine paternity, the procession and the eternity of the Word, the divinity of the Holy Ghost: each and all of these will clarify for Origen the origin of rational beings and will enable him to define the relations uniting rational beings to God.

This theological enterprise starts from the consideration of the Father. Divinity is in Him at its source. His superiority to every nature can be affirmed. Negative propositions used in regard to Him are merely a means to express His greatness, His supreme majesty, His excellence which necessarily surpasses in a thousand ways the feelings or the ideas we may have about Him. The eminent majesty of God is a kind of postulate from which are derived all the notions we have of His nature, of His intelligence, and of His perfection.[1] To adopt this fundamental attitude and to develop within ourselves the divine feelings of the heart are to repeat in another form the conversion to the invisible, which is necessary as a preliminary to the interpretation of Scripture. The method of each conversion is the same. It consists in a search for God where we pass through various phases in our transition from the contemplation of the things of earth to that of the things of the spiritual world and where we finish by passing beyond all that we can attain of the spirit itself. Thus the theology of the divine attributes is not an illusion. It rises toward the ineffable but not toward the irrational. This theological inquiry dazzles human thought, not by reason of its essential obscurity but by the excess of light with which it floods the soul.

[1] *Ibid.*, I, i, 4 and 5.

Suppose that we desire to explain the splendor of the sun to a man who has difficulty in seeing a beam of light or a momentary flash. In such a case the only thing to do is to tell him that the sun surpasses beyond description the feeble light which his eyes see. "But among all intelligent beings, that is, incorporeal beings, what is so superior to all others—so unspeakably and incalculably superior—as God, whose nature cannot be grasped or seen by the power of any human understanding, even the purest and brightest?" Thus Origen refutes the false interpretations of Scripture on which certain of the heretics based their assertion that God possesses a body, that He is a fire or a breath. "It is the custom of Sacred Scripture, when it wishes to designate anything opposed to this gross and solid body, to call it spirit, as in the expression, 'The letter killeth, but the spirit giveth life,' where there can be no doubt that by 'letter' are meant bodily things, and by 'spirit' intellectual things, which we also term 'spiritual.'" God is spirit. With the reservation that He infinitely surpasses the power of our intelligence, the treatise tells us that we can advance from the knowledge of the soul to the knowledge of divine being.

The reason given for this power of ours is that there exists, even in us, an incorporeal nature. When we move from place to place or live in a diversity of locations, our mind and its workings are influenced in what is merely an accidental manner, and the sole reason for this is that we are living beings composed of body and soul. Certain circumstances may arise in which the body is thrown into such confusion that it no longer functions according to the rules which are normal to it but in a way that is disturbed and disorderly. But the mind is independent of place. We must also note that the development of the mind does not follow the same rhythm of growth as the body, for the mind is sharpened by exercises of learning. When the body has already been in the enjoyment of its full growth for a long time, the mind can still continue to grow by meditation on the knowledge it possesses or newly acquires. In particular, the exercise of memory, which is capable of retaining ideas that are difficult and subtle, cannot be explained by a disposition of the corporeal nature, for the body is incapable of the vital movements adapted to such a diversity of objects as the memory holds.

THE SON OF GOD

In a concluding remark Origen confirms our notion of the soul. Understanding and perception, as we have said, can be compared with each other. There underlies every perception a certain peculiar sensible substance on which the bodily sense works. For example, colors, form, and size underlie vision. The sense of mind is superior to all the other senses of man. Now, is it not absurd that under this sense of mind nothing at all of the nature of a determined subject should be placed, but that a power of an intellectual nature should be an accident, or consequent upon bodies?

If intelligence, then, is incorporeal, God, who is the source and, as we shall soon see, the model of all intellectual life, has far greater reason to be freed from the limitations of the physical world. Therefore, when any man wishes to study the second article of our faith and to know who and what is Christ, the only-begotten Son, he must remember always the incomparable dignity of God. However, the series of names or of notions on which is founded the theology of the pre-existence of Christ shows immediately that the Son does not possess the divine attributes under the same relation as the Father. In God the Father the divine attributes are absolute. In Christ the Son they are regarded as goods in the enjoyment of which creatures participate. The Son is pre-existing wisdom, containing the principles and ideas of all reality.

There are still other titles which make Him the eternal Mediator. He is also called the way, the resurrection, and the life, because His mission is to restore imperfect creatures who do not understand how to maintain themselves in possession of the Good. Numerous passages of Scripture are to be interpreted in this way. Thus, when the Apostle says of Christ that He is the image of the invisible God, he describes Him in this manner not only because of the likeness owing to His sonship but also because there resides in Him the supreme image of all the images whereby we may understand something of God. The Apostle also calls Him the brightness of God's glory, because in Him and through Him the rational creation accepts the divine order which is imposed on it, not by force but with reason and wisdom.[2]

The second chapter of the first book insists less than Origen's subsequent works on the subordinate majesty of the Son, on His function as creative wisdom, and on His mission as mediator. At this point the text is concerned mainly with the eternal generation of the Son, because the function of the second principle rests upon this generation. He is different from beings such as angels and men in this respect: there was no time when He was not. To assign to Him a beginning would be a belief contrary to the divine dignity, an impiety. Can we suppose or believe that God the Father ever existed, even for a moment of time, without having generated this all-powerful wisdom? Those who claim that God the Father adopted the Son ignore the fact that the divine generation is incapable of any comparison, not merely in created things, but in those which cannot even be conceived by thought. Let us admit that the will of God suffices to give subsistence to whatever He desires. It is not fitting, nor is there any reason for it, that God has not always been able to possess what is good. He wished to beget wisdom, with a will that is the expression of His intelligence. The Son has no other principle than this eternal origin. He proceeds from the Father, as an activity which would be derived directly from an intuition of Himself: a divine necessity, all-knowing and all-willing, which must be placed at the point where perfection is realized without let or hindrance, contrary to the inferior necessity from which the personal will is excluded.

In this manner Origen repudiated not only Adoptionism but every theory and every corollary of that heresy which might divide the divine substance and introduce degrees into it. There is no other second goodness in the Son, except what is in the Father; but that goodness is essential to the Son, whereas angels and men can possess it only *per accidens* and are liable to lose it.

[2] *Ibid.*, ii, 2–6.

THE HOLY GHOST

When he came to consider the Holy Ghost, Origen found it agreeable to follow the same method. He made the starting point of his study the effects which the Holy Ghost produces in souls, and he decided to explain its function by a consideration of the Trinity as a whole. However, certain conditions of this particular inquiry are different. The Father and the Son can become in some measure the object of philosophy. Every system of thought that admits the operations of providence is led to affirm the existence of an uncreated God, a Father of all things. By means of the visible creation and the natural feelings of the human mind we can discover that this God possesses a reflex idea or Logos, although our unassisted human reason does not comprehend the transcendent wisdom which expresses itself in the universe. But we are unable even to guess at the existence of the Holy Ghost unless we appeal to the Old Testament and unless we believe in Jesus Christ. The scriptural texts will be called upon to confirm the doctrine and also to give it the basis it requires.

The dignity of the Holy Ghost appears in a number of passages of the New Testament where He is associated with the Father and the Son in the sanctification of souls. An outstanding example is the baptismal formula. Since the Spirit shares in the work of creation, He is not to be confused with any of the beings that have received their existence. In the Book of Genesis the role assigned to Him is exclusively divine and implies no suggestion of passivity. When the Scripture states that the Spirit of God moved over the waters, it does not imply that the Spirit is incorporeal matter, a mass of light common to all spirtis, eternal but without form, by means of which the demiurge would have introduced order into the universe for the purpose of drawing therefrom the world and the minds that would dwell therein. The Holy Ghost is of the same rank as the Son, exercising the ministry of eternal life, without any dependence other than that which unites Him to the Father as to His origin. He has no need of being instructed by the Word. He has perfect knowledge of the Father as principle, and it is impossible to suppose that there is in Him either acquisition of new knowledge or progressive advancement in the knowledge He eternally has.[3]

One of the most striking passages in the treatise is that in which Origen, in all the power of his Alexandrian theology, sets forth his views on the function of the Holy Ghost. Since creatures depend totally upon God, they can make no progress in the direction of perfection except by sharing more and more in His gifts. From the Father they possess the essence that makes them what they are. From the Son or the Logos rational beings receive the enlightenment of conscience, the seeds of wisdom, by which they are made capable of knowledge when the reason implanted within has suggested to them the difference between good and evil, and by which also they are capable of merit or of choosing the errors of ignorance. From the Holy Ghost, spiritual beings draw the power that produces in them a new life and assists their moral development. Thus we can say that the divine operations, in the measure in which their effects approach perfection, influence a progressively smaller number of created beings.

Since this theory seems to give a superiority to the Holy Ghost, Origen does not wish to adhere to it without some further explanation. He warns us that the progress of the soul to perfection is not a matter of such logical divisions as he has enunciated. In the work of sanctification the Father has His particular function also, and the Logos, in implanting reason within us, gives us the immediate means of living in a holy manner. Besides, the Holy Ghost not only is the source of extraordinary gifts but must also be considered in His habitual manifestation—the operation of grace, given by the Father and dispensed by Christ.[4] Therefore the simple distinction, given above, of the divine operations is merely a starting point. More profoundly, the creature must become what he is, and his progress consists in the development of a unique gift which is no less precious in its lowliest beginnings than in the full glory of its

[3] Ibid., iii, 4.
[4] Ibid., 7.

final achievement. Every phase of this progress bears the mark of the Trinity. The three divine Persons, exercising the different operations which are peculiar to each of them, are united and mutually compenetrated as far as the term of their action. Everything comes from the Father, and everything returns to the Father. Such is Origen's manner of presenting the theory of recapitulation familiar to St. Irenaeus and to the theologians of the period. "The working of the Father, which confers existence upon all things, is found to be more glorious and magnificent, while each one, by participation in Christ, as being wisdom and knowledge and sanctification, makes progress and advances to higher degrees of perfection; and seeing it is by partaking of the Holy Spirit that anyone is made purer and holier, he obtains, when he is made worthy, the grace of wisdom and knowledge . . . that the being which exists may be as worthy as He who called it into existence. For, in a way, he who is such as his Creator wished him to be, will receive from God power always to exist and to abide forever." [5]

Expounded in this manner, the theology of the Trinity leads to the principal theme of the treatise, an inner view of spiritual progress. In many a passage of his *Commentary on the Psalms*, Origen had already studied this way of perfection. But he was forced to defend it against the false theories of progress proposed by the heretics. In their eyes moral advancement was a discontinuous drama in which the fitful interruption of striking events dispensed from the gradual inner transformation which the Christian knows conversion to be. The treatise was about to link the different phases of the spiritual life to their principle and to show the conditions that must be postulated for its final success.

THE ORIGIN OF RATIONAL NATURES

Every good comes from God. Being is the first of all goods. The dependence of the creature is the inspiring theme of the simple and powerful emotions that find expression in the cry of the psalmist. The Greeks called this dependence by a special name, participation, but they never succeeded in developing the notion into a definite

[5] *Ibid.*, 8.

theory. At Alexandria, on the other hand, the word was royally welcomed into the domain of Christian philosophy, for only in that domain, it seems, was it possible to employ the expression to full advantage. It is a compound word, being derived from *pars* and *capere* in the Latin. The Hellenism of the third century threw the emphasis on the first half of the word, *pars*. It vexed itself unceasingly with the problem of how the divinity could subsist in itself and simultaneously communicate itself to the manifold world of created beings, how it could diffuse itself and yet remain itself. Christian thought, on the contrary, instantly gripped the other notion in the expression, the notion of receiving, and regarded the sharing and the limiting as a consequence of receiving. Christian thinkers saw from the first that creatures possess what is merely a received being, and they argued that this is the reason why creatures are limited and contingent and why they must grow gradually by a slow appropriation of the good. Further, the creature can either retain this good with God's help or lose it through his own fault.[6]

But this total dependence immediately raises a second difficulty, one more serious in the eyes of all thinkers whose primary concern was the study of the life or the mode of spiritual beings: whence comes the imperfection of creatures? The treatise recognizes this imperfection under two forms: a limiting of duration and a limiting of the good. Since it is easier to see a new idea than to elaborate its consequences, the solution is in each case a hesitant one. Instead of going direct to the heart of the theory, the notion of participation, Origen makes concessions to a method of argument which he should never have considered at all.

Take first the limiting of duration. In the Trinity, considered as principle, two powers are distinguished, a creative power and a beneficent or providential power. These two powers have, for their object, the totality of created or transient beings, since the Trinity, being uncreated and eternal, cannot exercise those power upon itself. Now, if creatures have a beginning, are we to admit that the divine poet remained for aeons without a poem, that the King was without a kingdom, that Providence was without any good that He

[6] *Ibid.*

might accomplish? We cannot imagine that there is in God any impediment to His actions or that the powers which are His—or, to speak more accurately, which are His very essence—were ever, for any period of time, idle and useless. No, says Orgien, the demiurge is not such as the heretics imagine him to be, the irrational author of an accidental and unexpected creation. His skill is supreme, unlimited by any preliminary condition. God's infinite intelligence has always had for its object a clearly defined world, the world of the ideas and species contained in that wisdom which is the joy of His eternity. There exists, then, an invisible universe of intelligences where the Creator's reign is more comprehensive than elsewhere, a kind of spiritual matter on which He acts with an action that knows neither beginning nor end.[7]

In this guise we find, under the oldest dress with which it is clothed by a Christian theologian, the classical notion of the universe of ideas, of a totality of intelligences eternally present to God, of a pre-existing world in which this present world is prefigured. But now there is another difficulty which prevents Origen from developing his thought. This pre-existing world is already the object of divine intelligence, already the object of divine power. It is composed of invisible beings, and their number is fixed in advance although the world in which they live gives the illusion of infinity. Those intelligences, so intimately associated with the Word as to be able to enjoy with Him a unique discernment of wisdom, remain nevertheless distinct from Him by nature and constitute a kind of ethereal heaven with Christ at its head, a heaven in which God finds His glory in His saints. If we remember, in addition, that every spiritual being is corporeal in some degree, with the unique exception of the Trinity, we may well ask if those essences do not constitute a higher universe. Are they creatures or are they eternal ideas? Between this semi-participation in which total emanation is halted in its stride and the radical participation implied in the doctrine of creation, Origen makes no definite choice. As a result of this indecision, his system suffers from a number of weaknesses.

[7] *Ibid.*, iv, 3-5.

THE IDEA OF TWO CREATIONS

One way of escape was open to him. He might have awakened to the fact that this new philosophy of his was making undue demands upon him. Seeing this, he might have boldly reduced this intelligible world to an eternal thought by removing from it every aspect of duration, even of indefinite duration, and every character of a pre-world, since the words "before creation" were words without meaning. Instead of grasping this possible solution, he let himself be influenced by the fashion that prevailed at Alexandria. In his efforts to throw light on the problem, instead of reforming his ontologism he pushed it to extremes. The ideas became higher beings in a celestial universe. There were two creations, one superimposed on the other. One creation was perfect, the other imperfect and inferior. The transition from eternity to time was the effect of a defection or falling away on the part of those higher beings. This fall is described, in more than one passage of the treatise, as having despoiled the life here below of its proper character and of having had the same injurious effect upon its means of salvation and its holiness. The general result is that nothing remains of the celestial city but a nostalgic memory of its glories. Between the beginning and the end, between the primal dignity and the final consummation when, thanks to the Mediator, God will shine forth again in every creature, Origen saw only a dispersion and a search for a unity that had been lost.

THE PROBLEM OF EVIL

Another difficulty presented by the imperfection of creatures was the problem of evil. It brought out even more strongly than the preceding problem the inadequacies of Origen's metaphysical system. On this point also he seemed incapable of bringing his universe into harmony with the spirit of the new philosophy.

He begins with the statement that, since the creature has received his being, he possesses the good in a manner that is limited, partial, and imperfect. In this participation Origen will seek the cause of sin and evil, which, according to the heretics, are caused by God.

To refute this pessimism of theirs, let us begin by taking a less lofty view of man and by estimating at its real value the immutable virtue which adorns all the sages and wise men of this world. Their well-known perseverance is rendered possible, first by God's primary gift; then by wisdom, which undertakes the education of the soul; and finally by the Holy Ghost, who makes the soul perfect. These are the only terms on which the soul is granted the gift of perseverance, described so eloquently by the first psalms in the recital of all the struggles it involves and all the joys it brings. The created being is divine in the measure in which God resides within it. If it ceases to desire God, to possess Him and to hold Him, it can become sinful and evil.

Our reason thus proves to us that God is not the cause of evil, and the truth is confirmed in those passages of Scripture where we find descriptions of the management of souls, the origin of the spiritual life, the powers of good and the hostile powers. Meditating on this truth, we learn the meaning of Satan's fall, the first of all sins. "Spotless purity exists in the essential being of none save the Father, Son, and Holy Spirit, but is an accidental quality in every created thing. Since what is accidental may also fall away, and since those opposite powers once were spotless and were once among those that still remain unstained, evidently no one is pure by essence or by nature, and also no one was by nature polluted." [8] The causes of evil are, then, the feeling of satiety, the diminution of love, the forgetfulness of the teachings of intelligence, the negation of the good.

The rational being's own initiative is responsible for evil. The free will with which we are endowed involves two possibilities: the possibility of making progress in wisdom and love by developing the germ of intelligence, and the possibility of falling away and, so to speak, of making progress in the neglect of the divine teachings. He who can persevere to the point of acquiring virtue for himself, can also refuse this benefit; if he does this, he becomes, by default, a principle of evil "in standing aloof from participation in spiritual gifts." Thus the conditions imposed by God for the greatness of a

[8] *Ibid.*, iii, 8. Cf. *In Psalm.*, 4, 7; *P.G.*, XII, 1161.

rational creature are mirrored in the experiences of our ordinary personal lives, but those same conditions also make us responsible for all the disorder that may mar the plan of the divine work. So the "free choice" of classical ethics acquires a new meaning. It becomes an option on salvation, and the two conceivable terms of the option are by no means of equal value. One such term is the very foundation of our being. The other term is the privation of God, a metaphysical void, a not-being, but also a not-being which affects the rational creature by depriving him of his good.

Not quite content with this solution, Origen put forward other solutions in the course of the treatise. As if the contingence of the creature did not suffice our author in his effort to explain the imperfection of created beings, he reacts to the pressure of several academic theories which concur in representing the created universe as a diminution or a degradation of the divine power. In his first description of this notion, the origin of evil appears as a gradual retrogression which begins almost insensibly. A theory of semi-emanationism safeguards the majesty of the Creator by postulating, as a link between Him and the universe, a defection or falling away which is composed of many phases; and the entire process of defection was the reverse of what could have been, for the rational being, a process of advancement in spiritual progress.[9] When Origen found that such expedients as these did not correspond with the scriptural idea of sin, he abandoned them, and they disappeared from the second book of the treatise. They were superfluous in his philosophy of participation. He decided that a sudden sin and a gradually progressive indifference were different effects of the same cause: the weakness of free will.

Another wrong notion, which Origen was at great pains to refute, was derived from the view that the inequality of created beings is an imperfection. If created beings have their origin in divine intelligence wherein there is not the slightest shadow of inequality, how can they form the hierarchy that constitutes the universe? By what falling away does the primal unity become so widely differentiated? How can souls which once possessed the love of God lose that love?

[9] *Ibid.*; "He must decline gradually and little by little."

The philosophers endeavored to solve the problem by supposing that the inequality was owing to a providence, which they deliberately confused with an immanent justice, a law of Adrastes, by which each created being is allotted the rank befitting his dignity.

DIVERSITY OF SPIRITS

It was agreed that the diversity of spirits could not emanate from God. But the origin of those diverse spirits was not clear to the philosophers in their descriptions of the plan of the universe. Origen holds that the explanation of their failure to meet the problem lies in the fact that they have a wrong notion of the condition of creatures. In the psalms and especially in the epistles of St. Paul he found the elements of a conjecture which any unprejudiced philosopher must consider. The end, or consummation, of the universe is like a returning to unity. At the name of Jesus every knee shall bend, in heaven, on earth, and under the earth. Since the end and the beginning are always the same, it can be supposed that at the beginning there was neither difference nor variety of any kind among created beings. All were equal, but they removed themselves from God unequally; and each, according to the diversity of his conduct, received his rank in the universe.

Thus Origen extended free will to the entire creation of rational beings. There is no inequality in their origin, and when they enter the realm of time there is no inequality established among them by fate. A metaphysical threshold, so to speak, separates unity from multiplicity, and divides the Creator from his differentiated work. Free will sums up the contingent nature of the universe and makes it logical. No rational being is, at any moment, incapable of choosing between good and evil. This is axiomatic in Origen's explanation of the order of the universe.

In the eyes of the philosophers who remained loyal to the classical cosmology, this was a novel theory of the universe. Clement had divided the world into two cities, one fixed and immutable, the other destined to make progress only through incessant struggle, but a recent Alexandrian theory had given to the law of nature a paternalistic slant. What Origen did was to take the universe of

Ammonius, which was marked by a wise disposition of rational beings, and to enliven it with a spiritual life of unending stress and
strain. He placed men at the very center of the universal struggle;
they were souls in an intermediate state, halfway between the angels
and the evil powers. He considered that the higher beings themselves had, for the most part, fallen away in some degree and were
capable of falling even more. On the contrary the most perverted
beings are never, he held, utterly delivered to sin or utterly lost to
hope.[10]

This anxiety to avoid the slightest admission of an original inequality shows that Origen's mind did not yet reach the level of
the Christian philosophy he had in view. The Alexandrians believed
that, if necessary imperfections exist in creation, they must be an
affront to the divine nature. Such imperfections would degrade the
dignity of God, as if creatures were attached to their principle by a
bond which is a kind of extension, like the ray that comes from the
sun or the overflow from a river which bursts its banks. Some of the
heretical sects seemed to push this notion to a point where wisdom,
in consequence of its relation with the world of men, was not really
transcendent. Apparently Origen reacted to this atmosphere, for
the first book of the De principiis shows evidence of the unconscious workings of emanationism on his mind.

When he pushed his theory to its logical consequences he found
himself confronted by Christian beliefs. He based his theory on his
concept of the heavenly order, but the mind of the Church held
that the order of heaven is not alone in proclaiming the immutable
laws by which rational beings must live. By arguing from the obedience of the purest and holiest souls, he had little difficulty in explaining the glorious liturgy with which those highest beings praised
God. But he held that they could fall away. Christianity, on the
contrary, taught that the happiness of those holy souls is immutable
and that their spiritual life is something fixed and certain. Against
his bold statement that not even the most perverted being is utterly delivered to sin, the Christian teaching was that there is a point
where the turning away from God becomes a radical aversion, an

10 Cf. *ibid.*, vi, 5.

evil inveterate and irreducible. All those teachings of Christian orthodoxy seemed to be called in question by Origen's cosmology, and serious critics asked themselves if Origen really meant that the devil could be converted. More than all the censures, and even before a single censure was launched against him, this inner departure from Christian thought ruined the cosmology of the *De principiis*.

He described, sometimes with grace and beauty, the operations of the three divine Persons. He laid the foundations of a Christian philosophy in his idea of a total participation by which the creature is dependent upon absolute Being and absolute Good. But apparently he confused the origin of created things and the eternity of the creative thought, and he failed to draw a clear distinction between their primary goodness and the perfections of God. The world was not placed in its actual setting of reality as a work created for a limited perfection; on the contrary, it was an idea of wisdom. Its basic dependence, according to the theory of participation, would have justified the welding together of a notion of time and a notion of evil. But the only use Origen seems to have made of this radical dependence of created being was to hide it at once behind the oldest dreams of Alexandrian thought.

II. THE SPIRITUAL WORLD

THE UNIVERSE

In the first book of the *De principiis*, Origen considers the source of being, of good, and of holiness; and so, throughout the entire book, he discusses the world and the created beings that inhabit it. Having discovered their principle in the divine intelligence, he devotes the second book to the study of the actual world, which is composed of those created beings. He considers the universe a community of distinct spirits, a city of obedient souls; as a necessary consequence, it is a vast living thing, with a unity that is moral rather than physical. The individual souls, which are not parts of a total soul but natures or essences irreducible one to another, work together for the general harmony, each according to its own personal value.

The physical universe has been not only organized but created for the hierarchy of rational beings. It is adapted to the peculiar capacity of each spirit. Matter is something that changes, and it lends itself to the most diverse transformations. Gross elements pass into a more subtle state. Thus, wood becomes fire, and fire ends by being changed into smoke or air. From all this Origen argues that spiritual activity, when it is associated to the body, can receive an appropriate setting and a natural object, in some such way as the divine understanding has the Word as a term of its activity and even, so to speak, for its matter. He does not push this comparison very far, remarking that probably no created being ever becomes completely incorporeal.

This kinship between rational natures and bodily matter is proved in the Scriptures, if they are examined with care and diligence. The Apostle says: "for this corruptible must put on incorruption; and this mortal must put on immortality." The detractors of matter interpret this passage as if the physical world must disappear, being swallowed up with death in the triumph of Christ. By dint of purifying itself, matter would be reduced to a quintessence and would finally disappear; and the soul, thus rendered incorporeal, could receive totally the immortal life of grace. But this notion cannot be admitted, because a higher life would not destroy what it absorbs or swallows up. In the better world that will follow this world as it has preceded it, the body will be conserved and enveloped by the soul, the power of which will grow under the direct influence of justice and wisdom. The participation will become so perfect that it will establish a union between the entire human being and God.

It is a long step from this belief to the theory of an eternal returning, with its irrational hypothesis of several successive and identical worlds. Those who uphold this theory point out that, in a process that goes on and on, the ear succeeds the grain, and the grain succeeds the ear. From this they argue that in a perpetual cycle the degradation of natural energies would find its compensation in an equivalent restoration. Origen meets this view by asserting that, although it is easy to conceive of an idea repeating itself indefinitely, we must remember that the universe is an ensemble of ideas, a system. Let us suppose a sower who is never weary, an eternal god Pan. This sower, without ever resting and without ever finishing his work, casts his seed upon the ground. But that the seeds should be thrown in the same order and in the same direction in each successive sowing is an impossibility. The world that is to come into existence after this world may be better or may be worse, but it will never be identically the same as the world which it replaces.[11]

Besides, we know from our faith that a unique event has occurred in history, an event that had no precedent and has had no renewal: the redemption. "But now once at the end of ages, He hath appeared for the destruction of sin, by the sacrifice of Himself." [12] This decisive moment marks the fullness of the ages in the passage of indeterminable periods of time. It proclaims the end, a better world, the "forever" which the psalmist longs for and to which he offers his song of praise. Such a future can be imagined as a series of ages, but in itself it is far more than that. It is the unity of the kingdom of God, the house invisible not made by hands. Men may flee from it to the delusion of a perpetual cycle of worlds or to the hypothesis of an eternal returning. But all created things must ultimately reach their consummation in God, however indefinite the course of time may seem to be. Likewise the plurality of worlds may be true; but even if it is true, it is no obstacle to the existence of one whole, one more general universe of which each of the worlds can be only a part.

Thus Origen refuted simultaneously the philosophers who believed in the eternity of created beings and the gnostics who denied it. Each of those non-Christian groups divorces the work from its principle, and ignores the truth that time is dependent upon eternity. Time derives its limitations and its value from eternity. Never has the doctrine of the Fall led to less pessimistic conclusions. Ori-

---

[11] *Ibid.*, II, iii, 4: "It seems to me impossible for a world to be restored for the second time, with the same order and with the same amount of births and deaths and actions."

[12] Heb. 9:26, quoted in *De princip.*, II, iii, 5.

gen would almost apply the words *felix culpa* to the souls that have
come into this world to animate matter and that dwell in this harmonious purgatory where the holiest among them find a fertile field
for their spiritual activities.

THE PLAN OF PROVIDENCE

The unity of the world being thus safeguarded, the providential
plan, the work of the Trinity, can be recognized therein: one only
God, the author of the Old Testament and of the New Testament;
one only Christ, the eternal Word-made-man; and the same Spirit,
equally present throughout the entire history of revelation, but dis-
pensing His gifts according to the capacity of each recipient.

Disdain for bodily creatures and for their author is, then, denial
of God. Marcion represents the Creator as a secondary and visible
divinity. His disciple Apelles makes this divinity a kind of angel.
Certain Valentinians conceive of him as a petty king who did not
know the smallness of his own empire. The Father to whose goodness the Gospel bears witness would be a higher God, reigning on
high and far removed from our state of misery. These apostates do
not see how intimately the religion of Christ is rooted in the religion
of Israel. Jesus speaks of "the Father who maketh the sun to rise
upon the good, and bad," and nature, in its noblest and lowliest
parts, glorifies the Father. This was the God of the patriarchs, and
the Temple is His dwelling place. Undoubtedly the Old Testament
presented Him under carnal images which seem to be out of harmony with the religion of the New Testament. But all such anthropomorphism cannot mislead us, any more than the parable
which tells us that God planted a vine. Such descriptions are merely
figurative, making an appeal to the feelings of our hearts. Are we not
aware that we are incapable of forming an idea of the Creator
through the eyes of the body? We can know Him only through an
inner sense, and even then we know Him imperfectly.

Origen argues that we must follow the same process of thought
when we consider the attributes of justice and goodness. The Marcionites portray their just God in colors so dark and gloomy that He

appears to be almost an evil genie. Their example is followed by the Valentinians who take their stand upon a wrong interpretation of the Gospel and refuse goodness to Jesus since He is a human creature. Logical astuteness makes it only too easy to put two divine attributes in opposition to each other: justice and goodness, for example. A possible answer to those sophists would be that both justice and goodness have evil for their contrary, and that they constitute one virtue in their opposition to evil. Besides, we know that providence undertakes the education of souls. Providence sends temptation as an occasion of possible victory, and punishment as a remedy for sin. If the idea of heavenly vengeance is repugnant to our feelings, it is especially incompatible with the sovereign Good, in whom justice is merely an aspect of goodness.

The work of providence, we have said, is almost as mysterious as God Himself. At every step of its study of that work, the human mind must pause and take its bearings. Despite the fact that we are continually observing things, we see little of the universe; the weakness of our powers is brought home to us even more eloquently when we reason about the invisible world. In any such inquiry we must resort to faith, for we are the lowliest and weakest among all rational beings. But the Word-made-man has come to us as a guide and a mediator. Let us join with the psalmist in proclaiming his two-fold royalty, human and divine, and then let us go more deeply into the study of this great plan and contemplate the abasement of the ineffable majesty, of the Wisdom known only to God the Father. To reveal the Father to men, the Word dwelt among them in the narrow and limited guise of a little child who was born of a virgin in Judea. He suffered death. More astonishing still, He endured distress of soul. But it was ordained that His presence among men should be marked by brilliant signs of His power, that His coming upon earth should be heralded by the voice of His prophets and succeeded by the mission of His apostles. "We are lost in the deepest amazement. . . . The spectacle is to be contemplated with all fear and reverence, that the truth of both natures may be clearly shown to exist in one and the same being; so that nothing unworthy or unbecoming may be perceived in that divine and ineffable substance, nor yet may those things that were done be supposed to be the illusions of imaginary appearances." [18]

This mystery, which is a mystery even to the angels, is the very heart-beat of Christian holiness. The soul of Jesus can be considered as a guide-soul united to wisdom so closely that it is capable of communicating wisdom to other souls. From the very first instant the soul that belonged to Christ was bound to the Word with such firmness of purpose and immensity of affection that it has chosen the good without ever having had experience of evil. On account of this intimate relationship an inextinguishable warmth of love has become part of its nature. Thus we can say that the soul of Christ is filled with light and love unchangeably, by an anointing which consecrates it forever. It has become, as far as possible, like the divinity which resides within it, like the Word in whom the good is not accidental but essential. So close is this union that we can compare the soul of Christ to a bar of iron which is thrust into a blazing furnace; the bar becomes red hot, it burns, it is so transformed that it becomes wholly fire. The attributes of God are inseparably united to the human body and soul of the Savior as in a *compositum* where the properties of two beings seem to be blended. The odor of the ointment has penetrated the material of the vessel, which contains the substance of the ointment, to such a degree that the odor is never lost. Other souls receive the perfume, it is true; but if they depart a little way from its fragrance, its beauty is gone. Souls hide themselves in this incomparable soul. They are enveloped in the Spirit of the Lord which overshadows it. In Jesus they find their primal unity. Through Him they obtain a share of the life which is superabundant in Him.

THE NATURES IN CHRIST

There is little in this theological disquisition to herald the historical crisis that tore the Christian world asunder two centuries later. Is Origen the precursor of Nestorius or of Eutyches? Did he

[18] *De princip.*, II, vi, 2: "If it thinks of a God, it sees a mortal; if it thinks of a man, it behold Him returning from the grave, after overthrowing the empire of death, laden with its spoils."

separate the two natures in Christ or did he blend them? The former interpretation has a greater number of adherents than the latter. If the soul of Jesus really merited by its virtues and its love to be "taken" by the Word to form the Christ, then the union of divine and human is merely moral, such as is found in a supreme degree of holiness. God resides pre-eminently in a man of whom the Scripture says: "Thou hast loved justice and hated iniquity; therefore God, thy God, hath anointed thee." The application of these words to the incarnate Word comes very close, it seems, to the teaching of Nestorius. Taken in this sense they would mean that the Son of God and the historical person of the Messias could be considered separately.

But let us note what Origen means here by merit. He speaks of it as something anterior to this present life, something acquired by the first act of love, without effort or deliberation. Is this a real merit, in the proper sense of the term? Is is not rather the nobility natural to a soul specially prepared by God in view of the Incarnation? If Origen's theory is examined thoroughly from this standpoint, it will be found free of any suggestion of Nestorianism. The divinity of Jesus is not reduced to the Father's delight in the goodness of a privileged soul. The union of the two natures is so complete that Origen calls it a blending. "Throughout the whole of Scripture, not only is the divine nature spoken of in human words, but the human nature is adorned by appellations of divine dignity." This communication of the idioms, as the theologians call it later, would be the watchword of orthodoxy.

Moreover, the human nature of Jesus is far from being absorbed in God. The soul of Jesus remains specifically a soul like other souls. It is capable, as they are, of good and evil; but it is the first of all souls. We must not be misled by the notion of blending. Plato employed it when he tried to fashion his city after the divine model, using it to signify the intervention of the ideal in human affairs. With Origen, it expresses the mystical union and the superabundance of divine good that filled the soul of Jesus. He clarifies his meaning by the example of a life of love from which is excluded every imperfection and every inconstancy. The attitude of soul which produces, in the case of a number of the saints, a practical impossibility of committing grave sins must be, in His person, a conversion of the human nature that is united to the Word in an unceasing intuition of love.[14]

If the critics desire to find in this theory any suggestions or warnings of future disturbance in the traditional balance of Christian beliefs, it would be well for them to remember that Origen was an Alexandrian. That being so, his thoughts would naturally have inclined toward something like Monophysitism, that heresy of the fifth century which affirmed that Christ had but one nature, the divine alone or a single composite nature. But, as a matter of fact, the great defect of the theory is not in the way Origen describes the soul of the Savior but in his ready use of the myth of pre-existence. Does a transcendent history admit of a time and a series of distinct acts? Origen's adherence to the old classical myth is the sole cause of the obscurity of his theory. The Platonist fable of the daemon who is the intermediary between two universes is employed by Origen against not one background but two, the temporal and the eternal. He would not have resorted to it if he had not considered the Logos exclusively as mediator. Reduced to this role of an intermediary between the Good and the created world, the Logos had to choose, from the beginning, a particular soul from rational natures. With this chosen soul it had to form the pre-existent Christ, the eternal High Priest already united to the spiritual world before making His appearance upon earth.

But when the mists were cleared away, Origen's inquiry would survive. It led to an inquiry that was eminently fruitful, to an interpretation of the soul of Jesus in accordance with Christian mysticism. At every step of that inquiry the mystic saw what made this soul infinitely superior to the souls of the holiest saints. Thus is shown, more appealingly than by any other means, the solidarity which ensures that other souls, even the most wretched, can have Christ for their model. Beneath all the flaws of this first effort to formulate a theory of the Incarnation there was the great theological

---

[14] Cf. *ibid.*, 5: "So that firmness of purpose and immensity of affection and an inextinguishable warmth of love destroyed all susceptibility for alteration and change."

truth of the imitation of the Word-made-man, our perpetual Mediator with the Father. Origen would later bring forth that same truth in his homilies and would affirm it in his treatise on prayer: "The Son of God is the High Priest of our offerings. . . . He prays for those who pray." Like well beloved children, those who resemble Him have a share, in a measure, in His sonship. His Father is the Father of all who follow in His ways.[15]

THE DESTINY OF SOULS

The destiny of souls becomes clearer to us as soon as we recognize the guide and shepherd given to us by the mercy of God. Two problems are involved in this study: first, the value of souls; and secondly, the limitations of the rational person.

In a broad sense, every living thing possesses that imaginative and impulsive substance which philosophers call the soul. On this animal life, on this blood which the Bible calls the life of the flesh, reason imposes its special form. The angels also have souls. We even speak of the soul of God when we wish to imply that He possesses in an eminent degree the faculties that we see manifested in the minds of His creatures.

Our soul is the link that binds us to the ensemble of living things. We know that it can pass beyond this present state of existence. What seems to us to be its nature is merely a transient mode of existing. The word "anima" proves this, for it summarizes the wretchedness of its actual condition and the nobility of its destiny. It is a spirit that has waxed cold from the fervor of holy things and from participation in the divine fire. Every power it possesses aspires to a consummation essential to it. It was created for the life of the spirits, and its progress implies nothing else than a continual realization of the perfection of its primal state. It needs to be enlightened, and it must enlighten in its turn. Ignorant and obscure it may be, but it always aspires to more knowledge. Waxed cold though it may be, it seeks to be warmed anew by the fire that warmed it in its beginning. Although it has turned away from the good and is now weak and enfeebled, it longs to be restored to the good and to find

[15] Cf. *De oratione*, XVI.

therein its lost substance and its vaguely remembered joys. Two passages in the Scriptures express the two modes of the soul's existence, at once the richest and the poorest among all beings; they are passages recounting what Jesus said: "My soul is sorrowful even unto death," and "Father, into Thy hands I commend My spirit."

Every good has its source, we know, in contemplation, and every good returns there. This is the same as to say that the history of the spiritual world dominates the history of created things.

Through weariness, negligence, and lack of attention, the soul loses its habits of vigilance. Then the evil inclination, taking advantage of this heedlessness and inadvertence and being allured by opportunities to assert itself, turns the soul toward the darkness where it can no longer perceive the good. The soul falls and loses its fervor. In the darkness and silence into which it is cast, there follow the estrangement from God, the sleep of laziness, and the death of the soul itself. On the other hand, the germs of reason which every creature made in the image of God possesses always within its own being offer a perpetual possibility of restoration, and are therefore the ground of a hope that the restoration can be achieved. By the practice of self-denial, by assiduity in prayer, and by the faithful performance of the duty of meditation and study, the fallen soul can regain the mental attitude enabling it to fix its attention on salutary things. As there are occasions which lead to a fall, so also there are things which are favorable to growth in holiness. Among the latter we include texts from Holy Scripture or the symbolical occurrences described in the Bible. These things cause the inner powers of the soul to lift themselves upward, so that the soul is no longer greatly concerned with material things. Then the road to spiritual progress opens before the soul, a new feeling of life is experienced, a hunger and thirst for God is felt, and a progressive enlightenment pours into the mind. The soul sees and understands. Gradually it discovers the hidden truth, with which it gradually learns to commune. Finally it begins to grow as its faith develops more and more and as it advances in the practice of contemplation. Thus, refined and purified, it is introduced at last to eternal wisdom.

Deep within our own hearts we can discover the restlessness at the origin of our diversified and unstable world, a world always either progressing or declining. To understand this world we must study our own inclinations and the consequences they involve. Within the recesses of our own being we must seek the cause of the inequalities that fill us with astonishment when we contemplate them in the behavior, the qualities, the destinies of mankind. Nothing is left to chance. A law of justice operates among created beings, however mysterious its effects may seem to be. This law is the wisdom through whom God has created everything that is.

RACISM

The city of Alexandria lay on one of the frontiers of the Roman Empire. Its great port was the gateway to the main roads of Syria. When the Christian citizen of Alexandria looked out upon his immediate environment, he was faced with the problem of different races trying to live together. The nationalities that were subject to the empire of the Caesars remained unchanged by the culture and the laws of their conquerors. On the contrary, they evinced a tendency to maintain their own national individualism, at least to the point of reviving a number of their sacred traditions. How could the upholders of Christianity maintain that there was no longer either Greek or barbarian, Roman or Jew?

This social setting gave the philosophers food for thought. As a result of anti-Semitic disturbances, a theory of racism came into fashion, as is evident from a study of Marcion's teachings. That heresiarch's followers believed in the existence of inferior races, and their theory was accepted by all the other heretical sects that shared with the Marcionites a belief in fate. Natural inequalities are obvious, said the heretics, even in the moral conscience and in the workings of human reason. No law exists that cannot be violated in some country or other by inhuman and bestial practices. The reports brought home by men who have traveled in distant lands testify to the fact that parricide, cannibalism, and even the sacrifice of human victims are accepted as lawful among entire peoples. There are many races of souls in the world. Some constitute a spiritual aristocracy by birth because they are specially prepared by God. They are a privileged class and are necessarily saved. Other souls are created for the carnal level and are destined to live as members of unrighteous nations.

We find the earliest refutations of this racial theory in the Christian literature of Syria. The Christian was quite ready to admit that every people has its own law of development, its peculiar genie, its angel good or bad. But it maintained that the relative order of souls depends on merit, on the freedom of the individual will. God, foreseeing the worth of each soul, arranges for each individual the helps by which it can profit on this earth. The fact that this apologetic was called forth by the passing problems of the day did not deter Origen from fashioning it into a more general notion applicable to the spiritual order of the universe. He argued that every soul in the world is placed in the rank best fitted for its capacity, and that in a forgotten past each soul's freedom of will either incited it to progress by imitation of God or reduced it to failure through negligence. In this way he explained why a harmony exists between the inner life of the rational being and the outer circumstances that move him to action. Divine providence continues to regulate each soul according to its needs by preparing for it occasions or circumstances which correspond to the variety of its movements or of its feelings and purpose.

The equality of souls is demonstrated by the consummation common to all of them. In the course of the spiritual struggle in which they are now engaged they never lose the possibility of attaining it ultimately. The fact that brutal or perverted beings exist in this world must not cast doubt on this truth. A single act of free will is sufficient to manifest the immortal destiny of a savage and to show the kinship he enjoys with the holiest spirits. In the unenlightened minds of rude and unlettered men as well as in the minds of those who possess a refined feeling for things invisible, there is revealed a mode of participation proper to all creatures whom God has endowed with intelligence.

DESTINY OF SOULS

In a system like this, which completely subordinates matter to spirit, proofs of the immortality of the soul are unnecessary. Their only purpose is to recall the common origin of all rational beings and to provoke us to reflect on the destiny to which God calls all of us. But it is easy to deduce such proofs from the different aspects of participation. Every intelligence has its own share of divine illumination, according to the needs arising out of the condition of the created being. Every created being must receive wisdom from God in order to be enlightened and sanctified. On this point men are no different from the angels, who are immortal. But beings are similar in nature when they share similarly in the source of their good. It follows, then, that God confers incorruptibility on human souls as well as on the highest spirits.

To be assured of the truth of this conclusion, all that is necessary is to consider the inner life of the individual. In every soul there is some feeling, or some vague knowledge, of its destiny; there is always a germ of spiritual progress; in the words of Holy Scripture, there is an image or likeness of God which can never perish. Thus our real home is in the life of eternity. The Logos, God's own perfect image, has placed within our being the reflection of Himself. Every virtue we acquire makes that reflection sharper and clearer. Our efforts to imitate the Father's perfection bear witness to our immortality. Mind is heaven's own mark placed by providence on the breast of creation, and it possesses a value surpassing all the changes of material things. It summons us, each in his own measure, to turn aside from the things of this world that will pass away and to seek our treasures in the world of the invisible.

Origen's study of the soul leads him to the consideration of the final things, judgment and sanctions. To formulate his opinions on those last articles of the faith, he prepared himself by establishing that souls are immortal and that providence calls us to salvation by various means. Relying on the Bible, he would now be confronted with Christian beliefs that were part of the Christian tradition.

Therefore he must define his views on the future life where each rational being is to achieve its appointed end.

Although sin leaves its final marks even on matter, the *De principiis* discusses an inner chastisement only. The reason for this is that we are thus given a better understanding of what "sanction" means. Sanction is not a vengeance inflicted from without, but is the achievement of a destiny that is fixed forever. Personal memory persists after death, and all our acts leave on our minds, at the moment of commission, their peculiar signs or impressions by means of which they are recalled to us. The pain of loss can come from a memory to which, by an effect of divine power, all former states of the individual soul would be presented simultaneously. Such a picture of the accumulation of sins would generate a kind of fever, the intensity of which would vary in each sinner according to the quality of his memories. This inner fermentation, induced by the object of conscience, would be the gnawing worm of which Scripture speaks. The suffering of the wicked has no other cause than this. The sinner is his own accuser in the inner court where he must defend himself against the testimony of his own heart. When this condition reaches its crisis it has something analogous to the violent sufferings that are to be seen in cases of demoniacal possession. The morbid exaltation of sensuality, the madness of jealousy, the darkness of melancholia, that immense and terrible sadness which tortures the soul and robs it of the courage to live, all these abnormal feelings take possession of the sinner who, while existing in this life, has neglected to procure any amelioration for himself.

If our thoughts turn from the consideration of conscience to that of the harmony of the world, it is certain that sinners are excluded from that harmony and have no part in it. Since every soul is created with the responsibility of adjusting itself to the order of the world, the condition of sinners has in it some disorder and unreason. This lack of outer adjustment is translated into an inner anguish. The restlessness of sinners becomes an impossibility of achieving the peace of a mental balance; they are ever in a state of disturbance, and their minds are filled with a sterile homesickness. As in the case of evil powers, they reach the point where their inveterate wickedness forms a second nature in opposition to the nature with which the Creator endowed them. Thus they become divorced from the source of good and of holiness, separated from the image and likeness of God that was a part of their spiritual life at its beginning, and deprived of the ordinary or extraordinary gifts of the Holy Ghost, which were intended to unite them to God. This is why they are spoken of in Scripture as cast into the outer darkness. They have buried their talent in the earth or tied it up in a napkin.

In this chastisement, which is perhaps only a purifying fire for those who are subjected to it, we can discern the promises which God has made to him who seeks Him. We must, however, be on our guard against the paradise of carnal delights that some of us imagine. Those who have such thoughts about the resurrection after death offer an incontestable proof that an exegetical literalism always conceals some element of sensuality, for there is a gluttonous manner of interpreting the Scriptures. But the soul which has a real knowledge of its own nature cannot assign to itself a paradise where bodily pleasures will be satisfied. It is filled with the desire to know, with the longing to possess knowledge and wisdom, to eat of the bread of life and to drink of the chalice of our hopes. "We have received this desire from God, not that it should never be gratified or be capable of gratification. The love of truth would seem to have been implanted by God in our minds to no purpose, if it were never to have an opportunity of satisfaction." [16] Here on this earth we understand little of the mechanism of things. We burn to discover their matter and form. We wish to learn the purpose for which they were made. In a word, we are consumed by a desire to know the divine efficacy by which they exist. All these are things which we are ignorant of. To speak more correctly, our faith makes us surmise what can be the joy of contemplating the wisdom of God. It gives us a first draft, a preliminary sketch in outline that prepares the way for the laying on of the true colors of the painting. It accustoms us to the thought of the divine object on which our mind works. By permitting us to study this outline of knowledge and truth, it grants us a foretaste of the beauty of the heaven we yet shall know here-

[16] *De princip.*, II, x, 5 and 6.

after. "To every one that hath shall be given, and he shall abound."

Origen's belief that the veils would be withdrawn in the heaven to which he aspired led him to reduce his theological enterprise to the most exact limits. His work as a theologian became a modest introduction to his magnificent perspective of heavenly life. Without renouncing his desire for knowledge in even the slightest degree, he learned to arrange the immediate results of his theological inquiry in a transcendent order that surpassed in every way the hopes with which he had embarked upon the inquiry.

III. THE WORLD OF NATURE

Up to this point Origen has considered the rational being under two aspects: in the life of union with God, and in the life of the world of spirits where the soul indicates the lines along which its destiny will be realized. He now turns to the study of the struggle by which the soul is delivered from the power of its lower nature. The third book of the *De principiis* is dedicated to the human heart and to the conflict always raging in the terrestrial city.

This conflict, he points out, we have already seen as a transient mode of a higher activity. But he is far from satisfied with this incomplete method of considering the human act as if it were wholly independent in its decisions. He warns us that, in any such view, we must not forget that the free choice of the will is the lowest form of contemplation. Only in diminished power and strength do there exist within us the intellectual light and the fervor which the holy spirits owe to participation with God and to the mediation of the Logos. If the universe, in this third city, seems to be shared between divine influences and human decisions, we must remember that, on this level of terrestrial being, we are unable to go beyond the data of our ordinary experience, such as we hear discussed in every sermon we listen to. The Church teaches simply the collaboration of grace and free will, without penetrating to the ultimate cause of our acts.

In the city of the purest spirits the free will of the rational being was interpreted as a power to appropriate a good which did not belong to the rational being by reason of its essence. It manifested, then, the contingent nature of the creature. In the middle city it was interpreted as the means whereby the rational being linked itself with the plan of providence and became a member of the great company of incorporeal existences. But in the present study Origen considers free will from the angle of philosophy. An immanent movement distinguishes the rational will from the impulsions of an animal sensibility. This movement permits a choice between phantasies of desire or incitement, making the rational creature fully responsible for its good or evil decisions.

PROVIDENCE AND LIBERTY

Before studying the role of temptation in the spiritual struggle, Origen decided to analyze the general conditions of the conflict. This he did in his third book, where he discusses the relations between providence and the freedom of the will. He was aware that the critics would inevitably attack the philosophical presuppositions of his moral theology. In the view of the majority of the heretical sects, providence worked as a necessity or an inexorable law of nature. By a certain predetermination or by their very constitution, souls were conditioned for salvation or for eternal loss. This meant that, as human beings are either male or female, there are spiritual souls that are constitutionally different from the common run of mankind. Marcionism derived this doctrine from certain Pauline texts that would continue to hold the interest of the theological mind. The third century is the scene of the first of the three great struggles waged about the Epistle to the Romans. Alexandrian humanism, Augustinian mysticism, and the Counter Reformation represent three periods in which theological warfare was fought on the basis of the teachings of the Apostle. Each of the three movements is marked by its own view of Christian tradition.

Marcionism took its stand on a Pauline text that later became a favorite with St. Augustine: "Therefore He hath mercy on whom He will; and whom He will, He hardeneth." [17] Because of this apparent link between the heresiarch and the great Bishop of Hippo, historians are tempted to regard the gnostics of the third century

[17] Rom. 9:18–21. Cf. *De princip.*, III, 1, 21.

as the hidden precursors of St. Augustine. But we must not forget
that every theological controversy owes its special character to a
certain mentality. Verbal resemblances are of little account in such
matters. The full meaning of a theological attitude is to be found
in the profound thoughts with which that attitude is expressed. In
judging the value of this particular link, we do well to remember
the maxim of the Gospel: "By their fruits ye shall know them."

Alexandrian humanism was concerned with problems that pertained to the beginning of religious experience. St. Augustine, on
the other hand, discussed religious experience when it was already
in full flower. The very argument used by Origen against fatalism
was later twisted by Pelagius into an argument against grace. The
doctrine of the third-century gnostics contains nothing that suggests the principles of St. Augustine's theological system. When
the Marcionites said that a soul is saved or lost through a necessity as inexorable as a natural law, they were simply borrowing the
naturalism of antiquity. Divine efficacy thus became, in their view,
an organic disposition operating like a germ hidden in the recesses
of the rational being. The effect of this predestination was to ab-
solve the soul from the obligation of perseverance. It tended to
render prayer an empty gesture. It destroyed the taste for research
and nullified the value of all studies on the inspired words of Scripture. St. Augustine's theology produced results quite opposite to
those, for it exalted the inner life and discovered the all-powerfulness of grace in prayer, in the sense of satisfaction that spiritual
victory brings, and in the wealth of spiritual enjoyment that throbs
in a heart overwhelmed by divine law.

Origen harmonized the freedom of the will with the plan of
providence. In doing so, he constituted himself the defender of
free will. As he expounds his theory, providence envelops free will,
impels it in the direction of good conduct, disciplines it, and heals
it. If we contemplate this help as it comes to us from God, we
cannot understand it. But the Christian teacher or the spiritual
director is not without evidence to convince him of its value.

The heretics, when confronted with the obduracy of the sinner,
had the habit of using three words to explain it: chance, justice,

and fatality. Origen insists that they have a wrong concept of God's justice; the justice they invoke is shortsighted and resembles wickedness rather than goodness. Sin, he says, is never a necessity. We have all seen examples of unchaste and intemperate men who were aroused to enter upon a better course of life, thus becoming sober and gentle and even persevering in that way of living. Despite evil incitements, such men persist in their salutary efforts to overcome their baser instincts.

Turning to the Pauline text and to similar passages of Scripture, he says that when we read of God hardening the heart of the sinner, we are dealing with a line of thought which is expressed in tropical or figurative language. A master says to his servant: "My patience has ruined you," thus confusing two notions, producing and permitting. But even if the Scriptural expression is interpreted in the strictest literalism, it is no argument against free will. On the contrary, it proves that this hardening of the heart was not natural and that it happened as punishment for a willful sin. The divine intervention is still going on and the action of providence does not cease. Every evil, and consequently every punishment, is subordinated to a higher end. The world is a vast purgatory in which, as we know, the soul never ceases to be provided with the particular set of circumstances appropriate to its inner dispositions.

GOD THE FRIEND OF MAN

To understand how God regulates souls according to their attitude, let us observe, first, those blessed souls that yield entirely to His influence. They become so docile that they no longer have the power to resist Him. On the other hand, the heart of stone resisting every influence of the Logos and resenting its every approach soon builds up within itself such a power of resistance that it seems, strange to say, to possess a certain strength against God. This false appearance of energy conceals the inner distress of a soul that is dragged down to earth by it own absorption with material things. But the appearance suffices for the sinner, enabling him to "attribute to himself the principle of his good and to render thanks to himself for his talents." Thus he believes that he is independent of his Creator. If the matter is thus examined, we see that the sinner hardens himself. In its extreme form, this is what Satan did. Such a process of hardening the heart has the effect of reversing the very condition of morality, because morality is founded on the dependence of rational beings upon God. Hardness of heart is a direct denial of the creature's own being. By a metaphysical falsehood the sinner is guilty of the grossest self-deceit when he seeks to persuade himself that he has not received from God his substance and his principle.

God applies a remedy to the disorganization of the soul. He leads the sinner to recognize his dependence and his need of grace. That is why He sometimes seems to abandon the sinner, who soon learns in bitter sorrow that not only his being but even his power of accomplishing good has been received from God. The hardened sinner is thus taught the value of the gifts he has rejected, and the full consequences of his mistake become obvious not only to others but to the sinner himself. Sin is destroyed only when it is dragged forth into the light of day and when the hour comes for the sinner to acknowledge God's power and to yield to the benefits that come from Him.[18] In some cases this hour is long in coming, and a temporary conversion not followed by perseverance leads the sinner into a darkness worse than before. But there is a definite moment for every human soul, a moment that is not to be measured in terms of our brief human delays. When that moment is to come God knows by His foreknowledge. He hides the healing message from those who are not yet ready for it, so that "seeing, they do not see." He is content to wait for the moment when the sinner is filled with loathing for his sins. That is why certain of His threats do not seem to harmonize with the general plan of providence. There are times when God's forbearance takes on the quality of silence. He no longer speaks to the sinner, and that is the worst punishment of all.[19]

Nothing is outside the plans of providence, not even our sins or our efforts at resistance. We can say with the Apostle that all

---

[18] *De princip.*, III, i, 17; III, i, 12.
[19] *Ibid.*, 13–16; cf. *In Exod.*; P.G., XII, 270.

the work of salvation is God's. God has endowed rational beings with the gift of free will. He imparts His enlightenment to them. He implants in their souls the germs of good and of perfection. Yet all the while He leaves them free to reject His gifts, even while He regulates the circumstances in which the soul lives and breaks down the obstacles the soul encounters. Do we not render honor to the architect who builds a house after many others have offered to build it? Is the leader who has saved a beleaguered city not given a triumph by the grateful citizens? Similarly, without further considering our very small part in the work, we attribute our salvation to the divine mercy, through whose goodness and forbearance the work is brought to completion.

Undoubtedly there was a deeper significance in St. Paul's words: "It is not of him that willeth, nor of him that runneth, but of God that showeth mercy." But that deeper significance was not excluded from Origen's system of theology, and it is worthy of note that St. Augustine never considered Origen one of the enemies of the doctrine of grace. The theologians of the seventeenth century, too anxious about this question, showed an undue severity in denouncing him as a semi-Pelagian. There are times, however, when he seems to hew too close to the line of common sense and when he appears too easily satisfied with the solutions he proposes for the great problem of predestination. But he considered his task to be completed as soon as he established against the fatalists the right to invoke the authority of Scripture. Because of his passion for exegesis, he thought he had solved the difficulty as soon as he could interpret the Pauline passage. He seems not to have realized that it was at that very moment that his task as a theologian was laid upon his shoulders.

This doctrine was not the road by which he reached the profound knowledge of the religious experience at the moment when the mystic realizes, without the smallest shadow of doubt, that he has received not only an inner fountain of God's grace but even his own desire for the Good and his own thought of asking for grace. That all perfection depends upon the Logos, was a truth that Origen acquired in his chosen domain of the contemplative life more than anywhere else. Only in his study of the illuminative way did he approach Augustinianism. His analysis of the act of virtue taught him nothing more than God's collaboration with man. It was difficult for him, as for all the men of his time, to believe that in every action there is already something of contemplation and that the saints are inspired in their works as in their thoughts. Was this because of his own fondness for speculation? Was it merely his Oriental distrust of external effort? Was it the prejudice of the Platonist against the world of sense? We do not know. But it is certain that the freedom of the will, if thus separated from its sources, could become, for him, a little world that was quasi-autonomous and capable of imposing its own conditions on the grace of God.

Perhaps for the same reason—because he failed to affirm the entire gratuitousness of salvation and because, in reducing predestination to a providential system of healing, he despoiled the mystery of much of its dignity—it was repugnant to him that salvation was not universal and that every evil did not possess the character of a test or a remedy. On this point St. Augustine parted company with him. The Bishop of Hippo had, like Origen, a soul that was sensitive to the way God works among men. Unlike the Alexandrian, he did not believe that providence, to achieve its ends, had need of any special pleading on our part.

TEMPTATION

Under the guidance of providence, life is a continual trial by which the wicked man is corrected and the righteous man is granted opportunities of showing his merit. In conclusion, then, we must explain what temptation is. We have seen that it is something from which the spiritual man is never exempt, however advanced he may be. St. Paul says: "For the flesh lusteth against the spirit; and the spirit against the flesh." Why should there be this struggle, if matter is not intrinsically sinful? Evil is neither in the flesh itself nor in the spirit itself, but is to be sought in the fall. Let us concede that it is in the flesh, so far as the embodied soul is a spirit that has fallen from its high estate and lives now on a

lower level of being than that for which it was created. In the past
the soul was capable of entering into the enjoyment of a life of
contemplation. It preferred, however, to turn toward perishable
things. In that wrong choice we have the origin of the darkness,
of the heavy weight of the body, and of all the other causes of desolation in which the soul now lives.

Now let us consider the ready answer of those who say that the
devil is the cause of temptation. This answer fails to take account
of the fact that the devil's power is derived from the weakness of
the soul. Is that power ever exerted unless the soul is off guard
and lacking in vigilance? Does not the devil take advantage of the
lowering of our resistance owing to luxury and sloth? Seizing the
occasion of the first transgression, he presses us hard in every way,
seeking to extend our sins over a wider field. He knows how to
profit from sin, for he was the first sinner on this earth. He exploits
the threefold temptation of the body, of external things, and of our
thoughts. He turns a man of uncontrollable anger into a murderer.
He takes full control, we know, in the morbid states of obsession,
of madness, and of melancholia. He offers such incitements to sin
that even the purest soul must be vigilant against the merest defilement from his assaults. But his attacks are never greater than our
powers of resistance. No being, except the Savior, has ever had to
withstand the attacks of all the powers of hell.[20] Therefore the
great occasion of sin is the flesh itself, with its instincts that turn
the soul away from its true end. Within our body there are germs
of evil, opposed to the germs of good which God has implanted in
the mind. The human will, which of itself is weak to accomplish
any good, readily yields to those instincts. Then the memory, in
its weakness to hold fast to good, makes the sinful impressions
even stronger.

But the most subtle of all temptations are those arising from
intellectual concupiscence. This we understand to be such as the
secret and occult philosophy, as they call it, of the Egyptians, the
astrology of the Chaldeans, the knowledge of high things promised
by the Hindus, and the many other kinds of opinion which are

[20] *Ibid.*, ii, 2–6.

nothing but the deceitful wisdom of the devils, the wisdom of the princes of this world. To this we must also add the common opinions prevailing among the Greek about divine things. A consequence of this so-called wisdom is to be found in the heresies, which are the degenerate offspring of minds unable to accept the truth or to reject it. As we cannot doubt the sincerity of those heretics, we must conclude that they are the dupes of their own wild imaginings. Moreover, as there is a peculiar energy or power which is the inspirer of poetry or of the arts, so also there are energies or powers of sinful inspiration. These latter energies or powers have no purpose but to ensnare and injure men who are engaged in searching for a truth that would uplift them and ultimately save them.

Thus we see that there is within us a warfare of thoughts, an inner conflict, as if we possessed both a spiritual soul and a carnal soul. The human will is unceasingly torn between the spirit that adores and the flesh that lusts. But perhaps the Apostle, in speaking of the wisdom of the flesh, was using a metaphor, as when we say that blood cries out for vengeance. The human soul possesses, in addition to its spiritual functions, the power of animating matter. It lends a voice to the appetites when it submits to them. Therefore the Apostle says that all the passions, the rivalries and jealousies and so forth, are "works of the flesh." In the lukewarm soul those works of the flesh are multiplied. A sort of animalism with which it has let itself be endued makes conversion a slow and somewhat difficult undertaking, as we so often see in the case of the libertine. Such a condition of things places all the faculties of the rational will at the service of the irrational animal within the soul.

Temptation is the conflict between these two inconstant factors. On the one hand there is the body, with its appetites always crying out for satisfaction, because it is not sufficient to itself; on the other hand there is the soul, always in a state of unrest because it has lost the perfection in which it was created. Further, the elements of matter are unstable, and therefore the body is ceaselessly undergoing changes in its substance. But the mind is subject to change only by accident, when it is affected by the privation of good. Its substance is then veiled, as it were, in some such way as the beauty of a painting is hidden by a cloudiness of the atmosphere or by the dust adhering to it.

The purpose of this mobility on the part of the soul is that God should be, in the Apostle's phrase, "all in all." This does not mean that God's perfections are achieved by the transformations taking place in the world. It means that rational beings—the part of creation which is made specially to receive God and to which matter is subordinated—transform themselves at the end of the world by completing themselves in God. The sufferings and temptations which rational beings must undergo in this life are to convert them, to purify them, in a word, to give them back to themselves. God becomes really all in them, if they feel, think, see, and hold Him. Then they achieve their perfection. As soon as the full measure of the soul's capacity for God has been satisfied, nothing more can be added to it.[21]

Thus we see that Origen's doctrine remained true to itself throughout the long disquisition on rational beings. The fundamental dependence of the creature is affirmed in its primal perfection, in its fall, in its rise, and finally in its consummation and end. When Origen first studied the theology of the inner life, he saw that, if it were to convey the opulent hope of Christianity in all its fullness, it stood in need of a profound analysis that could make known the weakness of the flesh and the all-powerfulness of God's grace. Sometimes his exposition of the wisdom of Christ, that wisdom which is foolishness to the Gentiles, was too much a matter of reason. But in a day when the philosophers taught that man's highest wisdom could be attained only by escaping from all the toils of evil matter in favor of the immutable insensibility of the gods, the treatise gave a new and tremendous impetus to the work of the Academy of Alexandria.

[21] *Ibid.*, vi, 3: "so that when all feeling of wickedness has been removed and the individual has been purified and cleansed, He who alone is the one good God becomes to him 'all' and that not in the case of a few individuals, or of a considerable number, but He Himself is 'all in all.' "

CHAPTER XIV

The Effects of the Treatise on Origen's Teaching

THE subsequent history of the *De principiis* throws light on Christian tradition and on the trend of Christian theology in the period when Origen lived. It was a historical period in which the inner forces that were guiding Christianity were revealed more clearly than at any other time in the history of the early Church. The value of such a work as the treatise is enhanced when the author, as in Origen's case, is quite aware of the implications of the task to which he puts his hand. "And I may tell you from my experience, that not many take from Egypt only the useful, and go away and use it for the service of God." [1] Knowing the scruples that challenged his own faith, he understood the resistance of his hearers. His immediate public were members of a Christian community which, with the possible exception of Rome itself, paid more attention than other Christian groups to the quality of the teaching offered to them.

When he set out upon the task of formulating a Christian cosmology, he foresaw that a number of his followers would consider it superfluous to embark on even the smallest inquiry on the order of the universe. In all the chapters where he treated in any way of the relations which matter and soul bear to the physiology of rational beings, he left his readers completely free, without hiding his own preferences. He took this attitude partly from prudence, but chiefly to maintain a principle that was very dear to him: a respect for other minds which had equally a right to the truth, to be attained by them in their own measure and perhaps in ways different from his. In imitation of providence, that is in itself the divine system of teaching, he held that "whoever discusses mys-

[1] *Epist. ad Greg.*, 2; P.G., XI, 89.

terious things ought to choose the moment to introduce new concepts without doing harm to him who listens to the lesson." So he
instructs the reader gradually, and always within that reader's capacity. When he stands at the threshold of an ineffable mystery,
he imposes no conjectures, but says just enough to stimulate his
hearer to further inquiry, to help in the growth of faith, and to
increase the desire for God. Thus he avoids both timidity and presumption. But in free questions there is a wrong direction and a
right thought, both of which the master perceives in the soul of
his hearer. By observing his pupil, he knows whether the teaching
will become fertile or will perish. In such matters Origen had a
kind of instinct which was the assent of Christianity, the agreement
of all those who believe the Church's message.

In the course of the successive dissertations which compose the
treatise, he found it necessary to give further explanations of his
ideas. In the first book it seemed that the universe was an emanation of the divine ideas, a sort of diffusion to which matter lent its
inexhaustible diversity. The beginning of things in time was a
question that was passed over in silence; at least his followers had
not recognized it. In the third book he definitely states that "this
world was created and took its beginning at a certain time." [2] This
is one of the points defined by the Church when it teaches the
history of origins. The Mosaic account permits of no doubt on
the matter, even if it contains a more profound meaning.

SCHOLARLY OBJECTIONS

The objections he had expected were not confined to those first
reactions on the part of his own followers. As soon as the consequences of his doctrine began to be manifested in such important
things as scriptural interpretation and the Christian way of life, he
had to meet criticism from circles outside his own school. Those
objections came from the learned and also from the public opinion
of the Christians. Under this pressure he took care, in his succeeding works, to revise his doctrine more and more. The result of

[2] *De princip.*, III, v, 1.

all this correction and adjustment was a real reform of his system without his ever acknowledging any change.

At the time when he composed the treatise he had not yet written his commentary on the creation of man according to the Mosaic account. The first man, the body made of the slime of the earth, the tree of life which was to be cultivated, all the realism of the Bible was quite forgotten in the transcendent history portrayed in the first book of the treatise. The Academy at Alexandria had not quite parted company with the literal sense of the words of Moses. A very powerful tradition, going back to the time of St. Paul, rejected the symbolism associated with the name of Philo. The famous Jew of Alexandria had been successful in finding the fable of Plato in the Book of Genesis; according to him, the skins with which Adam and Eve had clothed themselves before going forth from Paradise represented bodies; they were crude and perishable coverings wherein the souls of the two sinners were imprisoned because of their sin. This was something the Christians had never admitted. St. Irenaeus, Hippolytus, and Tertullian spurned this interpretation. But, if Origen were to adhere to his own system of origins, he should have accepted it. That, however, he did not care to do, for he recoiled from asserting that corporeal life was a punishment for sin as soon as he perceived the pessimistic consequences of any such proposition. Other retractions would follow, and they were of greater importance than this.

His theory of pre-existence was definitely Platonist, and he worked it into his interpretation of biblical passages that could have been explained easily without the use of any such profound conjecture. The divine vocation by which the prophets were set aside from the bosom of their mothers stood in no need of being explained by a theory of pre-existing merits. Indeed the theory is suspiciously like metempsychosis. As soon as he realized this, Origen repudiated all connection with the absurd and unholy doctrines which taught that human souls can be incarnated in animals. To meet the charge that he had been too hasty in his interpretations of Scripture, he promised to write a treatise on the soul. In fact, he never wrote it and left only the substance of it in his *Commentary on the Canticle of Canticles.*

At the Academy, in the period before his trial, he completed his work of interpreting the Mosaic account of creation, and he wrote his final opinions on that matter, probably in the fourth volume of his *Commentary on the Book of Genesis.* During that same period he was busy with the section of this commentary that included the part from the fourth volume to the end of the eighth. His explanation of original sin belonged to those last-named volumes.

During the years immediately following the publication of the treatise, he was content to impress upon his learned critics that his system was far from being a Greek philosophy in disguise. At that time, interest in the work was still confined to scholarly circles. But the sentence which expelled him from his native Church of Alexandria was not slow to affect a doctrine the novelties of which had been undoubtedly one of the inner causes of the trouble that came upon him. This time he was judged, as he had long been judged, both at the bar of public opinion and at the tribunal of authority. The first dogma with which he was formally reproached was that in which he laid himself open to the charge of teaching that the devil could be saved. In his *Letter to the Alexandrians* he defended himself against the charge of upholding this heresy.

POPULAR OBJECTIONS

Public opinion, which had no patience with subtle abstractions, interpreted his doctrine of indefinite liberty and universal salvation as leading to no other conclusion. On this point Origen made a genuine retractation. He warned his over-zealous followers against the applications suggested to them by the notion of final restoration. They imagined that beyond a future age there was yet another age when all punishments would end. But Origen said to them: "I know souls who remain so conquered by their own sinfulness that, if they are not pardoned in the next world, they will not be any more pardoned in the worlds that come after it."

His pupils and supporters glorified his writings. Thoughts that were uttered by him merely as conjectures were elevated to the rank of dogmas, and his interpretation of the Gospels was employed to give them authority. Origen was quick to decline this dangerous form of hero-worship. His enemies, on the other hand, excited by the mistakes and the exaggerations of those who supported him, made him the victim of their calumny. They even went so far as to express the tendencies of the treatise in a set of formulas, but only to condemn them. Here we see the beginnings of Origenism: propositions craftily strung together, questions transformed into categorical assertions, expressions surprised in the heat of controversy and clumsily forced by the zeal of his pupils or twisted by the malice of his adversaries. Where he had discussed an open question, his critics discovered unsound opinions. In his dissertations on other matters, they found heresies, and they were quick to make a list of them. Origen complained that his work had not been understood, that it had been misinterpreted by his inexperienced pupils and altered by his foes. The treatise was an object of calumny. He used to say that it was the cause of the misfortunes that befell him.

But he was not entirely free from blame for all this. He had applied to theology the peculiar method of a sort of veiled and esoteric teaching in which the master permitted his most advanced pupils to guess at the solution that fitted his system of thought. That being so, he should have known that the critics would attribute to him, instead of conjectures, undeveloped doctrines which would becloud his entire system. It was a simple matter of logic that his esoterism would lead to such a result. In more than one passage he had left himself open to charges that could not be called unfounded. In the end he was able to avoid heresy only at the cost of several inconsistencies. He is not a heretic. Undoubtedly he did not consider himself bound by conjectures he uttered in the heat of controversy or in the hours of burning ambition to arouse those around him to contemplation on divine things. Twenty years later all that he retained of his Alexandrian labors was the feeling that inspired it. Piece by piece, the complicated scaffolding of his cosmology had fallen away because the history of rational beings could be supported without it. The world or universe had become for him in the Christian way of life either the Church, the body of the faithful whom Christ, the Light of the World, has saved; or it was "a part of this earthly place, the men who dwell here with us and to whom the Church is a stranger"; [3] or it was the multitude of those who are still in ignorance of Christ's message and before whom the light begins to shine, men who dwell within the fringe of a shadow that will soon retreat before the light of the Church.

So we find him two decades later when he has forgotten "the compacted whole formed of heaven and earth, and those in it." He has long since crossed the threshold of wisdom. All that remains of his early work is the natural elan, the plan laid aside, the spirit that impelled him in those first labors. In his eyes, nothing has changed, for he holds little account of what he borrowed from pagan learning. His preoccupation with divine things has never been interrupted. In commenting on the kingdom of God, he still asks himself the old question: Why are the angels unequal? And the answer is always the same: each in his measure and according to his progress. But the vast theater of the universe and the succession of ages are forgotten. A single thought dominates him, the thought that was undoubtedly the inspiration of the treatise written twenty years before: the diversity of souls. In the Christian assemblies, in the net that was cast into the sea, how diverse is sin, how many kinds of men, good and bad! There are those who content themselves with the mere observance of the law. Others go as far as the precepts of the Gospel, and such men are of Christ but are not yet truly Christian. And there is a third class of men who think with the apostles and are really of the Church. To be held by some meshes of the net is good. To be enveloped and enclosed within the net itself is a far better thing.

Later still, when he meditates on the prayer of the woman of Canaan, there emerges the second problem: How is progress possible? Again, the answer is unchanged. The rhythm of his early teachings is repeated in a page that is like a spiritual translation of

[3] *In Joan.*, VI, 38; P.G., XIV, 301; *In Matt.*, XIII, 20; P.G., XIII, 1149, 1152.

the treatise, except that it in no way recalls the pre-existence of souls or their successive incarnations. No soul is ever so debased as to be utterly without hope, for the restoration can compensate for the fall. "The more rational condition changes into one more irrational, undergoing this affection in consequence of great sloth-fulness and negligence. But also, in the same way, a will that was more irrational, because of its neglect of reason, sometimes turns and becomes rational, so that what was a dog, accustomed to eat the crumbs that fell from the table of its masters, comes into the condition of a son. . . . He who is reproached as a dog and yet is not indignant at being called unworthy of the bread of children, will obtain the gentle answer of Jesus, saying to him, 'Great is thy faith.' " [4]

The author of the treatise has passed beyond the anxieties of theology and history. He has stripped away the perishable gar-ments that hid the immortality of his work. His love of humanity, his optimism, his dislike of sloth, his appeals for the conversion of the Christian, his hope that is stronger than every evil—all this has survived in a philosophy that has been nurtured in wisdom, deep-ened by experience, and freed from the ambiguities that vexed him in the writing of the treatise.

[4] *In Matt.*, XI, 17; *P.G.*, XIII. 964.

CHAPTER XV

The Prologue of St. John

THROUGHOUT the whole course of the *De principiis*, Origen kept the Bible in the forefront, appealing to its authority to support his dogmas and to prove his conjectures. In the third book, which is devoted to an analysis of free will, he sought to correct the erroneous interpretations proposed by the fatalists about certain biblical texts. The fourth book is more constructive, for in this section of his work he transformed the symbolism that had long been fashionable at the Academy of Alexandria into a genuine technique of biblical research. He illustrated the value of this exegetical method by a choice of examples where the boldest application of Alexandrian symbolism seemed to be successful in uncovering the spiritual meaning beneath the words of the text. Since the whole of Scripture is inspired, he held that its apparent contradictions and obscurities are a challenge to the inquirer to dig more deeply into the mine of significance hidden beneath the apparent meaning. We cannot have too lofty an idea of the greatness of God or of that mysterious wisdom that is so far above the wisdom of men.[1] If we wish to let the divine wisdom speak to our hearts, we must put aside the simplicity of our mental adolescence; we must remember that, as there are degrees and ranks in the order with which the Holy Ghost regulates the Church, so there are degrees in knowing. Thus arises the necessity for us to pass from the mere wording of Scripture to the deeper sense which the words envelop. Since the Gospels also have their symbolism, they are no exception to this rule. "The historical order of the narrative is often interrupted by numerous lessons presented under the covering of the

---

[1] The first chapter is devoted to the inspiration of the Scriptures; the second shows the dangers of literalism; the third draws its arguments from some obscure passages where the literal sense is impossible. Cf. *De princip.*, IV, ii, 9.

letter. Divine ordinances and commandments are not always given under the form we would naturally expect." [2]

Origen held, therefore, that there is a spiritual Gospel which contains the higher teachings and that it is hidden beneath the words of the four Evangelists. He drew its outlines toward the end of the *De principiis* when he expounded his doctrine of the Logos and discussed the appeal of that invisible Wisdom which assists the Father and has created all things. But the treatise did nothing more than prepare the approaches and construct the foundations of the great system of theology which he proposed to formulate. His *Commentary on the Gospel of St. John* would finally give expression to his theological project. Better than any other of the four Evangelists, the apostle who announced the eternal gospel would allow Origen to satisfy, in one great effort, the impatience of his admirers and especially of his dear friend Ambrose. In the Gospel of St. John we read of Jesus as the light of the world. In the inspired words of that message Origen was able to find the real meaning of Christianity.

I. THE JOURNEY TO ANTIOCH

Origen was returning from a journey when his friend imposed this new task upon him. "Our whole activity is devoted to God, and our whole life, since we are bent on progress in divine things. . . . In what must our first fruits consist, after the bodily separation we have undergone from each other, but in the study of the Gospel? For we may venture to say that the Gospel is the first fruits of all the Scriptures." [3] There is nothing in these words to suggest an absence of Ambrose, as has sometimes been supposed. Assuming that they refer to a journey on Origen's part, we must establish what journey it was if we are to discover the date when Origen began his work on St. John's Gospel.

[2] *Ibid.*
[3] *In Joan.*, I, 4; *P.G.*, XIV, 25.

DATE OF THE COMMENTARY

The first conjecture is that Origen's reference to a journey was made after his return from Palestine, where he had gone on the occasion of the riots in Alexandria. This leads one historian to assert that the date of the composition of the first book of the *Commentary* was about 218 or 219, the period subsequent to the disturbances. But we know with certainty that Origen's exile interrupted the beginning of the sixth volume, and it is unlikely that he took twelve years to write the preceding five volumes. Those volumes form a unity; they are written from the same standpoint and deal with the same doctrine. Without curtailing his other activities and in spite of the persecution, Origen took less than five years to produce the twenty-five volumes that follow.

The account given by Eusebius suggests a much more probable hypothesis. That historian assigns the beginning of the *Commentary*—which he erroneously thought was Origen's first work—to the period of his sojourn at Antioch. Origen had been invited to that city by the mother of Emperor Alexander Severus. Her name was Mamaea, and she was the granddaughter of Bassianos, high priest of the Sun at Emesus. The imperial dynasty to which she belonged was disgraced by the fact that a murder had been the means by which the ruling power passed from one cousin to another. Only the women of the imperial family were outstanding. A sense of priestly royalty marked their mentality. They were superstitious and cruel, ambitious for power, devoted to the religion and philosophy of the paganism in which they were reared. Julia Mamaea, however, was distinguished for her loftiness of character. She heard reports about Origen from the members of her retinue. Eusebius tells us that during a visit to Antioch "she desired greatly to see the man and especially to make trial of his celebrated understanding of divine things."

It was a matter of public knowledge that the Academy of Alexandria did not condemn Greek philosophy completely. The Christians of that center of learning were somewhat tolerant of the worship of the Sun, a learned and philosophical religion. They preferred an enlightened and educated paganism to a worship of idols, never foreseeing that this new mysticism, at that time almost official, would soon gather around itself all the foes of Christianity and put the Church in great danger. "A third class worship the sun and moon and all the host of heaven, wandering, it is true, from God, but with a far different and a better wandering than that of those who invoke as gods the works of men's hands, silver and gold—works of human skill." [4] Before the coming of the true religion the stars were offered as objects of worship to beings who were incapable of making the effort of abstraction needed for the act of contemplating the spiritual world. The human mind was content with this visible kind of providence and failed to penetrate beyond the region of the stars where the majesty of the divine Reason is more manifest than elsewhere.[5]

Alexander Severus was a priest of the Sun. But he had created for himself a personal religion by joining together all the forms of worship that had ever been used by learned men, for he believed that all such men were enlightened by the Sun of intelligence. He included Christ in his list of sages. Besides, the persecution of the Christians had been slackened under Caracalla and had now become a sort of tolerance. Sometimes the official attitude was one of benevolence, which occasionally was interrupted by sudden bursts of cruelty. Because of the changed conditions Origen accepted the invitation extended to him by the mother of the gentle and religious Emperor. The historian Eusebius in his loyalty to the Caesars does not fail to recall with admiration that the imperial lady sent a company of her military guards to escort the theologian to her palace. It almost seems that the historian is anticipating the terrible happenings of the following century and is presenting the incident of Mamaea's reception of Origen as a ray of sunshine that would quickly disappear in the darkness of the persecution marking the end of the century. After the peace which the Church has enjoyed, the memory of the Christians will no longer go back to the preceding century and consider it an era of

---

[4] *Ibid.*, II, 3; P.G., XIV, 112.
[5] *Ibid.*

persecution. The faithful will forget the triumphs of the Church's martyrs and the sufferings inflicted upon them a hundred years ago.

Eusebius goes on to say: "With her he stayed some time, exhibiting innumerable matters calculated to promote the glory of the Lord and to evince the excellence of divine instruction, after which he hastened back to his accustomed engagements." If the historian's account is correct, Origen's visit to the Emperor's mother took place after the accession of Alexander Severus to the imperial throne and after the election of Urban to the Roman pontificate. Those two events belong to the year 222 or 223. If we are not prepared to accept this date as it is implied in the account given by Eusebius, we have no historical foundation for the alleged visit, for there is no other evidence to show that the Empress was at Antioch during her son's reign. On the other hand, she was certainly absent from Rome at this very time, as we know from a letter which the Emperor wrote to her and in which he sought her advice about certain matters. The problem is even more difficult if we place the visit in the year 218, on the occasion of Origen's sojourn in Palestine; in that year the imperial family was engaged in the grim struggle of protecting itself against its rivals. It would be even worse to assign it to the years 230–31, when Origen was visiting other parts of the East, for at that date the Emperor was at Antioch in preparation for his expedition against the Parthians.

When everything is considered, it seems most likely that the visit to the Empress took place about 224 or 225. This hypothesis agrees perfectly with the account given by Eusebius. According to him, the beginning of the *Commentary on the Gospel of St. John* —or the beginning of Origen's writing career, in his opinion— must be assigned to the early years of the reign of Alexander Severus. The first four volumes of the Commentary could have been written between 226 and 229, the fifth volume could have been composed during the voyage in the East in 230–31, and the sixth was interrupted by his exile in the subsequent year.

II. THE GOSPEL AND THE GOSPELS

No single work of Origen's was so intimately bound up with his life as his *Commentary on the Gospel of St. John*. Not only did he dedicate it to a personal friend, but he actually wrote it to that friend for the purpose of imparting to him the higher knowledge to which every spiritual Christian was entitled. It is the obligation of every Christian engaged in the service of the New Testament to seek out the most advanced souls, the firstlings who are to be gathered out of the tribes and who are marked with the seal of the true life of contemplation. Origen recognized his friend Ambrose as being of this chosen number, and to him he confided all his ideas. Without any effort to force them upon Ambrose, he would again bring forth the boldest speculations of the *De principiis:* the procession of Wisdom, the pre-existence of souls, the allegorical meanings hidden in the Bible. Not quite content with this, he would incur the risk of giving some applications of those conjectures. Laying aside his professorial habits of detachment, he weaves into his Commentary a number of discreet and personal confidences. In his preface, for example, we find gentle hints of all that he expects from his system of Christian gnosis, and in the pages that follow we meet references to the great quarrel that culminated in his banishment from his native diocese; later still, we encounter also avowals of his disillusion and regrets that are somehow fired with a new boldness.

CHARACTER OF THE COMMENTARY

The teaching which he sets forth is, at first, almost entirely intellectual. But in the course of those years, as volume follows volume, he seems to develop the habit of writing for the human heart, and the delicacy of his emotional approach gives us a foretaste of the most beautiful pages of his Homilies. The volumes written in exile show more adjustments of his doctrine than do those composed in Alexandria. In those later volumes we see the yielding of the gnosis to the power of his theological genius, we witness his cosmology giving place little by little to the study of the soul and of prayer, and we perceive his vast knowledge of religion abasing itself as he grows into an ineffable intimacy with Jesus Christ. As the work approaches its conclusion, Origen the theologian yields to Origen the mystic, and the final pages become almost a part of his *Commentary on the Canticle of Canticles.*

He had not yet studied the New Testament in itself. Suddenly he saw its grandeur, for he found in its pages something more than theological arguments and something richer than principles of biblical interpretation: the presence of Jesus, the concrete vision of the fact of Christianity, the good tidings. For him, those three things surpassed everything else. "The Gospels are four. These four are, as it were, the elements of the faith of the Church, and out of these elements the whole world that is reconciled to God in Christ is put together." [6] But what are these good tidings, and what do they announce? Origen answered his own question by becoming the brother of the God-man. The good tidings are everything in the coming of the most precious of all good things. With a realism rare in Origen's writings, this is the thought that vibrates through the opening pages of the *Commentary on the Gospel of St. John.*

The work begins with an exaltation of the Old Testament prophets, for the Marcionites and the pagans held that prophetical inspiration was something akin to the unconscious delirium of the soothsayers. The great figures had come in their appointed time. They were men of purity and holiness, souls filled with the divine light, bearers of a message which was obscure for other men only and which they themselves saw fulfilled in the glory of Jesus Christ. In a certain sense, they were greater than the apostles, for the light of their holiness illuminated the darkness of the times in which they lived. They were the mystical ambassadors of the Savior, delegated by Him to take His place before He assumed our human nature.

Assuredly, if we consider merely the message itself, the Old Testament was incomplete. It needed to be clarified. But, according to Origen, the function of Jesus in fulfilling the Scriptures was

[6] *Ibid.,* I, 6; P.G., XIV, 29.

nothing else than to make manifest the truths that were already there. Had the Gospels, then, no other purpose than to justify a method of Scriptural exegesis which had been, up to that time, a matter of dispute? Did they announce to mankind nothing else than the logic of the method of biblical study employed at the Academy of Alexandria? Origen preferred, above every other technique of biblical interpretation, the method that enabled him to interpret Scripture against a background of timelessness. This depreciation of the historical elements of Scripture exposed him to the grave danger of missing the full import of the message and of robbing the Gospel of the privilege of being the announcer of a new order of men. Fortunately his intellectualism was conquered by his deep feeling for the proved and tested fact of Christianity. He discovered a way of escape from the difficulty. It was a narrow way, but it sufficed for him.

EXPECTATION OF THE PROPHETS

The New Testament would bestow upon men an incomparable gift: a presence.[7] Generation after generation of men had waited and longed for that presence. The Messianism of the Jewish people is expressed in that question of John the Baptist, when he sends his disciples to ask the Savior: "Art Thou He that art to come, or look we for another?" The Samaritan woman made confession of her belief in the great promise when she said: "I know that the Messias cometh (who is called Christ); therefore, when he is come, he will tell us all things." Of Moses and the prophets it would be nearer the truth to say that they awaited and expected the mystery of the incarnate Word. That mystery was something they had already seen, at least in the brief flash of an intuition or in the recesses of their own souls. The ancient days had witnessed, then, an annunciation, but not the proclamation, of an actual good already foreseen with the eyes of faith; but it had not been granted to them to receive the glad tidings that caused joy in the hearts of all who were disposed to listen. To fulfill a prophecy is the same as to make it manifest, to express it on the plane of reality. "The

7 *Ibid.*, I, 9; P.G., XIV, 36.

Savior, when He sojourned with men and caused the Gospel to appear in bodily form, by the Gospel caused all things to appear as gospel (good tidings) ." [8]

But if we follow the development of the message from its first flowering up to its fruit, which is the Gospel, we are confronted with a new question. Do the good tidings not continue to bear fruit in the Acts of the Apostles and in the canonical Epistles? Is not this last part of the New Testament the most perfect part of the Bible, as was the belief of certain heretics who made the *Epistle to the Romans* the norm of all Scripture and considered St. Paul the type of the predestined soul? It would be easy to reply that these final books of the New Testament are of lesser inspiration than the writings of the Evangelists. Paul and Peter speak in virtue of the apostolic power which they have received and not in the simplicity of prophetical inspiration. They are not on the same level as that, "Thus sayeth the Lord Almighty." They rely on their own authority, or they quote from other parts of the sacred writings. Their works constitute a kind of Christian wisdom, it is said. But, although their teachings are wise and worthy of belief, their place is in tradition rather than among the writings that form the foundations of the Christian faith.

Origen, however, prefers to hold that "all the New Testament ought to be called the Gospel." Every page of it has the sweet odor of the presence of Jesus, and "it also contains many praises of Him and many of His teachings, on whose account the Gospel is a gospel." [9] Every written account which establishes the coming of Jesus and inspires faith in His person deserves this name. Even when the apostles and their companions are not recounting His actions, His discourses, or His passion, they are carrying on, in a wide sense, their work as evangelists in pursuit of their task of preaching the Christian faith. Thus they fulfilled their providential mission, which is the same for all the writers of the New Testament and which can be abrogated only by the coming of the spiritual gospel at the end of time. As disciples of the Savior, they

[8] *Ibid.*, I, 8; *P.G.*, XIV, 33.
[9] *Ibid.*, I, 5; *P.G.*, XIV, 28.

carried out that mission to an eminent degree, and the Epistles are the echo of their preaching. So we find St. Paul speaking of his own gospel, although he left no work under that title. The entire New Testament is the first fruits of the Bible, and the Gospel of St. John cannot be separated from it.

EXCELLENCE OF ST. JOHN'S GOSPEL

If we are unable to distinguish differences of degree in inspiration, it is quite otherwise in the case of revelation. St. John's Gospel is the first fruits of the New Testament. No other Evangelist enables us to see so clearly the divinity of Christ. It almost seems as if the other three writers had left to him who reclined on Jesus' breast the greatest and most complete discourses about the Savior. His account speaks of Him whose genealogy had already been set forth, but it begins to speak of Him at a point before He had any genealogy. In the beginning was the Word; that is, in divine Wisdom and at the beginning of every created thing was (or is) the Word. The Word was with God, and the Word was God; the reason being that the Word was the expression of the divine ideas. The same (this Word-God) was in the beginning with God; in an intimate and necessary relation which united Him to the divine intelligence. All things were made by Him, and without Him was made nothing that was made; without Him was made sin and evil. In Him (without any development whatever) was life: what was made by Him shared in this life which He alone essentially possessed with the Father. In Him was life: with all its perfections. The life was the light of men: the participated life was, in the highest degree, the light of men. The light shineth in darkness: among imperfect and sinful beings. And the darkness did not comprehend it: however ruthlessly the darkness pursued the light, it could not overtake it.

The first book of the Commentary is devoted to the elucidation of one phrase: in the beginning was the Word. A preliminary definition explains the different meanings of the word "beginning" (*principium* or *arche*), as those meanings are applicable to the Son of God. Then there follows a study of the names of Christ, the titles by which He is referred to throughout the Scriptures. The purpose of this study is to distinguish the Son from the Father. Origen points out that it is difficult to establish this distinction if the inquirer adheres to the custom of the majority of theologians and is content to build up his argument solely on the title of Logos or Word. If any such procedure is followed, it is impossible, he warns, to avoid the foolish and superficial systems of theology that lead to heresy; moreover, it is impossible to understand what is behind the meaning of Logos. It is wrong, then, to omit consideration of the numerous titles that Scripture has given to Christ or to say, without due examination and in a casual manner, that such titles are used figuratively. Why prefer the title of Logos to that of Light or Life, as if that one title were more important than any other? Origen insists that in the case of all those other titles we should turn from the title to the concept it suggests, and apply and demonstrate how the Son of God is suitably described by it. This method of research, which is useful in the theology of the Trinity, becomes vitally necessary if we are to know the mission of Christ and to understand His work of salvation.

The titles can be studied in a list which suggests their diminishing importance, and the titles at the bottom of the list are contingent and refer to the sacrifice of Jesus. Origen begins his study of the Logos, only when the attributes proper to the Son of God have been protected against the assaults of the adversaries of the Trinity. Usage has given to the Logos the office of the demiurge. But this is a secondary role; it is based on the relation by which the Son is one with the Father and to which the creative act merely gives a new expression. The conclusion of the first book affirms the distinction of the Logos, a divine personality superior to every other. The second book, a commentary on the subsequent verses of St. John's prologue, affirms this theological viewpoint, and then proceeds to consider the relations of the Logos to men, the office and the mission of the Logos in the world, and finally the confirmation of all this that we may gain from the precursor.

III. THE ONLY-BEGOTTEN SON

At this stage of the Commentary we perceive Origen's purpose: to establish, before everything else, the distinct subsistence of the Logos. It was a purpose common to all the theological efforts that marked this first half of the third century. There were two dangers in the enterprise. On the other hand, there was the danger of affirming, after the manner of certain Pythagoreans, the existence of a second God who would be the Son. On the other hand, the effort to safeguard the oneness of God exposed the theologian to the possibility of denying the Trinity. This latter error was by far the more threatening. The contemporary heresies had forced the Christian theologians to clarify, first of all, what was later called the distinction of persons.

TRINITARIAN HERESIES

Among the adversaries of the doctrine of the Trinity, Origen considers two groups, which he sometimes confuses with each other. He knows the extremists who reproach the Christian theologians for teaching the existence of two gods. In the West they were called partisans of the one God, in the East they were known as the friends of God. In their fear of a doctrine which they interpreted as ditheism, they contented themselves with formulas that were false and wicked. They said, for example, that the Father suffered the passion.[10] This was the error of the simple and illiterate Christians, but it was evidence of the fear prevailing in Christian communities, particularly in the main body of the faithful, of every suggestion of pagan philosophy.

The second group of heretics was more cultured. They were content to deny that the Son possessed a subsistence or an essence proper to Himself. They confused Him with the Father in the divine substance and reduced Him to a power or a particular causality that could be readily distinguished in an analysis of the notion of God. This theological viewpoint must inevitably end by disturbing the entire plan of salvation. If the Logos did not really pre-exist,

10 *Ibid.*, II, 2; P.G., XIV, 108.

the divinity of the Father is what is united to the soul of Christ. The Son is, then, merely a divine sort of man, a hero adopted by God for deification. He has a distinct existence, but His divine dignity is lost.[11]

Thus the Trinity and the Incarnation, or, in the technical language of the schools of the day, theology and the plan of salvation, were intimately bound together from the beginning of this third century. It is not difficult to understand the reason of this close association. The chief obstacle encountered by the adversaries of the Trinity was the traditional belief in the Word-made-flesh. This dogma, one of the focal points of Christianity, protected every other teaching of the Church. Christians found in it the source and object of their love of God. But the heart does not reason by a process of deduction. The faith of Christendom did not imagine the descent of a second God upon earth, nor did it consider the coming of the Son as the consequence of a transcendent genealogy. On the contrary, when the Christian saw in the Gospel the figure of Him who alone knew the Father and who had come upon earth to make the Father known, he readily passed, with the élan of the beloved disciple, from the God-man to the only-begotten Son, the first-born of creation, eternally the offspring of the Father. Certain attitudes and certain sayings of the Master allowed men to guess the intimate and ineffable relations within the bosom of the one God whom Israel adored. Truly, the whole mission of Jesus put those relations on the plane of feeling. His prayer, His miracles showed Him at once as having been sent by the Father and as being united to the Father in a mysterious way without any confusion of persons. By coming among men, the Son of God proved the existence of the Father. Faithful Christian souls could not and would not see the splendor of the Father or the glory of the Logos begotten before all the ages of time except in the figure of Jesus of Nazareth as He was seen and heard and touched by His own. When the apostle cried out those words, "My Lord and my God," he was merely giving expression to the spontaneous emotion of the Christian heart.

[11] On Adoptionism, cf. *In Joan.,* II, 2; P.G., XIV, 109.

For this reason the champions of the faith of the apostles always defended the doctrine of the Trinity by recalling the mystery of the Word-made-flesh. What made them even more inclined to that apologetic was the fact that the God-man was at the very center of the purest theology. St. Irenaeus, probably under the influence of the school of Antioch, had given to this dogma a glory that was new to the apologists of the second century. Hippolytus, his disciple on many counts, found in that same dogma a ready argument against the so-called partisans of the one God. The office of the creative Logos, the mission of the incarnate Word, sufficed to reveal the distinct subsistence of the Father. "The Logos was begotten as a first cause, a counselor of the divine thoughts, a maker of created things. . . . In sending Him, the Father has shown to men what is the power of the Son." Thus the design of providence for the salvation of mankind showed forth the intimate life of God, and indeed it can be said that the providential plan and the divine life were scarcely distinguished from each other. The word "economy," which up to that time was reserved for the dogma of the Incarnation, was now extended to include the Trinity considered in the missions of the three divine persons.

TITLES OF CHRIST

Origen is far from repudiating this system of theological thought. He seems indeed to develop it when he insists that, in order to know the Son, we must consider the titles which He bears in the Scriptures and which are connected, for the most part, with His work of salvation. Before inquiring why He is called the Word, Origen devotes many pages of his Commentary to a discussion of the expiatory sacrifice of the Lamb, the good Shepherd, the true vine, the arrow that wounds every heart with divine love. Moreover, he does all this in a manner which opens a new period in the theology of the Trinity. He not only proposes to show that the Logos is distinct from the Father, but he seeks to define, by a theory of greater depth and wider sweep, the procession of the Son.

In one of his early controversies Hippolytus said: "You desire to know the genesis of the Word, how the Father begot Him by

His will. . . . Is it not enough to know that God made the world? . . . Is it not enough to learn that the Son of God came for our salvation if we have the faith? But we fall into confusion, inquiring how He was begotten." When the question became more insistent, the theologian resorted to an old metaphor that had been dear to the early Christian apologists. The Logos was uttered by divine power. He is a kind of expression that has fallen from the lips of the Father. Origen took issue with this metaphor, denouncing it as a wrong comparison, which was the cause of much of the disability afflicting the theology of his day. "They imagine the Son of God as the utterance of the Father deposited, as it were, in syllables." [12] Who could recognize in this utterance of the Word the Son of God in whom we believe?

The theologians who omit consideration of the other titles of Christ and regard this as the most important one make great use of it against the heretics. Without the slightest effort at interpretation, they bring forward that passage from the Psalms: "My heart hath uttered a good word," as if the meaning of it were obvious. Changes of person occur frequently in the psalms, and it is not certain that those words are to be attributed to God. If, as the psalm goes on to say, He spoke His words to the King or to the Son, we should have to assume that the Son did not exist before the works or at least that He did not know the creation of which He was the artisan. It is probable that the words of the entire verse were spoken by a prophet, whose soul was filled with the Spirit and who is the voice of the Logos. But, even if we admit that the words are to be attributed to the Father, the meaning is not as clear as those theologians believe. God has not a heart or a faculty of speech such as we have, and it is not enough to add that the Word is an animated Word. If that Word is not an entity from the Father, it has no subsistence and there is not a Son. On the other hand, if it is separate and has a distinct reality of its own, it can still be divine; but is it clear that it is God? To understand, then, the utterance (prolation) of the Word in a manner worthy of the perfect principle, we must inter- pret "heart" as meaning the power of intelligence and decision

[12] *Ibid.*, I, 23; P.G., XIV, 65.

which is in God; and we must recognize that this power proclaims, by the Word, the multiple aspects of Truth, instead of keeping them locked within the recesses of the primal unity. But this method of interpretation implies the abandonment of metaphor and founds the generation of the Word on an act of the divine intelligence.[13]

THE WORD

Origen's philosophical researches had trained him to think of providence as the totality of ideas presiding at the creation, the organization, and the history of the world. This eternal wisdom assists the divine will, maintaining order among beings, and reigning over the spirits it has created, by assuring them of their salvation and their ultimate union with their principle. In the *De principiis,* this wisdom appears identical with the Word, an activity issuing immediately from divine intelligence. But it remains for Origen to demonstrate that this intellectual begetting implies a real distinction between the Father and the Word.

Origen starts with the notion of divine generation. It consists in the act by which God contemplates Himself. The intuition of the primal unity is analyzed in the divine wisdom and is expressed in the Word. To this first truth there corresponds a system of diverse truths, known and comprehended in the unity which binds them all together. Such is the mode by which the only Son proceeds from the Father, and we are able at once to deduce that the Son is distinct from the Father and that the Son is God. The Son has His own subsistence, His own definite place and sphere as one who has life in Himself because He is constituted by an act immanent to a subject. Let us suppose that the faculty of understanding truth is not a created power, as it is in us; and let us suppose, further, that this faculty is exercised on an object that is fully intelligible. With these two thoughts to help us we can obtain a dim understanding of what this distinct being is. "He has His subsistence in the divine wisdom." [14]

[13] *Ibid.*
[14] *Ibid.*, I, 42; P.G., XIV, 104.

But not only is the Word distinct from the Father. The Word is also God, subsisting in the divine essence since it expresses the accord between the Father and creative wisdom. From all eternity God exercises His omnipotence through the Son, and in this unity of operation we find a second proof of the divinity of the Son. Do we not call the Son equally omnipotent? But in this recognition of His glory we do not make Him a second God. Instead of considering the primal source of being, we distinguish in divinity a being in which creatures participate, a light of all lights, an image-type of all images, a reason of all rational beings, the God of all the natures that are capable of being gods.[15] In thus demonsrating how God is united to intelligences, we can affirm His distinct reality as the supreme intelligence which finds within itself a perfect object; and we can also maintain the dignity of the Word, the dignity of God Himself inasmuch as His ideas exist on the plane of reality and are diffused thereon. Far from being opposed to the notion of procession, the two theses are woven into the very texture of it.

It is now possible for us to have a much higher notion of the manifestations of the Word and of creation in particular. What is at the origin of things if not the accord of divine power and divine understanding, when this accord is indicated and expressed by the creation of multiple beings? "Christ is demiurge as a beginning, inasmuch as He is wisdom. It is in virtue of His being wisdom that He is called beginning." [16] In this case, to speak of the mission of the Word would be to employ an incorrect term. "When He came among us and was born of the Virgin, we can say that He was sent by the Father; but when He made the world, not doing so as one delegated, these words alone are to be used of Him: 'He was with God, and He was God.'" Let us realize how poor is our metaphor if we compare God to an artisan. In the case of other artisans, their technique is called upon as soon as the hour to begin their work has struck. But the Son of God is not distinct either from His technique or from His wisdom, and therefore He is called Word or Reason. His thought is, in itself, the constructive element, and the act of

15 *Ibid.*, II, 2; P.G., XIV, 110.
16 *Ibid.*, I, 22; P.G., XIV, 56.

creating adds nothing to Him. He has merely consented to the existence of creatures, and His act of consent established a new relation by which contingent beings were united to their principle. His truth made them exist. So wonderful an artist was He that He could bring His work into the sphere of reality merely by conceiving it. That work would be independent of all material conditions; and His mere idea of it would be, in itself, a power of being, a creative decision. His intuition suffices, then, to give existence to all creation.

In Origen's view, therefore, the procession of the Son does not depend upon His office. In the theology of Hippolytus, the Word seemed too often to exist solely in virtue of the power that came upon Him at the right moment, making Him not unlike a laborer who is hired for a week's work. The Word was uttered when the Father created the world, for the simple reason that creation was established in the Word. The purpose of that utterance was that He might draw mankind to Himself and that His love might dwell in the hearts of men. By substituting for this divine action an act of the divine intelligence, Origen avoided the grave dangers implicit in the theology of Hippolytus. The Alexandrian started from the principle that the Word is anterior to creation since it is He who has made heaven and earth. This makes it incumbent on us not to base His existence on the birth of the God-man; indeed, when the Gospel tells us that the Word was made flesh, it clearly indicates that "He was God by His essence, and already existed as the Son of God." The nobility of the Son is clearly shown in one single word of the phrase used by the Father: "This day have I begotten Thee." "This is spoken to Him by God, with whom all time is today, for there is no evening with God, as I consider, and there is no morning, but time that stretches out, along with His unbeginning and unseen life. The day is today with Him in which the Son was begotten, and thus the beginning of His birth is not found, as neither is the day of it." [17]

In the study of the Trinity the theological genius of Origen saw that the person of the Word was not reduced to a role or an office.

[17] *Ibid.*, 32; P.G., XIV, 77.

His notion of person was not, however, very clear, and it is not astonishing that the simple faithful were unable to recognize the only-begotten Son of God in an intellectual act which had for its subject the divine wisdom. An office and a substance were not sufficient to assure the distinction of the Word. The Son of God was still quite relative to creation, and Origen's theory seemed sometimes to degrade, in a way, the divinity that was in Him. Undoubtedly he himself perceived that the study of the divine titles gave him merely a knowledge that was fragmentary and always incomplete, for there is much more in the Son of God than the highest human intelligence can understand. As soon as he had accepted these limitations to his theological research, he was able to realize his desire of considering the Son as the life and truth of created beings. But this did not prevent him from sometimes mistaking his speculations for definite knowledge, and his study of the titles of the Son claimed to solve the entire mystery. His *Commentary* might very well provoke the reader to ask if divine wisdom is not reduced to the level of the intelligible world. Although Origen proclaims wisdom as necessary and eternal, in several passages he seems to be thinking of it as nothing more than the ensemble of the ideas of created things and as the rationale of things yet to be.[18]

[18] *Ibid.*, 22; P.G., XIV, 36.

CHAPTER XVI

The Word and the Lamb

I. THE WORD WHICH ENLIGHTENS

THE first two books of the Commentary are devoted, for the most part, to the discussion of the relations by which creation is united to the Son of God. The treatise had given a glowing picture of the spiritual city from without. The Commentary, on the other hand, studies it from within, seeking to reveal the hidden forces that operate in the minds of men, the life and the light which are ever at work in the world of souls. By the Word all things were made, and life that was in Him was the light of men. So Origen's spiritual city is now the world. We know that there is no created thing that cannot serve in the work of spiritual progress. We understand also that created souls form a vast community and that the more advanced members of that community help their weaker brethren. The hidden author of this good is the Word. His action extends to all created beings: to the angels, to heavenly spirits, to men. He illuminates and purifies and saves the whole of creation.[1]

Thus Origen begins his Commentary. Its opening pages represent his boldest effort to link the physical universe to the spiritual world. To establish and to explain the connection between those two forms of existence was a problem that challenged all the thinkers of his day. He endeavored to solve it in a Christian way by excluding pantheism and by placing in the forefront the mission of the Savior.

THE HOLY GHOST

To those who were inclined to believe that the Holy Ghost is created and is the link between the Word and the less perfect spirit-

---

[1] The first two books of the Commentary contain a cosmology more forceful than that of the treatise. At many points Origen suggests that salvation should extend to the universe; cf. In Joan., I, 17 (P.G., XIV, 52); I, 24 (P.G., XIV, 72); I, 40 (P.G., XIV, 93). Hence the two books are the ones most tainted with gnosis.

ual beings who inhabit the earth, he replied that the Trinity is absolutely separate from creation. The order of the hypostases is not governed by a law of emanation, in virtue of which the Son would be the first worker and the Holy Ghost the worthiest of creatures and the most perfect of the heavenly spirits formed by the Word. We must conceive of the Trinity in another manner, by taking our stand, as does the *De principiis*, on the divine operations such as they can be deduced from our knowledge of the plan of salvation and of spiritual progress. Thus the Holy Ghost will be seen to be neither a useless entity nor the supreme revealer. He is the third of the divine persons, it is true. But He is mentioned last because He completes the work and because, in the life of religion, perfection comes only at the end.

This was Origen's way of meeting the difficulty that in Scripture at times the Holy Ghost seems inferior to the Word and sometimes superior. Since the Spirit is the substance of grace, He maintains the life of the soul, that inner life that has been given by the Father and dispensed by the Son. His operation is, in a way, a dependent one. He comes from the Father through the Son in a way peculiar to Him, and that way is not filiation. But, in spite of those textual difficulties, the Scriptures uphold the dignity of the Spirit. Christ declares in the Gospel that there is no forgiveness for blasphemy against the Holy Spirit, and the reason of this is undoubtedly because the rational beings who are most favored by the Spirit are those who have been found worthy of it and because there cannot well be any forgiveness for those who fall away in spite of such powerful cooperation, and who defeat the counsels of the Spirit who is in them. Scripture tells us also that the Messias was sent by the Spirit, but this declaration refers to the incarnate Word and to His abasement. Perhaps the work of our salvation is befitting to the Son only, but the uncreated Spirit would assist in the struggle as a divine power equal in divinity but subordinate in operation. Hence there is no need to suppose a genealogy of created essences as a consequence of the Word. All things were made through Him, the exceptions being Wisdom, the Life that was the light of men, and the ensemble of divine life which was in Him and with Him.

THE WORD

The Prologue of St. John's Gospel draws a distinction between created beings and the Mediator; it says that they were made and that He was life. The good which He possesses by His essence, He shares with them. If the author of the Fourth Gospel did not wish to insist on His pre-existence, he would have written more accurately that He is life. The Word lacks nothing, and nothing can be added to His substance. The Prologue does not tell us how new natures would be begotten by the divine Word in the passage of time. We cannot discover a time when things were not, although the gnostic fables incline toward such a belief. But the existence of different beings determines the relations that allow us to study the Son and thus to learn some of the attributes of Him who is in the beginning of angels and of men. He gives them life, and in this word the notion of virtue is included. But, above all, He gives them light. This is the privileged relation. It is, so to speak, the type of all other relations, since the Word is Wisdom.[2]

This illumination is not total in any created being. In heavenly beings, that have the purest bodies, as well as in the prophets and the apostles, the solar rays of divinity are received directly. Less perfect beings need the help of intermediaries. For these there are the saints, who ascend the mountain with Jesus and spend their days in prayer. But Jesus does not remain there. He goes down to Capharnaum. With His mother, His brethren, and His disciples, He walks among the poor and lowly. Under the glow of His illumination, the soul awakes, gross and material thoughts disappear, and the fluttering wick that His coming has lighted casts its reflections even on the body, the vessel of clay which contains it.[3] Christ humbles Himself for human souls. St. John tells us that the Light shineth in darkness. Their struggle with sin is merely another aspect of His mission upon earth. The prophets in an intuition compounded of faith and hope, the martyrs in the shedding of their blood, all the faithful in their words and acts, render a testimony that is

[2] *Ibid.*, II, 12; *P.G.*, XIV, 145.
[3] *Ibid.*, 4; *P.G.*, XIV, 121; *ibid.*, X; *P.G.*, XIV, 321.

merely an imitation, under different forms, of the witness borne by the Father Himself.[4]

There exists, so to speak, a metaphysics of conversion, which the treatise had already expounded for Origen's disciples. When Christ is afar off and when men have deprived themselves of their share of divinity, we can see them ruled by ignorance and the not-being of intelligence. Sinful influences have power and strength only in the measure in which the soul is weak. It is wrong to attribute unbelief to the soul of an entire race or an entire nation. Lack of God is never natural to any human soul. For the soul to be re-established, it is enough that the light comes to it. Always the light can come without harm or loss to itself, for it comes only in the measure of the needy soul's capacity to receive it. When it has once been received, it must be kept alive by holy practices and by attendance at salutary instuctions, for all around it there is the darkness of evil thoughts affecting even the actions. This explains why the light is wisdom first and justice afterward.

LIGHT AND DARKNESS

"It drives away darkness, ignorance, and sin, and causes them to disappear before it. . . . As wisdom, it dispels the ignorance of the intelligence. As justice, it corrects the errors of the heart. It can shine in the darkness by throwing forth without hindrance rays that are really its own and by causing them to fall upon him whom it would illuminate. So the darkness does not know it; by the mere presence of the light, it is dispelled and disappears. It is wrong to think that the darkness vainly tries, like an active substance, to overtake the light. On the contrary, it always disappears and ceases to exist. In order that falsehood and imposture should be dispelled, is it not sufficient for the light of truth to appear? However strange it may seem, the darkness must be far away if it is to try to reach the light. The nearer it approaches the light, the more quickly it is dissolved. We can say, then, that error has strength and movement within us only when we are far removed from truth. Only then does it move forward to come to grips with our understanding; and each

[4] *Ibid.*, 28; P.G., XIV, 176.

time it approaches the enlightened intelligence, it shows its own nothingness." In the wide sweep of this passage, written in the loftiest terms of Alexandrian thought, we see the reflection of all the vital elements of the Academy over which Origen presided: the rejection of gnostic dualism, the high regard in which intellectualism was held, and the glowing optimism based upon the feeling that the religion revealed by Christ could be preached to all men.

Light comes to the Christian from on high. It operates in the heart, and its work is not accomplished without preparation. In attributing this illumination to the Word, the Academy of Alexandria showed that the light comes from God. The coming of the Word complemented natural reason at the same time as it revealed in every man an elementary word. This elementary word is reason, enabling man to participate in the Word, as the early apologists had often said. Tertullian, indeed, had appealed to the soul, that was naturally Christian. Origen returned to this concept and gave it supreme importance by explaining it in a doctrine of the unconscious, although he did not use this modern expression.

In this world the Word has never ceased to be. It is manifest not only in our innate notions of right and wrong but also in the highest forms of natural religion. It is present in every rational being. Acknowledged by the just man and ignored by those whom Origen calls "irrational reasons," it stamps the mark of its presence in every soul.[5] It is lacking only to those who are lacking to it, those stupid minds that have wandered from their natural mode of life. Our Lord Himself said: "If I had not come, and spoken to them, they would not have sin." When the inner voice speaks, he who disobeys it commits a sin, being guilty of voluntary blindness. He sins against this ordinary grace, which is the natural gift of the Creator.[6]

But, no less truthfully and somewhat paradoxically, we can say that the saint alone is rational. Our innate notions of morality, those germs of contemplation, are deficient and are disobeyed as long as they are not divinely complemented, in the order of miracle, by the extraordinary grace of revelation. The same Word that enlightens

---

[5] *Ibid.*, 3; P.G., XIV, 112.
[6] *Ibid.*, I, 42 (P.G., XIV, 97); II, 9 (P.G., XIV, 140).

every man, ends by molding the soul to truth as soon as it makes the Father known to that soul. Intelligence, like reason, is the daughter of God; and, like reason, it tells what it sees in God. Moreover, there is in the world a diffuse kind of revelation: traces of primitive contemplation, concepts taken from the Bible, flashes that for a brief instant have illuminated the mind of some genius. Revealed Christianity alone can discover this other Christianity which does not know its own identity: wells of living water which the Philistines have filled up, divine colors which have been gradually covered with dust. "There is work for those who dig the wells of living water, wherever they labor; that is, for those who teach the word of God to every soul and draw from it its salutary fruit. . . . Let us dig those wells that are within us and throw out the earth that chokes them. We shall make the waters come forth again, even unto overflowing, because the Word of God is within us." [7]

Undoubtedly the germs of wisdom are, of themselves, capable of some growth, in the measure in which the individual observes the laws of natural righteousness. But indeed they never come to growth. They fulfill their purpose only when the soul is raised to perfection by Christ. At that moment the soul comes to life and becomes aware of its destiny. It receives the light of baptism, it hearkens to instruction in the faith, and it finally learns the royal rules of contemplation so that it no longer leaves the Word unregarded.[8]

A man must question his own heart as soon as he hears the message of the Church. Christ is found by those who are determined to find Him. He does not impose Himself upon us. "He knows by whom He is likely to be repulsed and by whom He is to be welcomed." At the moment foreseen by providence, He makes Himself known to the heart that longs for Him. "As long as a man preserves the germs of truth within himself, the Word is never far away from him. Such a man can always nourish the seeds of hope." [9]

If we consider the history of the world, we can perceive even there

---

[7] *Hom. in Gen.*, XIII, 3 f.
[8] *In Joan.*, I, 42; P.G., XIV, 97.
[9] *Ibid.*, XIX, 12; P.G., XIV, 548.

the hidden presence of the Word. From age to age the Word has spoken to His own chosen ones—to the prophets, who were as blessed as the apostles. Even if they knew nothing of the sonship of the Word, they already received, in the Messianic hope, "Him who would communicate His spirit of adoption to those who believed in God through Him." The long years of waiting were illuminated by an implicit revelation.

ORIGEN'S HUMANISM

In the wide sweep of Origen's theory there seems at times to be a confusion of two concepts which others of that time had clearly distinguished: the natural participation of the divine reason and the Christian imitation of the Savior. In Origen's thought the Gospel appears to be the natural fruit of philosophy. To express it more accurately, our natural reason is presented as a dimly conscious illumination or an obscure presentiment of the revealed religion of Jesus Christ. Despite this criticism, it was possible to mark the limits of the theory. When this was done, Origen's humanism possessed an incomparable strength, both by reason of its boldness and by reason of its respect for the individual consciousness. These two elements enabled it to have a place in the rapid propagation of the new religion during the first half of the third century. Without any derogation of the mission of the Savior, the Academy of Alexandria discovered in every individual a sense of divine things and the hidden image of God.

II. THE LAMB OF GOD

In considering the mediation and abasements of the Word, Origen was led to make a study of the redemption. There were many obstacles in his way. In the first place, his philosophical mentality filled him with repugnance for the unheroic and humiliating Passion of the Savior. Secondly, his intellectualism inclined toward the revelation of the eternal Christ rather than toward a God whose appeal would be felt by the human heart. And lastly, in his preoccupation with the illuminative way he naturally relegated the process of purification to the elementary stages of the Christian life. He had made his first commentary on the mystery of divine love when he was studying the cry of the spotless victim in the Psalter. He had been frightened by it to the point of exempting Jesus from every physical emotion. This, indeed, was in line with the tradition of the Academy of Alexandria, which endowed the incarnate Word with certain privileges of immunity from suffering. Thus it happened that Origen, studying the agony in the Garden of Olives from the narrow perspective of his school, regarded it as something occurring outside the soul and body of the Savior and reduced it to a passing disturbance of the imagination.

But now, when he set forth the titles by which the Savior is known in the Gospels, he comes to the lowliest title of all. Christ had been a servant, He was a propitiation for our sins, He was our Redeemer. When Origen stood on the frontier between the world of feeling and the world of knowing, between the visible cross and the eternal mediation of Christ, he became more and more interested in the meaning of the great sacrifice. The ultimate abasement of the God-made-man was presented to him in the passages that tell of the distress of Christ's soul and His death on the cross. In this matter Paul and John were in agreement. The one had said: "He humbled Himself, becoming obedient unto death, even to the death of the cross." And in the Fourth Gospel we read: "Behold the Lamb of God, behold Him who taketh away the sin of the world."

We need feel no shame of the Savior's Passion, for it had its source in His voluntary abasement and in His extreme desire to serve. "We do not hesitate to say that the goodness of Christ appears in a greater and more divine light, and more according to the image of the Father, because 'He humbled Himself.'" [10] His acceptance of servitude was but a small part of His sacrifice. In His sufferings, in His silence, in His agony, the Word-made-flesh experienced all the sorrows that afflict the human heart. In Him their domain was limited, because He was without sin. But in another sense His afflictions were total, since He who was always the Savior and even in His transcendence and in His divinity willed that it

10 *Ibid.*, I, 37; P.G., XIV, 85.

should be so. He was silent before Pilate. "He desired to suffer for all mankind. If He had spoken, He would not have been crucified because of weakness. There was no weakness in what the Son of God said." [11]

REDEMPTION

We cannot have too lofty an idea of this sacrifice, offered unceasingly to the Father for the redemption of the world. But we must understand the word "redemption" in a manner worthy of God. Souls, it is said, are ransomed from the power of the devil. Origen has sometimes been represented as the author of this doctrine, but he seems only to have reproduced it, for he brings it forward with a number of reservations. No Christian thinker perceived more clearly than he that a real redemption must be something more than a matter of barter. Jesus yielded to the devil nothing more than His blood and His life, and He yielded that for a time only. How could the devil have taken possession of the God-man? The acceptance of such a ransom would have crushed the creditor, and he was not even capable of keeping the price paid to him. In accepting the challenge to pit his strength against the Messias, he merely succeeded in being destroyed in the end. Assuredly, in this mystery the devil does not fill the part assigned to him by certain formulas accepted by the theologians. Christ's sacrifice is a remedy; if He lets loose the powers of evil, His purpose is to encourage the faithful soul with greater assurance against the hidden enemy, which is sin. Salvation works invisibly. Jesus allowed darkness to descend upon His soul in order that it might be dispelled from ours. How could the darkness have overtaken Him? The Word is quicker than the evil powers, and they are always outstripped by Him. If He waits for them, as He did in the drama of His Passion, they are entrapped. When they approach Him, they are certain to be destroyed. Redemption is, therefore, only the first aspect of illumination. It is a struggle in which Truth confronts the powers of darkness before vanquishing them utterly.

To understand the various explanations that Origen gave of the

[11] *Ibid.*, XIX, 2; P.G., XIV, 544.

mystery of redemption, we must never lost sight of the first two books of the Johannine *Commentary*. The principles of his mystical theology are set forth there, as the more general principles of his entire system are set forth in the treatise which preceded it. With Origen, the Passion is always bound up with the mission of the Word. The suffering Christ is the horseman of the Apocalypse, riding on a white horse. The horse is white as a symbol of the truth proclaiming His glory, and the rider's garments are sprinkled with the blood with which He triumphed. Christ's sacrifice is a preparation for the spiritual progress of the Christian soul. His extreme abasement is the beginning of holiness for a multitude of men.

Thus Origen found that an intellectual study of the crucified Savior is possible. This was the great discovery with which the *Commentary* endowed the Academy of Alexandria. In his preface he had promised his friend Ambrose to leave the physical facts of the Passion to the simpler class of Christians; he proposed to hurry on from this external Christianity of the unlettered to the study of the spiritual gospel. Some pages later he contemplates the blood of Christ bespattering the ground, and immediately theory yields to fact. "Of that Passion, even should it be our lot some day to come to that highest and supreme contemplation of the Logos, we shall not lose all memory, nor shall we forget the truth that our admission was brought about by His sojourning in our body." [12] Years later, he would tell the more advanced of his pupils that a study of the crucified Jesus was the means of reaching the highest degrees of the spiritual life. He warned them that this mystery of the Savior's Passion would give them a knowledge of Christ that would be far from imperfect, and that it was so difficult a mystery that even the Apostles had to be instructed in its meaning before they could understand it and before they could see that it meant our salvation.

[12] *Ibid.*, II, 4; P.G., XIV, 121.

CHAPTER XVII

The Conflict

ABOUT the year 230, when he was engaged in the composition of his *Commentary on the Gospel of St. John,* he was again invited to leave his native city to deal with some pressing difficulties of the Christian communities outside Egypt. The occasion of this summons was probably the need of replying to the heretics.[1] Marcionism in particular was still in a strong position, and in Syria its Churches were described as spawning like a race of serpents. In some communities the heretical groups were in the majority, defaming the Christians and even maltreating those who ventured to preach the Christian faith. One apologist for Christianity was, however, the victim of his own zeal; thinking to convert a certain heretic in a public debate, he was vanquished in the discussion and renounced the Church.

MARCIONISM

We have already seen that the Marcionites, having first adopted astrology, employed the logic of Aristotle as a technique of biblical criticism. It was useless to quote texts against them. They had the knack, without completely destroying the authority of Scripture, of breaking a passage into little sections and of distinguishing a different source of inspiration for each such fragment. According to Apelles, who had given Marcionism a new lease of life, Moses, the prophets, and Christ were so many separate compartments, each a spiritual world in itself. It was argued that the ancient laws of God's chosen people had not been given by the prophets and that, therefore, it was illogical to assume that a new religion could have been promulgated by Jesus, even though the force of His words was

[1] Eusebius, *H.E.,* VI, xxiii, 4: "The Church of God, e.g., which is at Athens, is a meek and stable body, as being one that desires to please God, who is over all things."

sufficient to produce miraculous effects. Apelles and his followers claimed the right to sift and winnow the Old Testament as much as they pleased.

For some year Origen had been acquiring a more comprehensive knowledge of this school of heretical thought. In his early years he was satisfied with refuting its doctrine of fatalism. Then he turned to its exegetical technique, refuting it in several chapters of the *De principiis* and in the second book of the *Commentary on the Gospel of St. John.* He had now all the equipment necessary for victory: a flexible system of logic, a thorough knowledge of the Bible and of the spirit that maintained its oneness even in the most profound passages, and a philosophy of providence which he had extended to every degree of being that is manifested in the universe. Hence it was natural that the Christian communities should turn to him in their hour of need. Furnished with a letter of recommendation from Demetrius his bishop, he set forth in answer to their call.

ORIGEN'S ORDINATION

In the course of this journey, he proposed to buttress the defenses of the Christian faith against the attacks made by the various heresies. His particular foe, however, was Marcionism, for its adherents claimed to establish Churches by setting up their assemblies in opposition to the orthodox Christians. Origen was not a priest. But his ordination to the priesthood at Caesarea, which fulfilled a desire he had for some time, gave him the necessary authority to speak for the Christians. He thus became an accredited representative of the Gospel, a role which the prudent Demetrius had not appeared inclined to give him.

After his ordination he left Palestine, but before his departure he engaged a champion of the Marcionites in public debate. Then he proceeded to Greece, perhaps stopping for a brief period at Ephesus. One day soon after his arrival at Athens some Christians from Palestine brought to his notice a falsified digest which the Marcionites of that country had made of his public debate. They

had given their own version of his teachings, applying to his words
and phrases the mischievous technique that Marcion had used on
the Gospel and on the Epistles of St. Paul.

The new and many interests of this apologetic activity did not
take him away from his chosen work or make him to forget his
promise to Ambrose. He continued his labors on the *Commentary*,
composing the third and fourth books. In the latter he explained to
the Greeks that they should not be offended at the rudeness of language they might find in various passages of the Scripture, reminding them also that the apostles had been able to convert cultured
men by a form of speech that was without any artifice and that they
had resorted neither to the literary style of the period nor to the apparent sequence and splendor of language which the scholars of
their day affected.[2] Perhaps at his public conferences in Athens he
may have detected a smile here and there throughout his Greek
audience. Looking out upon a sea of composed faces, perhaps he
knew that those Greeks were afraid of being dupes and were steeled
against the possibility of accepting anything he said. But he told
them that the apostles were men of humble speech, who used no
tricks of eloquence but spoke straight to the point. In his lectures
in the famous universities of Greece, he deliberately adopted that
apostolic technique, and in every scholarly gathering he was always
the soul of simplicity. His Christian acquaintances considered him,
on the contrary, to be lacking in that virtue. Criticized by Christian
and pagan, he pursued his chosen way, realizing its difficulties but
being always ready for battle.

OPPOSITION AT ALEXANDRIA

On his return to Alexandria he encountered the open hostility of
a number of Christians who were men of no small importance in
the life of the community. They were the survivors of those who,
a generation before, had considered it blameworthy for a Christian
to write treatises after the manner of the Greeks. Clement had been
obliged to meet the same criticism thirty years previously. In Origen's case they seemed to have a certain amount of right on their

[2] *In Joan.*, IV; P.G., XIV, 184.

side. Five books on the Fourth Gospel had come forth from his pen, and in them he had given his interpretations of less than ten verses. Those books were full of a new system of metaphysics which, on many points, was open to question. The hierarchy of the divine attributes, the procession of the Son issuing from eternal intelligence, had more than one resemblance to the teachings of the Valentinian heretics. There were also parts in which the Word was called a begotten being. Did Origen wish them to believe, like Artemon, that a created spirit became the Son of God?

Disposing of the *Commentary on the Gospel of St. John* as being tainted with heresy, they hurried on to his other writings. In his *De principiis* he certainly seemed to teach that the devil would be saved. There was, besides, the digest of his public debate with the Marcionite in Palestine, a document that could not have been lacking in the formulas, the abridgments, and all the other things which Origen avoided in his written works. Although his enemies made those charges against him, they did not yet reach the point of setting forth a list of his errors. But the public opinion of the entire Christian body entertained a vague suspicion of Origen's orthodoxy. Ordinary Christians were unable to follow the subtlety and learning of his philosophy, but certainly his teachings were being called in question. And the simple, in whom there was undoubtedly little simplicity, would soon quote against him the scriptural warning: "Of making many books there is no end," adding, for good measure, the veiled hint: "In the multitude of words there shall not want sin." [3]

When the storm broke he received encouragement, it is true, from powerful friends, from numbers of his pupils among the clergy, and even from some of the junior members of the episcopate. He felt that the criticism leveled against his teachings threatened the entire party of Christian culture and endangered the whole future of this enlightened Christianity to which educated Christians had a right and which the Church needed for her defense. His reply is in the form of a preface addressed to Ambrose at the beginning of the fifth book of his *Commentary on the Gospel of St. John.*

[3] Cf. *ibid.*, V, *Praef.*, 4; P.G., XIV, 185.

On this occasion he put subtlety aside and abandoned his preoccupation, as a grammarian, with the various shades of meaning in a word. With a stern determination to safeguard the hopes of Christian philosophers, he took up the gage of battle.

ORIGEN'S DEFENSE

His defense is worthy of quotation. Showing his talents at their best, it is marked by a charming grace of expression and is not without the sophisticated irony of the Alexandrians. Moreover, it glows with the scholar's sincere knowledge of his own limitations. In a word, it contains elements of loftiness that belong to the mind rather than to the soul steeped in holiness. The language is that of the theorist who has lived long with his own thoughts. He now discovers that his philosophy faces a real test as soon as its corollaries are contradicted. His school has been everything to him: his Church, his spiritual progress, his fountain of grace. But there are many others to whom it is neither Church nor perfection. The hour has not yet come for this master of the spiritual life to ask himself whether the frugal and unappetizing fare of uneducated and illiterate Christians, to whom tranquillity of conscience means everything, is not worth more than the learning of great scholars "who certainly understand theology but have no knowledge of the inner force that ensures harmony and peace to the whole community." In these circumstances he remains the prisoner of the enthusiasms he had fostered within his own heart in the years when he was fettered by his dignity as principal of a great school. His friends vainly urged him to conciliate the hostile critics. By his acceptance of the challenge he let loose the dogs of war.[4]

Here is what he writes to Ambrose: "You are not content to fulfill the office, when I am present with you, of a taskmaster to drive me to labor at theology; even when I am absent you demand that I should spend most of my time on you and on the task I have to do for you. For my part, I am inclined to shrink from toil, and to avoid that danger which threatens from God those who give themselves

---

[4] Origen's defense of himself is to be found in the preface to the fifth book of his *Commentary on the Gospel of St. John.*

to writing on divinity; thus I would take shelter in Scripture in refraining from many books. For Solomon says in Ecclesiastes, 'Of making many books there is no end: and much study is an affliction of the flesh.'

"I might take my stand on this dictum that now confronts us, and send you the text as an excuse, and, in support of this position, I might appeal to the fact that not even the saints found leisure to compose many books. Thus I might cry off from the bargain we made with each other, and give up writing what I was to send to you. On your part, you would no doubt feel the force of the text I have cited, and might, for the future, excuse me. But we must treat Scripture conscientiously, and must not congratulate ourselves, because we see the primary meaning of a text, that we understand it altogether. I do not, therefore, shrink from bringing forward what excuse I am able to offer for myself, and to point out the arguments which you would certainly use against me if I acted contrary to our agreement."

Since he has caught his adversaries in a flagrant example of literal exegesis, he in his turn appeals to Scripture; not, however, in their manner, by taking passages in their literal meaning, but by interpreting them in their deeper sense. His adversaries maintain that the Scriptures condemn long discourses. Did not Solomon avoid sin when he composed three thousand parables? And similarly St. Paul when he spoke until midnight? The scriptural maxims warning us against a multitude of words are not to be understood in a narrow sense.

"Now the entire Word of God, who was in the beginning with God, is not much speaking, is not words; for the Word is one, being composed of the many speculations, each of which is a part of the Word in its entirety. Whatever words outside of this one promise to give any description or exposition, even though they are words about truth, none of these, to put it in a paradoxical way, is Word or Reason; they are all words or reasons. . . . Whoever speaks the words of truth, even though he should go over the whole field and omit nothing, is always speaking the one word." It is error that is multiple. The saints were not mere babblers. Jesus speaks of all the

Scriptures as of one single book, and He refers us to that book as testifying of Him.

Origen's doctrine claimed nothing more than to be a reflection of this primal oneness. In looking back over his words, he saw in them an imitation of the Word, a continual commentary on reason, as he was able to perceive it in the Pentateuch, in the Psalms, and in the Prophets, beyond the truth of the events and the words that signified it. In his own soul he has felt the joy of recognizing under its different forms the Wisdom who could prolong a discourse in order that men might give their attention to it. Origen feels that if he has succeeded in thus putting forth the true and saving doctrines, his work is not lacking in oneness. By this test he is content to be judged. "From these considerations, then, we learn what the one book is and what the many books are. What I am now concerned about is, not the quantity I may write, but the effect of what I say, lest, if I fail in this point and set forth anything against the truth itself, even in one of my writings, I should prove to have transgressed the commandment, and to be a writer of 'many books.' "

This preface was published at the same times as the fifth book, which Origen had promised to Ambrose. It has been written, he tells his friend, in the midst of the tempest at Alexandria. Only a fragment of it remains, containing a clarification of one of the most disputed parts of his doctrine. Although the Mediator is called a begotten being, we are to remember the very different sense in which that term is applied to creatures. He is the only Son by nature, not by adoption as are those to whom He gives the title of sons of God. Origen had no difficulty in clearing himself of the charge of the heresy of the Adoptionists, who had been recently condemned. But he was no longer concerned with matters of doctrine to which the conflict had given birth. Henceforth he was engaged in a wider field.

CHAPTER XVIII

The Church

I. AUTHORITY

IN THE eyes of the religious authorities, the Academy was merely a catechetical school, with the bishop of Alexandria as its official head, and it fell to his lot to appoint a new catechist whenever a vacancy occurred. Really, however, it was a Christian university. This development was mostly owing to the activities of Clement and Origen. Each of them became interested in the education of young men who wished to devote their lives to the study of Christian truth and especially of theology. But even this function had been outgrown, and now, for more than a decade, the school was recognized as a university. The fame of its head had gone far beyond the borders of Egypt, and his name was known in the Churches of Rome, Caesarea, Jerusalem, Antioch, and Athens. He was hailed as the great champion of Christianity against the heretics, the most scholarly and able controversialist, the instructor of those enlightened souls who, even in certain pagan centers, were interested in the Bible and the religion of Christ. He carried out this part with great devotion to the Church but also in his own bold speculative way. Now, for the first itme in Christian history, theology asserted its right to be considered a distinct branch of knowledge. The Academy, which had begun its life as a catechetical school dependent upon the hierarchy without ever being absorbed by it, began to ask itself what was its place in the spiritual life of the community. Needless to say, it was far from assigning itself to the lowest rung of the ladder.

THE TEACHING OFFICE

Ecclesiastical studies and ecclesiastical teachings were held to resemble the episcopate, the priesthood, or the diaconate in the fact they demanded virtues far above the ordinary.[1] In commenting on the Gospel, Origen was training men who would later be the ruling class in the life of the Church. He himself had not yet been ordained to the priesthood but he had long aspired to that grace. In the meantime he regarded his pedagogical functions as something sacred, seeing in them an image of the priesthood of Aaron. Let us remember that St. John represents the Christian people in his vision of the twelve tribes whom he counted around the Lamb. On one side he places the virgins, as first fruits of the faithful of Christ. They are the intellectual elite, the little group of true disciples who, by the study of Holy Scripture, by contemplation as well as by vigilance and perseverance, guard that purity of body and of mind by which the perfect are known. They can be called Levites or priests of Israel because they exercise an inner priesthood.

Thanks to this ingenious interpretation, the scholarly life, when it is united to prayer and mortification, is the highest form of Christianity. "Most of us devote most of our time to the things of this life and dedicate to God only a few special acts, thus resembling those members of the tribes who had but few transactions with the priests, and discharged their religious duties with no great expense of time. But those who devote themselves to the divine word and have no other employment but the service of God may not unnaturally, allowing for the difference of occupation in the two cases, be called our Levites or priests. And those who follow a more distinguished office than their kinsmen will perhaps be high priests according to the order of Aaron." [2] The life of contemplation is no longer merely a hidden end toward which perfect souls strive, each in his own measure. It becomes a real function of the Christian and ought to be given preference over other functions.

Passages such as this were not written to please the Bishop of Alexandria. If the good Demetrius was so unfortunate as not to belong to a group of scholars, his authority was a matter of trifling importance. The theologian will expound the consoling truths of

[1] *In Matt.*, ser. 24; P.G., XIII, 1629.
[2] *In Joan.*, I, 3; P.G., XIV, 25.

the faith and will be capable of denouncing sin, if the faithful need instruction.[3] The Academy can produce its interpreters of Scripture and its masters in the spiritual life, if the traditions of Christianity are to be analyzed and explained. Religious knowledge develops in the same rhythm as other branches of knowledge. It has its searchers, the prophets and the apostles, who discover the principles of the word of God. It has its young research-workers who study the tradition that is thus formed. From all this activity the various systems emerge. Then the masters who have received from God a higher faculty of discernment employ their philosophical learning to point the way to the unity of true doctrine.[4] As the successors of the apostles, they teach the Church instead of being taught by her. They are the prophets of the new Israel.

If Origen had been asked to write the history of theology, he would have distinguished three phases by three different words: apostles, priests, and scholars. He had an enthusiasm and a respect for religious knowledge, but his progressivism would have betrayed him. To reduce Christian tradition to researches and systems is to give too poor an idea of its vibrant perpetuity, too distorted an image of this priceless vessel which not only renews itself again and again but in each such periodic renewal revivifies the precious deposit of revelation which it contains.

In their attitude toward texts like these, our modern historians are somewhat at a disadvantage. We have had three hundred years of religious controversy, and in that long period we have seen a line drawn between the Church visible and the Church invisible, between ecclesiastical regulation and the inner life of the individual. With this background some of our modern critics are sorely tempted to isolate those phrases of Origen and to interpret them in a totally exclusive sense. If the true priesthood is to be found in the spiritual perfection of the individual soul, is it not logical to conclude that the spiritual life suffices to make every good Christian a priest? If the strongest impulsions that move the soul have their origin in

[3] *Hom. in Exod.*, XIII, 4; P.G., XII, 392.
[4] *In Joan.*, XIII, 46; P.G., XIV, 481.

theological studies and in spiritual training, is that not proof that these two disciplines confer on the clergyman or minister the authority without any other condition?

If this estimate of Origen is to be accepted, it means that the banner of the Reformation hangs from the walls of the great Christian university of Alexandria. Origen would then be the witness of a period when the episcopate was beginning to be no longer the custodian of apostolic tradition and when the bishops of the Christian Church no longer exercised any control over Christian teaching. Thus he would have summoned the saintliest men from the ranks of the laity and charged them with the spiritual care of the faithful. Of course he would have placed upon them an obligation of obedience toward the hierarchy, but that obedience would be purely external, for those saintly men would have known in their hearts that the members of the hierarchy were of less value than they. If this was really Origen's thought, Luther has been guilty of ingratitude in pouring his vituperation and scorn upon the name of the great Alexandrian.

MEMBERSHIP IN THE CHURCH

As a matter of historical fact, Origen never acknowledged any religion outside the Churches of God. He saw their origin in the coming and Passion of the Savior, whose dreadful sufferings were reproduced, in a measure, in the trials and tribulations of the apostles. To obtain eternal life a man must enter the mansion of God, and the moral virtues do not lead a man there for they are not inspired by love of the Savior. Origen's last commentaries were yet to describe this narrow world within a world, this great community of believers living in a world of unbelievers, this society of souls enlightened by the Word, immigrants who live in the world without becoming part of its life. Even before he encountered the armies of unbelievers who were bivouacked beyond the Church's frontiers, he knew from his life within the Church what separated it from the different heresies he met in the course of his studies. He knew that its peculiar characteristic was a message, and he judged it a gross impiety to allow his study of Scripture to lessen the value of that message in even the slightest degree. In his biblical studies his interpretations are guided and regulated by that message. If the Church in its schools has prophets like Israel, if sometimes one or other of those chosen souls has occasion to murmur the cry of the prophet, "The leaders of my people have not known me," it nevertheless remains true that the gift of prophecy can be exercised in that manner only which is conformed to the institutions of holy religion and under the guidance of authority. He proposed the life of contemplation especially to the clergy, as a sort of perfection of the sacred functions they perform. At the very height of his fame he himself believed that priestly ordination was necessary to him for the due fulfillment of the great tasks to which he had dedicated his life.

In the days of Christian antiquity the theologians were mainly concerned with two aspects of the Church's life: the faith which she taught and the sacred rites by which salvation might be achieved. Of these two Origen retains a preference for the first, for it touches more intimately his functions as a catechist and an expounder of Christian teaching. To become part of the Church is to think like the Church and to study her theology. But even during this period of his life we find in his writings echoes of the baptismal and Eucharistic liturgies.

Far from distinguishing the visible body of the faithful from the group of the elect, he leans to the other extreme. Deliberately he mingles them. The Church which he sees and loves is ever the ensemble of Christ's disciples scattered over the face of the earth. That great society can never be confused with the rest of the human race, although it never ceases to attract those who have need of belief and although the anxious crowds of those who are hearkening to its call surround it as with a radiance. He would sometimes think that this province of light, quite separated here on earth, had an opening which gives an unhindered view of the heavenly city and that it has the secrets and the rights of that celestial realm, that it is, as it were, the outpost of a mighty empire. When such thoughts come to him he forgets the earthly features of the Church, the veils of our faith, the continual warfare we are engaged in, the imperfections with which we strive. The Church becomes for him an emanation from the kingdom of the saints with little of its glory lost.[5]

In order that ecclesiastical powers should be efficacious, they seem to need, on certain points, a special communication of the divine will. It would not be enough to consider the Holy Ghost the normal atmosphere in which Christians live, the unfailing influence, the ever-present authority, the common fountain of life which re-animates human souls and never ceases to give healing to their wounds. The Holy Ghost ought to be visible in each of those who fulfill the functions of the priesthood. Bishop and priest are, in a way, of the company of those whom God has inspired. The voice of God designates His ministers.[6] If the head of a Church must choose his successor, he will not be able to trust his own unaided judgment. He must pray for the inspiration of God. He who is chosen receives the call by an inner revelation or by something ex-ceptional resembling the call to martyrdom. As there are false martyrs whose souls, deprived of virtue, are hostile to the religion for which they die, so also there are Christians who simulate the priesthood because they have not the spirit of it. The hierarchy of the Church must be founded on extraordinary gifts from on high.

PRIESTLY IDEAL

Because he considered priestly functions divine institutions, he had little indulgence for the clergy. Harnack's verdict is: "The de-fects which he discovered in them would not have had such weight with him, had he not been profoundly convinced of the value which such functions, and especially the episcopate, represent, and had he not recognized them as divine institutions and been able to imagine a Church which would be without them." Such as the Church was, Origen wanted it to be utterly spiritual. In this he fell into the venial sin of harboring a dream that causes little damage beyond impairing the vision of a Christian writer who has no de-sire, when he thinks about it, of sitting in judgment on the Church.

[5] *Ibid.*, VI, 38; P.G., XIV, 301.
[6] Cf. *Hom. in Levit.*, VI, 6; P.G., XII, 473.

The Church which he dreamed of had not the least resemblance
to the laicized religions that were the product of the Reformation.
He wished all bishops and priests to be monks, men of learning and
of lofty purpose, living a life of poverty in the presence of God. His
theology of the Church is one of the first demands for the monastic
ideal made up to that time. It was a period when the aspirations of
monachism tended to become confused with clerical life, before
the emergence of a way of life that was to be distinct from the priesthood while serving it as a model on a number of points.

The consequences of Origen's view were by no means of little
account. Even a cursory examination of some of his works gives us
vigorous declarations against unworthy heads of Churches, men
who were bishops in name only and who bore their title in the eyes
of men but not in the eyes of God. Preachers have always reminded
the clergy that the judgment of God establishes values that do not
correspond to the ecclesiastical dignities they hold here below. But
Origen affirms on several occasions that the validity of ecclesiastical
powers depends upon the priest's state of soul. "If he is tightly
bound with the cords of his own sins, to no purpose does he bind
and loose." [7] The right of forgiving sins committed against God is
reserved to him who "is inspired by Jesus, as the apostles were, and
whom we can know by his fruits as having received the Holy
Spirit." [8]

Origen does not ask himself whether ecclesiastical functions
have a virtue independent of the ministers who exercise them. Believing that Christ is an all-powerful mediator, he holds that His
first invitation does not await our merit. He fails, however, to see
the consequence of this view, not understanding that the means of
sanctification employed by the Church must have an efficacy in
themselves. He thinks that the divine will—the will in which the
theologians place the basis of the sacraments—is communicated
to the world only through the channel of the saints. Nothing gives
us a better view of him than his notion of uniting the priesthood to
a charisma, such as that of the grace of martyrdom. He views the

[7] *In Matt.*, XII, 14; P.G., XIII, 1013.
[8] *De oratione*, XXVIII, 8; P.G., XI, 528.

Church from the perspective of his own experiences. His ordination to the priesthood in Palestine has given a certain consecration to his genius, his success, his lofty purposes in writing his works. He wishes that his own good fortune should be the rule for ordinary men.

In such a perspective the things of religion—baptism, the Eucharist and holy orders—remain in view, but they are veiled in shadow and are intimately attached to the heavenly city. His allegorical method envelops them in paraphrases where they are not readily recognized. He separates them from the main body of the faithful and hides them in the holy of holies. The ritual of the Old Testament almost always gives him occasion to describe the inner progress of the soul. The most necessary task is to help the progress of souls that are already advanced along the way of perfection, while inviting the crowd to follow them afar.

We should like to think that things like these are but the clouds on the mountain top. But are they not sometimes the drifting fog of symbols, pressing upon him and confusing him? The fog will become less dense when Origen preaches in the presence of the faithful and sees Christian institutions other than in the exaltation of the martyrs or in the leisure of his books. He will then look out upon a Christian gathering in all its humble reality. On the edges of the crowd the deacons are standing, and the priests are seated apart, in the sanctuary. The Savior's power envelops all who assist at the ceremony. Whosoever has the right to join those Christians in prayer will find in that gathering a strength that is unequaled.[9]

II. ORIGEN'S DEPARTURE FROM EGYPT

On the initiative of two neighboring bishops, Origen received what he valued as the priestly consecration of his merits as a theologian. But his ordination took place without the consent, perhaps without the knowledge, of the bishop of the Church where his functions as a catechist had been exercised. In this way the privileges of educated Christians were thrown into direct opposition

[9] *Ibid.*, XXXI, 5.

to ecclesiastical authority, and the scene of this dramatic challenge was a disturbed city where preachers of many kinds held forth. Moreover, this ordination seemed to confirm, in a way, a doctrine whose novelty was beginning to disturb Christian opinion. Whenever Origen wished to avoid criticism, he never failed to take advantage of the authority conferred upon him by the oils of his ordination. This was the match that lighted the fuse. Soon an ecclesiastical conflict was raging, one of the most lively episodes in the crisis that began when it became necessary to adjust the traditional catechism to the efforts being made to formulate a doctrinal system. At Alexandria two special problems arose: to make the activities of the Academy subject to the episcopal magisterium and to adapt the emerging theological system to the common beliefs of the entire Christian community.

Origen's history is assuredly the best example we have of the authority exercised by the bishops in the Eastern Churches. In every dispute or doubt, approval or condemnation came from the episcopal see. The final opinion was always the verdict of the prelate who stood forth as the shepherd of the flock and who was acknowledged by the clergy as their prince or pontiff. His power was firmly established long before Christian scholars or Christian professors came upon the scene. Indeed it was difficult for the faithful to decide how to consider those luminaries, whether as workers in the vineyard or as princes of the blood.

ELECTION OF BISHOPS

In spite of this fact some historians have been at pains to find in the occurrences of the year 230 indications of a struggle undertaken by Demetrius and his successors to impose an episcopal monarchy on the Church of Alexandria. We are told by these historians that, according to a number of evidences, the most ancient of which is found in the works of St. Jerome, the bishop of Alexandria, from the earliest times in that Church, was one of the members of the local clergy; that he was chosen and delegated by the priests in some such way as the emperor was chosen by the army. This primitive custom, so we are told, ended only under the successors of Demetrius. Beginning with this post-Demetrius period, the "patriarch" was elected and consecrated by the neighboring bishops according to the habitual procedure; and they would have been under no obligation to choose him from the ranks of the clergy of Alexandria. Whatever may be the value of the tradition which, with a number of discordant details, reports this exceptional usage, there is little hope of finding in the life or works of Origen any contemporary testimony to confirm it. Although he does not study the sacerdotal office in general or discuss its relations with the holy sacrifice or with Christian liturgy generally, he is quite clear that there are two degrees of it, the priesthood and the pontificate. On this matter he never makes any distinction between the ecclesiastical institutions of his own country and the highly organized system of ecclesiastical government he must have encountered in Syria. His references to Egypt are sometimes marked with bitterness, but there is not a single reference to any peculiar innovation that would have lessened the authority of the episcopal see which had thrown suspicion on his teachings and had called down the thunderbolts upon his head.

On the contrary, the ecclesiastical procedure culminating in his dismissal from his native city contradicts one of the assumptions in this theory of the evolution of the episcopate. The theory assumes that, up to the period when Demetrius was bishop, there were no bishops in Egypt other than the bishop of Alexandria, an assumption which is used to explain why the members of the clergy elected the bishop; the new prelate is then assumed to have consecrated, for the first time, three other bishops. But the theory collapses before the fact: we know that the second synod, which declared Origen to be degraded from his priesthood, was composed of "some" Egyptian bishops, and there also exists a credible piece of evidence that shows the absence of others of the Egyptian episcopate.

Hence it follows that the history of the Academy at Alexandria does nothing to lessen the difficulty of accepting this modern theory of the origin of episcopal power. What is much more certain is that the trial of Origen afforded Demetrius the opportunity to assert his authority over the neighboring bishoprics, the number of which had increased during this period. Whether those bishoprics were created while he occupied the Alexandrian see or existed before his time, it is clear that the bishop of Alexandria had several episcopal brethren at that date.

IRREGULARITIES OF ORIGEN'S ORDINATION

Origen's ordination in Palestine suffered from two irregularities. First, he was ordained without an authorization from his own bishop; secondly, no consideration was given to the fact that Origen had already contracted a canonical impediment by his act of self-mutilation. In view of these facts, Demetrius convened a synod, composed of bishops and some priests. The synod did not depose Origen from the priesthood; but, by formally declaring him unworthy to be a catechist, it merely dismissed him from the Church of Alexandria. A hazy tradition tells us that he left Alexandria and went to Thmuis, where he was received by the bishop, Ammonius, a former pupil of his. He complained there to the clergy that his teaching had been deliberately misconstrued for the purpose of justifying an accusation of blasphemy. He further said that, seeing himself so sorely threatened, he had to take to flight.

CONDEMNATION OF ORIGEN

After Origen's flight Demetrius convened a second synod, composed exclusively of Egyptian bishops. This synod pronounced against Origen the sentence of degradation from the priesthood; when that sentence was formally signed, the exiled scholar had lost his last protector. Demetrius thereupon communicated to the Christian episcopate the findings of the synod, which were accepted by all the bishops, with four exceptions: the bishops of Palestine, Phoenicia, Arabia, and Achaia. It is thought that Ammonius was unable to challenge the authority of Alexandria; a short time afterward he was deposed by Heracles, who was the successor of Demetrius in the see of Alexandria.

In all this disturbance no condemnation was promulgated against Origen's teachings. But the convening of the synod produced the

most bitter criticisms of his work, a fact which he makes known to
us in his preface to the fifth book of the *Commentary* as well as in
one of the homilies he pronounced in the years of his exile. There
is no doubt but that the echoes of all this hostile criticism were
heard by the synod which forbade him to teach. The least harmful
rumor was concerned with the dangerous novelty of several of his
ideas. More harmful rumors would come later in his life, and perhaps their origin could be found in this troubled period. When
great men fall from their glory, the imagination of the mob runs
riot; the collapse of a mighty figure has a mysterious and dramatic
aspect for the crowds of lesser men. The great body of Christians
in Alexandria had little comprehension of the canonical trial, but
their minds were receptive to a popular version of it. This fiction
told of Origen's tears, of his weakness, of his excuses for his faults,
and of the misfortune which dogged him, all according to the popular taste of the day. According to this romantic story, the Alexandrian catechist had been guilty of blasphemy and had once been
prevented from committing an act of idolatry by the threat of con-
dign punishment. It seemed that once in a Christian assembly the
book of the Gospels had been handed to him, in the course of the
rite, and that the young Origen broke into tears and destroyed the
holy book. And so we come back to the Origen of the legend.

Origen in his exile was not insensible to this great change in the
attitude of the people of his native country. "The people of Egypt,"
he used to think, "were made for perpetual slavery." [10]

III. HIS FLIGHT TO CAESAREA

In great distress of mind Origen took refuge in Caesarea, where
he was received into the home of Theoctistus. His faith was unim-
paired, and the fundamental points of Christian belief were still, in
his view, the only possible object of theological study. His distress
came from a quite different cause. Looking back over his past life
and considering the principles by which he had lived, he asked himself if he had been too conscious of his own genius and had failed
to give due acknowledgment of his dependence on Him who alone

[10] *Hom. in Gen.*, XVI, 1; P.G., XII, 246.

illuminates the soul. Step by step he retraced his way. Had he been too presumptuous in yielding to the impatience of Ambrose? He felt that on that point he had made no mistake, for the enterprise was not a foolish one, as those around him had insinuated. He had faithfully observed the evangelical counsel: "For which of you having a mind to build a tower, doth not first sit down, and reckon the charges that are necessary, whether he have wherewithal to finish it." He had sat down and reckoned the cost, and all the materials were ready and in excellent condition. Further, he had trusted in God, for he had known that knowledge is something that comes after spiritual progress and never precedes it. He had written his commentaries so as to form them, little by little, according to the will of Him by whom we "are made rich, in all utterance, and in all knowledge."

In the midst of such musings he was informed of the verdict of the second synod and of the fact that it had been communicated to the episcopate of the Christian world. So Demetrius had reconsidered that older source of irritation which concerned the two episcopal protectors of the exiled man. "He has stated in his letter that such a thing was never heard of before, neither has hitherto taken place, that laymen should preach in the presence of bishops." [11] Alexander of Jerusalem and Theoctistus of Caesarea had been quick to defend themselves against a charge manifestly so far from the truth. Demetrius had allowed Origen to teach; even more, he had expressly authorized him to do so. Would he have casually recommended a man unworthy of the priestly office? The two bishops had merely drawn the natural conclusion from that recommendation.

The son of a martyr fell into discredit before all the Churches of Christendom. "The enemy assailed us with all bitterness by his new writings, so directly hostile to the Gospel, and stirred up against us all the winds of wickedness in Egypt." [12] He had the bitter memory of the defection of friends, among them Heracles, his old pupil and former colleague; and he thought of all those others

[11] Eusebius, H.E., VI, xix, 17.
[12] In Joan., VI, 29.

who had once sat at his feet. The prophet was right when he said: "Believe not a friend, and trust not in a prince." And we find Origen saying of his enemies: "We ought to pity them, not to hate them, to pray for them, not to curse them. For we have been created for blessing, not for cursing." [13] So he preferred to be silent in those hours of darkness when a man doubts even his own soul. Clement's admonitions on impassibility came back to him: beware of putting the imagination in motion, and do not add the tempest of wrong thoughts to the storm that assails you from without.

For some time he ceased to teach. His usual secretaries were no longer at his disposal, and he had left his last writings behind him in Alexandria. Perhaps when he fled to Thmuis he planned to return, believing that the storm would soon pass over. Those writings included the beginning of the sixth book of the *Commentary*, of which he had already composed the preface and several sections. As the days of his waiting lengthened, he began to feel the risk of leaving his work on the Fourth Gospel interrupted. Perhaps he thought he might weaken under the tension of other desires, the longing for retreat and solitude, the wish to put everything aside and to go away where he might have leisure to unravel the various strands of the failure of his work. "We, too, are exposed to the risk of learning, all too often, the bitterness of the trial that assailed the prophet Jeremias. When any one of us suffers in the cause of knowledge and finds himself incurring ill-treatment and even hate, many a time the thought comes to him: 'I retire, what can I do here?' Worries and troubles like these fall also to my lot, for I am a teacher and I allow my doctrines to slip from under my control and to go their own way. Is it not better that I retire into the desert where I shall find peace and calm?" [14]

If such a temptation attacked him, he must have resisted it, even in his hardest hours, for he had not the mentality of a hermit. Soon he was resuming his work at the point where he had put it down in Alexandria and, to avoid waste of time, was writing a new preface. In spite of his vague desires for silence and retirement, he had never

[13] St. Jerome, *Adv. Ruf.*, II, 18; *P.L.*, XXIII, 449.
[14] *Hom. in Jerem.*, XX, 8.

ceased to hold himself poised for the moment when his belief in himself should return. He confesses this himself, and now there is no trace of resignation in what he tells us: "Now that the many fiery darts directed against me have lost their edge, for God extinguished them, and my soul has grown accustomed to the dispensation sent me for the sake of the heavenly word and has learned from necessity to disregard the snares of my enemies, it is as if a great calm had settled on me, and I defer no longer the continuation of this work. I pray that God will be with me, and will speak as a teacher in the porch of my soul." [15] Let the attacks continue. Let those who strike a just man in the back make what they can of his mistakes. Their blows are no longer of any account and are quickly forgotten.

When he went forth from the land of Egypt, he was delivered from chains. He was beginning a new Exodus, not unlike that of Israel of old, whose spiritual significance he had so often contemplated. He was escaping from his enemies; better still, he was fleeing from the excitements of public controversy. He was delivered also from a more formidable enemy whom he had nurtured within himself, the impatience of his own thoughts. As the friends of his Alexandrian days left him, his old dreams fell away. He learned to be wary of his own genius. Little by little he began to understand that, even in free questions, research must be subject to guidance, and he realized that guidance as the part which authority must play in his life. One of those who have made a careful study of his mentality writes of him in these words: "Such discipline was needed before this high impatient spirit could obey with docility the bridle of God." Even so did Moses find a way across the abyss when all seemed lost:

"Strike with the rod of Moses the rising waters of contradiction. The word of the law and the careful study of Holy Scripture, if you ponder them deeply in the recesses of your own heart, will open a way for you through all your foes. The waters will suddenly roll back, and the way to victory will appear. Those who have been your most bitter foes will render unto you their wonder and astonish-

15 *In Joan.*, VI, *Praef.*, 1; *P.G.*, XIV, 201.

ment. Within the limits marked out for you by authority, you will follow the rule of faith in all your studies. You will become so proficient in the teaching of right doctrine that those who hear you, having been instructed by you according to the rule of faith, will rise against the Egyptians like the waves of the sea and not only will defeat them but will destroy them for evermore." [16]

[16] *Hom. in Exod.*, V, 5; *P.G.*, XII, 331.

CHAPTER XIX

Conclusion

IN THIS study we have followed Origen to a point where his work seems to have come to an end. The hostility of public opinion rather than that of ecclesiastical authority, condemnation, and exile, disapproval on the part of the Churches of the Christian world: such were the immediate results of his effort to formulate the theology of Christian beliefs. His work had reached a crisis, it is true; but it was a crisis full of rich possibilities. He emerged from it with his enthusiasm renewed and with a courage that was firmer and more vigorous than before.

When the effort is made to study the development of his thought during this first period of his life, we find a number of elements that combine to give us a clear picture of the road along which he traveled. It becomes obvious to us that his *De principiis* is the work of a mature mind rather than of a mind feeling its way. It was preceded by a comparatively long period, when Alexandrian philosophy held closely to the line of scholarly tradition. Neither the boldness of Origen's opinions nor the Greek molds in which they were cast suggest the primitive stages of human thought, and it is not illogical to pronounce a similar verdict on all the thinkers of Christian antiquity. The truth is that the early Christian thinker was not naturally a philosopher; he became philosophical through necessity and as a result of the influence of Christianity, a form of belief which is, as we have seen, the most metaphysical of religions. The Christian thinker of those first centuries became, in the measure of his opportunities and even a little more so, Platonist or Stoic, Roman or Athenian, inasmuch as he yielded to the atmosphere in which he lived or had recourse to the cultural advantages available to him.

At first Origen was merely a highly educated catechist. He had acquired the benefits of a literary training, and his philosophical equipment was that of an Alexandrian who had profited by his opportunities for study in the Greek classics. Moreover, he had inherited from his predecessors a predilection in favor of the Stoics. By his own personal desires he was led to a study of the soul as a means of achieving a knowledge of God. We see something of this ambition in his earliest work, his *Commentary on the Psalms*.

The resurrection of the dead was the subject that brought him into opposition to the Christianity of the illiterate mass of the faithful. He considered their ideas on this point gross and stupid, finding them a definite embarrassment whenever he had to defend them against the criticism of unbelievers. Discussing this handicap with his friends, he saw the need of assuring himself that the principles of his theology were sound. With this end in view he applied himself to the study of the philosophy of the day, the system of thought which we have called Alexandrian Neoplatonism. This new enterprise carried his inquiring mind far beyond the things of the soul, with whose rise and fall he had been concerned up to that time. New thoughts came to him, thoughts about the universe and the origin of rational beings. After some time his speculations on those subjects were worked into one definite system which had the novelty of being, at one and the same time, a cosmology and a treatise on the spiritual life. Thus was born his masterpiece, the *De principiis*. The work embraced the first causes of existence, of knowledge, and of virtue, the obstacles which the Good has to overcome and the way that victory is achieved. Then he turned to the question of the religion of the individual soul and applied his theological genius to a study of the inner life in his *Commentary on the Gospel of St. John*. This led him to dream of a Christian gnosis (higher knowledge) which should make the discipline of the intelligence the basis of spiritual progress and the purpose of which should be to give the educated Christian a purer knowledge of the nature of God. With a number of reservations and adjustments, he presented this program to those whose studies he directed and supervised.

From certain aspects there is nothing unusual in this history. Like all the young masters of religious philosophy, Origen began with his own prayerful thoughts, then came the testing of his ideas and the public controversies; finally a system emerged, to be followed by the spiritual applications of it. This is the highroad of Christian research. Today there may be obstacles different from those of Origen's time, but the direction remains always the same.

When we try to interpret this intellectual experience over the fifty years we have taken as their background, we refuse to be tempted by the easy solution so dear to many writers on the history of dogma. Of course Origen's intellectual adventures are part of the history of the age in which he lived. Far from shutting our eyes to that fact, we have been unable to escape the sharp feeling of something that has passed away, especially when we find how unstable and ephemeral the spiritual philosophy of the Academy of Alexandria proved to be. It would endure for only a brief period, the details of which are almost entirely hidden from the historian, so brief a period that men quickly forgot that it had ever been. Yet in that period the champions of the Gospel were too hasty in believing they possessed a philosophy of their own, and the pagan philosophers allowed themselves to be surprised into studying the Wisdom which has created all things. But if that Alexandrian effort represents a moment that was unique in the Church's history—something that shall never again be seen—and if its significance is studied against the background of all the attendant circumstances, its full and complete meaning can never be discovered by the hypothesis of the evolution of dogmas.

The enterprise to which Origen put his hand and the judgments to which that enterprise gave rise are an old and familiar story to the Church. It is a fact that on all the points in which Origen would offend Christian thought or Christian feeling today, the mind of the Church reacted instantly in a variety of ways. In the measure in which he had his scruples, because he knew quite well that he was expressing ideas that were rash and speculative, in that same measure anxieties and alarms disturbed public opinion within the Church. It is also a fact that the corrections imposed on him or suggested to him amended his philosophy in the sense desired by that Christian mentality of sixteen centuries ago.

In regard to the doctrines to which he gave firm expression, even those that would later be defined more accurately, they already had their value in the religious sentiments and pious practices of the Christian contemporaries of Alexander Severus. Under an aspect somewhat different from ours but in a manner quite in keeping with the needs of the time and the tendencies of the Academy of Alexandria, those truths were already sufficient. Nothing nebulous, no grave lack of precision, no inevitable occasion of conflict is to be found in his treatment of the Christian belief in the Holy Ghost or in the Incarnation. In the first three centuries that belief was able to nourish the religious life of Christians as it nourishes ours today. With the aid of a more precise theology of those mysteries, Christian philosophy later drew their lines more accurately. But the faith of those who listened to Origen was neither less perfect nor less delicate; indeed, in a number of instances we have found it more sensitive and more responsive than would be the common opinion in our own time. This explains why, without any disregard of the history of theological formulas, we have the right to assume the permanence of an idea. Further, we have the right to prefer the study of a man's personal development to the hypothesis of an evolution of dogmas which does not harmonize with the facts of this man's life. In the case of many Christian philosophers we can see an element of directed study. Origen's teaching is one of the clearest examples of it.

Less moving than that of others, the witness he bears to Christian truth is the more precious because it comes from the realm of his intellect. With the philosophy of St. Thomas, Origen's system of thought represents the most candid intellectualism that could be born of the Gospel. Origen always stands within the boundaries of reason and faith. Of all those who have written of his history, some lay stress on his argumentation alone, and others consider his piety exclusively. Actually it is wrong to separate those two elements in his life. No man has ever pushed the maxim farther than he, *intellige ut credas*. His system of theology is merely a sequence of speculations and arguments destined to justify Christian dogma without losing anything of its grandeur. Understand, see, contemplate: these were his favorite words. He never forgets his end, which is the ineffable union with God and the perfect intuition of His glory; therefore his intellectualism is not a rationalism. He understands also that as a theologian he works on a very humble level and that his foot is, so to speak, on the lowest rung of the ladder, where the knowledge of God is acquired gradually through the graces that are given in prayer. He knew that the husbandman who labors for the Lord must not be impatient with the pace at which the oxen draw the plow and that the grain must be sown year after year.

His concept of eternal bliss means, for him, leisure to contemplate God and the ineffable joy of knowing, rather than the revelation that must come at the highest point of ecstasy. His love of God is expressed in his insatiable desire to know. His faith is that of a seeker, although there flows in his veins the blood of a man who had died for his unquestioning love of Christ. He has even some difficulty in understanding the inner progress of divine love, in describing what new element the simple presence of Jesus brought into this world, in meditating on the mystery of Calvary. His knowledge is not always of service.

The historian who is satisfied to make a sort of inventory of Origen's philosophical ideas will find nothing there that would be unknown to profane philosophy. Theological reasoning differs from ordinary reasoning in its conditions, not in the manner of its application. It cannot claim to bring forward arguments that are not valid for every reasonable man. Right judgment does not act in two different ways, and a reason is good or bad universally. Origen's philosophical system is based upon a notion as old as Greek philosophy: the notion of participation.

When this notion is charged with all the energies of a life that is wholly spiritual, it acquires a deeper and more complete meaning. Because of this, Origen's philosophy is Christian, and Christian only. Origen tries, sometimes without success, to express the independence of creative Intelligence and the dependence of created being—with its perfection received, limited, and unstable. All being and all knowing come from God; and the only thing that does not come from God is evil, and evil is non-being. But we can go even further. Because God is good. He has not created evil, and evil

...ish into nothingness. He is the Father from whom souls ...re born, and the end to which they must return. He illuminates them, guides them, heals them, and re-establishes them by the coming of the Word, who bends down to the darkness in which they live and throws upon them the light for which they were created.

Origen has two viewpoints from which he sees the relation of the creature to the Creator. When he speaks of intelligences, he discusses participation; when he treats of the moral aspect of the relation, he says that the spiritual life is a struggle. From the angle of the creature, the limitations of a received perfection are shown by the need of spiritual progress, of conquest over sin, of persistent search for the perfect Good. Origen's insistence on the necessity of mortification is, together with his intellectualism, his personal mark on Alexandrian philosophy. His own teachers had already pondered over the mystery of the universe. What he saw in that mystery were the vicissitudes of sin, of repentance, and of final salvation. His universe was a world inhabited by souls engaged in a struggle that never ends, and the optimism with which he regarded that struggle is the most encouraging feature of all.

The whole of life is a temptation, but God is not the author of evil, and there is no soul lost beyond recall. Even the most sinful man can be restored to his primal dignity. Watch and pray. Are the lofty thoughts which have become familiar with us in this study of his life very different from the teachings of the Gospel? Has not this brilliant genius, this product of a learned and sophisticated city, become as much the disciple of Jesus as the humblest and most illiterate of those who strive to live by the Word of God? Happy the soul that has not to follow the hard road of learning! But that man is still more blessed who gives the example of personal conviction faithfully sought and finally acquired in the twofold joy of the mind and of the heart.

Index

Academy of Alexandria: commentaries in
  use at, 38; cradle of symbolism, 30
Action and contemplation, 74
Adamantius (i.e., Origen)
Adamantius, Dialogue of (apocryphal),
  100
Adoptionism, repudiated by Origen, 230
Alexander (bishop of Jerusalem): friend of
  Origen, 86 f.; historical interpretation,
  87; relations with Clement, 86; self-
  defense of, 321
Alexander Severus (emperor): Christ
  among sages of, 276; priest of the Sun,
  276; tolerance of Christians under,
  276
Alexandria
  attitude to intellectual leaders, 150
  catechetical school at, 21
  election of bishop, 317
  Gnostic infiltrations at, 104-9
  Gnosticism at, 145
  heretics in, 105
  looting of, 85
  martyrs at, 15
  Neoplatonism at, 182-85
  opposition to Origen at, 304
  Origen degraded by synod of, 318
  Origen's departure from, 316-19
  Origen's return to, 91, 304
  Platonism at, 140
  population of, 85
  study of creation at, 140
  superstition in, 106 f.
  terrorized by Caracalla, 85
Alexandrian Neoplatonism, 326
Alexandrian public, the, 105
Alexandrian School, Scripture exegesis at,
  34
Allegorical method of exegesis, 32, 35-59,
  199, 219
Amanuenses, Origen's, 67
Ambrose (friend of Origen), 16
  abjuration of errors by, 134
  commentary dedicated to, 278
  conversion of, 64
  financial assistance by, 67
  friendship for Origen, 64, 278
  preface addressed to, 306
Ammonius Saccas, 149-65
  doctrines of, 150-53

Ammonius Saccas (continued)
  Hierocles on school of, 151
  influence on Origen, 154
  the notes of, 153: on soul and body, 161
  Origen and, 186
  Origen pupil of, 206
  Origen's relation to, 154
  origin of name of, 149
  pupil of Origen, 64
  school of, 196
  theory of creation, 154
Angels: duties of, 122; function of, 196;
  inequality of, 271
"Anima," 249
Animism, universal, 180
Antioch, journey to, 274-77
Apocrypha, Origen's use of the, 62
Apelles (Marcionite), 108: on Christian-
  ity, 302; on Creator, 244; exegesis by,
  29; on Genesis, 23
Aquila's version of Scripture, 45
Aristotelianism, 23: influence on Origen,
  164; reconciliation of Platonism and,
  164 f.
Aristotle: heresy's use of, 23; influence on
  Plato, 164; Plato and, 164
Ascetical teaching, Origen's, 71
Asceticism, plan of Christian, 54
Astrology
  at Alexandria, 104
  baptism and, 110
  Neoplatonism and, 171
  Origen on, 168-71
  Plotinus on, 168 f.
  science of, 170
Athenians, intellectual attitude of, 150
Athens, Origen at, 303
Atlantis, myths of, 195 f.
Austerities of Origen, 22
Authority: of bishops, 317; of the Church,
  309-15

Banquet (Plato's), study of, 197
Baptism: astrology and, 110; faith and, 10
Baptismal formula, 215
"Beginning," meaning of the word, 282 f.
Being, Trinity the source of, 227
Bible; see Scripture
Biblical lexicon by Origen, 47
Bishop, choice of, 314

...thority of, 317; election of, 317; unworthy, 315

Body: contempt for the, 27; mind and, 228; the risen, 92; soul and, 161

Caesarea: Origen's conferences at, 85; Origen's preaching at, 88; flight to, 320-24

Caracalla (emperor): Alexandria terrorized by, 85; called the Getist, 85; tolerance of Christians under, 276

Catechetical school at Alexandria, 21

Catechist, Origen the, 21-28

Charismata: Clement on, 13; and the hierarchy, 8; Origen's knowledge of, 7

Childhood, Origen's, 1-28

Christ
appearance of the risen, 97
divinity of, 284 f.
the Lamb of God, 298-301
the names of, 283
the natures in, 246
the pre-existent, 248
of the psalms, 77-80
the soul of, 246 f.
titles of, 286
two natures in, 218
see also Logos, Son

Christian gnosticism, 116-35

Christian teachers in pagan schools, 21

Christian tradition, 60 f.

Christianity, conversions to: prohibited, 12

Christians: classes of, 9; persecution of, 12 ff.

Christological disputes, 51

Church, the, 309-24
authority, 309-15
membership in, 312
Origen and the mind of, 60
Origen's notion of, 127
teaching office, 309

Cities, the three, 195, 226 ff.

City: the natural, 226; the spiritual, 226, 256; the supreme, 226

Clement (of Alexandria), 1 ff.
Bishop Alexander's relations with, 86
on charismata, 13
conventual life not imposed by, 10
conversion of, 2
cosmology of, 159 f.
departure from Egypt, 12
esteem for contemplation, 71
influence on Origen, 4
literary projects of, 3-6
on martyrdom, 12-14, 27
on pagan philosophy, 24

Clement (of Alexandria) (continued)
paraphrase of Scripture, 30
on perfect Christians, 9 f.
spiritual teaching of, 6
Stromata by, 24
tract on martyrdom, 12-14
view of teaching, 7

Commentaries: of Origen, 42; in use at Alexandria, 38

Commentary on Genesis, Origen's, 269

Commentary on St. John's Gospel: character of, 278; composition of, 304; date of, 275; way of prayer, 40

Commentary on the Lamentations, 84 ff., 90

Commentary on the Psalms by Hippolytus, 50

Commentary on the Psalms by Origen, 50, 66-83: composition of, 67; date of, 66-70; influences in composition of, 77

Conclusion, 325-30

Concordance, Origen's use of, 57

Concupiscence, intellectual, 263

Condemnation of Origen, 319

Conflict, the, 302-8

Contemplation: action and, 74; Clement's esteem for, 71

Contra haereticos by St. Epiphanius, 191

Conversion, Origen on, 115

Conversions, laws against, 12

Copyists, Origen's, 67

Cosmogony of the Timaeus, 207

Cosmology: Greek system of, 144; Origen's, 157-61, 241; questions of, 155

Creation, 142-45
Alexandrian study of, 140
biblical account of, 137
emanationism in, 240
imperfections in, 240
Neoplatonists' view of, 177
Numenius on, 140
Origen on, 175
of physical universe, 242
Platonist view of, 141
problem of, 154
of rational beings, 147
view of, 146
the Word in the work of, 160

Creations, idea of two, 236

Creator, creature's relation to, 330

Creatures: dependence of, 234; inequality of, 238; relation to Creator, 330

Daemon, Platonist fable of the, 248

Damnation, eternal, 240